MIGHTY
MINIS

CHRIS HARVEY

The Oxford Illustrated Press

First published 1986
Reprinted 1987 and 1990
This edition first published 1993
Reprinted 1997

The Oxford Illustrated Press is an imprint of Haynes
Publishing, Sparkford, Nr Yeovil,
Somerset BA22 7JJ, England.

Tel. 01963 440635 Fax: 01963 440001
Int. tel: +44 1963 440635 Fax: +44 1963 440001

E-mail: sales@haynes-manuals.co.uk
Web site: http://www.haynes.com

Haynes North America, Inc
861 Lawrence Drive, Newbury Park, California 91320 USA

British Library Cataloguing in Publication Data
A catalogue record for this book is
available from the British Library

ISBN 1 85509 237 9

Library of Congress Catalog Card No 93-79174

Printed in Hong Kong

Contents

Acknowledgements

It gives me great pleasure to bring this latest edition of *Mighty Minis* up to date . . . not least because the Mini was heading for extinction so far as its makers were concerned when I wrote the original book. Sheer enthusiasm in the market place saved the Mini, which has become even more of a national institution than the first Austin Seven which started the small car boom in 1922.

I must thank my wife Mary for taking so many of our Hilton Press Services shots while I was busy writing, and for her seemingly endless patience in processing hundreds of rolls of film and printing even more pictures; and equal thanks to the staff at the Heritage Trust who, with Anders Clausager, produced such fine work. Special thanks also to Chris Cheal of the Mini Owners' Club for introducing members Hilary Ashman and family with their Mini 25 and other cars, David Bailey with his pick-up, Richard and Ann Horne with their late 1275GT and Sprite, David Humphreys with his Super de Luxe cover car, J. R. Marsh with his Cooper 1275S, Peter Muxlow with his 1071S, S. J. Plowman with his Riley Elf, Mark Smith with his Clubman, Les Stapleford with his Clubman estate, Konrad Thomas with his 1959 Mini, Steve Walden and his early 1275GT, Graham Thompson with his Wolseley Hornet, Riley Elf and mass of information on them, plus Dave Gilbert of the Mini-Cooper Club with his ex-works Cooper S and Moke, and Angela Wrigley of Austin-Rover for invaluable assistance. With photographers Paul Skilleter of *Practical Classics*, Bob Young and Gerry Stream, they gave me a lot of precious time, additional help coming from the Southern Electricity Board with their van and Rory Cronin of the Crayford club.

With this latest edition there are new faces on the scene, Denis Chick and Kevin Jones, at Rover's External Affairs department, proving exceptionally helpful, along with Paul Clark, editor of *Performance Car* and a former colleague at *Classic Cars* magazine. As a veteran of every Classic Marathon and Monte Carlo Challenge, I also have to thank organizer Phil Young for delving into his records at very short notice . . . and thank him, with all Mini fans, for organizing such wonderful events, which have taken the tiny terrors back to the top in historic rallying.

Here's to Mighty Mini motoring into the next century . . .

Chris Harvey, Hethe, Oxon, May 1993

Colour Plates

I

Mini: The Car That Charmed The Millions

For a car so small, the Mini, in all its forms, made an enormous impact on the world. It was conceived of sheer necessity during the Western world's first fuel crisis, and more than five million have been sold since to trigger a revolution in transport that will never be reversed. The Mini was the last great product of Leonard Lord, who realised that the world needed a car one step better than the

Below: The Mini introduced in 1959 was a delightfully simple vehicle that changed little in the decades which followed. This is one of the first production models, carrying a Morris badge.

Above: The key to the Mini's success was its space-saving front-wheel-drive formula, made possible by the development of these constant velocity driveshaft joints.

Above right: The efficient way in which the Mini utilised only ten feet of ground space was never better shown than by this demonstration model cut in half for the launch in 1959. For those with a fanatical eye for detail, this is a De Luxe edition with carpets and two-tone cloth upholstery!

Right: The Mini's makers, the British Motor Corporation, were anxious to emphasise the economical nature of their new car (a Morris in this case), created, as it were, by the recent Suez oil crisis ... so they commissioned this picture of a Mini at the fuel pumps in 1959, taking on petrol at the historically-high price of 5s 1d (25p) per gallon.

Right: BMC were also anxious to put over the sporting appeal of their new utility car (an Austin in this picture), so they required these two models to hold their pose with a fishing net and anchor against a suitable backdrop in 1959.

bubble cars that had abounded since an Arab dictator cut off oil supplies in 1956. It was designed by a stubborn genius, Alec Issigonis, whose brilliance had already been seen in the Morris Minor—the first British car to sell a million— and who would, by the late 1950s, brook no interference with what he wanted to do. The Mini has become a classic success story since then because, whether they knew it or not, it was just what the public wanted.

Back in the 1950s, following the upheaval of the war the average Briton's ambitions were modest: Small was secure and affordable and this spilled over into the fashion in cars, thereby benefiting the Mini. The Mini was fortunate during the 'swinging sixties' too, when the 'dedicated followers of fashion' decided the Mini was chic and bought them by the thousand. Abroad, it sold well everywhere except in America, where the long distances and cheap fuel were incompatible with the economic little car that many thought too cramped for comfort.

Top left: Having failed to sell the Mini Moke to the armed forces, BMC decided to promote it as a leisure vehicle, introducing this immaculate example, complete with equally- immaculate model, to a field some- where near Birmingham in 1964.

Top right: Alec Issigonis, the Mini's designer, had dreamed of a fully automatic small car almost since his childhood, and was gratified when brilliant engineers overcame technical problems to put the automatic Mini into production in 1965. BMC, not surprisingly, decided that it would be highly popular with women, more and more of whom were learning to drive during this era. But quite whether the women saw themselves having to do it in swimsuits is open to question. To the chauvinists' surprise, the average woman proved to be perfectly capable of driving any sort of car and the automatic Mini, saddled with a higher price than the manual version, died a natural death 15 years later.

Bottom left: Mini sales soared when it was found that it could convey enough power to win international rallies outright. Here three Cooper S cars (an Austin and two Morrises), of (from the left) Rauno Aaltonen, Paddy Hopkirk, and Timo Makinen, line up with one of the Big Healey sports cars they replaced in the BMC works' team. The departure point: the M.G. factory at Abingdon where BMC's competitions department was sited, and the Austin-Healeys and MGBs in the background were produced. The destination: the 1964 Alpine Rally.

Below: BMC became British Leyland, and eventually the Austin-Rover Group, to celebrate the Mini's 25th anniversary in 1983 with a special edition Mini 25 at the Birmingham Motor Show.

With the exception of the Americans, most people did not mind that the Mini was small inside—after all you could still get four people into this bargain box—nor did they care if they had an engine already growing old, gears that howled, and wind that whistled around windows which popped shut just when you need the ventilation most. They did not mind the spartan interior, the sit-up-and-beg driving position, nor the windscreen wipers which you had to park by yourself as you mopped away misty patches on the glass. Trendy young people in search of somewhere to park in bustling London had shown that these incredibly cheap and economical cars could transcend all class barriers. Racing drivers had shown that the Mini's amazing handling could turn it into a giant-killer; a veritable David among Goliaths.

In no time at all, this love affair turned into idolotry. Minis were adorned with all manner of accessories; decorations that demonstrated that although the owner was one of the people, he or she was really an individual. In extreme circumstances the new generation of pop stars turned Minis into limousines, as fans stuck imitation wicker panels on the sides, or fitted cheap wheel spacers and rorty exhausts, plus chequered tape, to demonstrate their passion in life: driving like a racing ace. More serious efforts with the Mini's gallant engine extracted as much as four times the original power to conquer pinnacles like the Monte Carlo Rally three times in a row when it was still the world's top motoring event. In exasperation, the French changed the rules to exclude it . . . and saw their event degenerate into an also-ran.

Nationalistic favour exploded into a riot of I'm Backing Britain Union Jack bedecked Minis, leading a fight to pull us out of economic blight.

By the late 1960s, the rest of the world had come to terms with the mystique needed to build a car expressly for those who could not really afford one. Still the Mini survived in the face of intense competition because it had become the devil people knew, with a recently strengthened transmission to iron out one of its last real weak points. The feeling of security that had been engendered by a small outlay and small fuel bills was reinforced by small servicing bills now that every village motor mechanic had grown up with what was at first a mysterious machine incorporating a revolutionary transaxle and rubber suspension. As we entered the 1970s, still on tiny 10-inch wheels that no longer looked strange, you could get a Mini fixed anywhere.

As small had been beautiful in the 1960s, a little bit bigger became even more attractive in the years that followed, leading to a new generation of super minis that would beat the old original in every aspect except size and price. You still couldn't produce a proper car smaller than a Mini. Owners continued to defend the whining gears, choppy ride—which had earlier been considered sporty—and infernal din from what was now a truly ancient engine. By the time the Mini's makers, British Leyland, had introduced their own super mini, the Metro, for the 1980s, the Mini seemed doomed. Most variants, such as the vans and pick-ups, were on their way out, and we'd even seen the last of the monkey-like Moke. Surely the basic saloon could not last much longer?

Since then the Minis have sold, maybe, another million to add to the four that have gone before on a combination that has not altered since the 1950s: extraordinary value, a size that cannot be beaten, and, above all, charm.

II
Enter the Mini

The original concept of the Mini was as delightfully simple as the car remains today. It was to be based on a box 10 ft by 4 ft by 4 ft with about 6 ft 6 ins of the length available for passengers and another 1 ft 6 ins for luggage. This, of course, left only 2 ft in which to instal the power train. Sir Leonard Lord did not mind what sort of engine Issigonis used, so long as it was on BMC's production lines at the time. This decision, born of necessity because so much money would have to be invested in other areas of the Mini's production, gave no alternative to the existing A-series unit used in BMC's small cars.

This power train measured 3 ft 2 ins from its front-mounted water radiator to the back of its gearbox—and early experiments in making a shorter two-cylinder version were discouraging. A 'big twin' quickly put together by sawing a normal A-series unit in half, ran so roughly that it dispelled any notion of developing it into a reasonably-civilised engine. Issigonis then decided that the only effective way to shorten the A-series power train would be to place the gearbox under the crankshaft rather than running it behind. Potential problems, such as lubrication, seemed minor compared to the contortions which would have been needed otherwise. The A-series power train could then be placed across the car with a driven wheel each side.

Even then this unit had a long history. It could be seen as a natural evolution of Austin's 1200 cc small car engine that was introduced in 1947. A four-cylincer in-line unit, it had a three-bearing crankshaft running in thinwall bearings, the first British production engine to do so when it appeared in 803 cc form for the new Austin Seven—or A30—in October 1951. This cast iron engine had water jackets running the full length of the bores. So far as dimensions were concerned, it was slightly more modern than the original Austin Seven unit of pre-war fame in that it had a 2 mm wider bore at 58 mm, although it retained the same long stroke of 76 mm. This was a relic of the days when British cars' taxation was governed by the size of their bores, but at least it gave the A-series unit a lot of torque.

It was decided to put the camshaft, pushrods, inlet and exhaust valves on one side of the engine, so that the pushrod tubes did not have to pass the sparking plugs which might be a source of oil and water leaks. This meant that

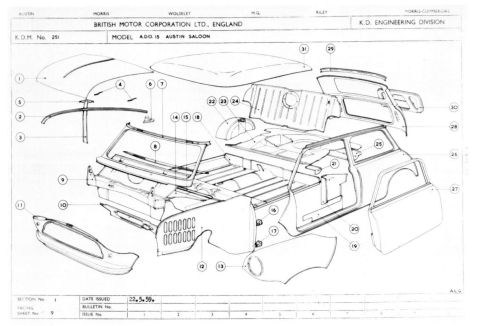

Above right/left: The Mini, particularly the 1959 model, was endowed with the minimum of adornment to keep down the price. Hence the discreet badging (Austin Seven for this car) neat slimline bumpers and exposed door and boot hinges. Only the corporate ruched rail radiator grille and stainless-steel finished lower body seam strips show signs of the embellishment so common of cars in the 1950s.

Left: By the time the Mini went into production BMC had become quite sophisticated in the way they made unitary construction bodyshells. This exploded diagram of the ADO15 (Austin Mini) saloon car body shows some of the relatively large panels which were stamped out by huge presses and then welded together to form the finished unit. The initial investment in such presses was colossal and required the use of basic mechanical components in the car, which were already in production for others, so that little additional investment was needed.

the inlet ports had to be cast together (siamesed) in the cylinder head with a siamesed central exhaust port. One side effect of this layout was that it put heavy demands on the exhaust valves and made the use of very high quality steel essential. But it was a very efficient cylinder head that had been developed by the legendary Harry Weslake. He discovered in wartime experiments with gasflow that a heart-shaped combustion chamber with a projection between inlet and exhaust valves promoted just the right degree of swirl to ensure complete combusion of the mixture. This Weslake-patented design also gave very smooth and economical part-throttle running on a small ignition advance.

The camshaft was driven by a roller chain from the crankshaft, with twin rubber tensioners. At the rear end of the camshaft was an oil pump and at the front end was the water pump, driven by a belt from the crankshaft, that also drove the dynamo. Production was simplified by the use of a split connecting rod, little end, which clamped on to the gudgeon pin. This meant that any pin which fell within the design tolerance would fit.

Right: The A-series engine which powered the Mini could trace its ancestry to 1947 and had tenuous links with the Austin Seven so popular before. This engine and transmission unit—or power train—was one of the first made for the Mini in 1959. It is pictured from the frontal aspect with sparking plug apertures on the cylinder head at the top, thermostat housing and cooling water inlet next to them on the right, dynamo mounting bracket below, oil filter boss to the right and below the distributor drive clamp on the side of the cylinder block. The starter motor bolted on to its gear housing at the extreme front of the engine, turning the ring gear concealed in the clutch bell housing at the left, with the clutch operating linkage and slave cylinder angled towards the back of the engine. One of the engine mounts can be seen on the left under the extreme end of the bell housing, with detachable lifting brackets for the power train on the rocker cover securing bolts at the top.

Right: Heart of the A-series engine was an appropriately-shaped combustion chamber designed by the gasflow expert Harry Weslake. It had the inlet valve on the right of the picture and the exhaust on the left, the sparking plug normally projecting through the hole shown in the bottom of the picture.

More than 500,000 of these engines had been made by the time BMC started to develop it for further applications, such as the Mini in 1956. In its initial single-carburettor form, it produced only 36 bhp, and more was needed if the performance of new cars was to keep up with modern trends. This meant that the A-series engine would have a larger capacity if it was to remain reasonably docile. The 803 cc engine had water all round its bores and its enlargement to 948 cc—originally visualised as the size needed to power the Mini—was undertaken with some trepidation because it meant siamesing the end pairs of cylinders. Early fears that bore distortion would result appeared to be well founded until it was discovered that a thick copper asbestos gasket was to blame and the problem could be cured by using a gasket of about half the thickness, 0.031 ins. White metal big end bearings had also proved to be a weak point on the 803 cc unit, so they were changed for the same lead indium as the main bearings in the 948, which, in turn, led to a change from a by-pass to a full-flow filter. The big end journal diameter was also increased by 0.0625 ins to 1.625 ins, and 0.125 ins was taken off the main bearing length and used to

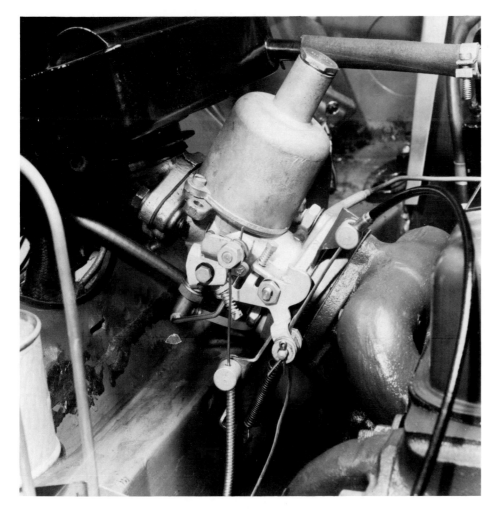

Left: One of BMC's strengths was that they made their own carburettors, called SU (for Skinner's Union, the original having been developed from a leather bag). This avoided having to pay a costly premium for what was a very efficient instrument. SU's 1.25-inch carburettor is pictured here mounted behind the Mini's A-series engine to shelter it from icing during exceptionally-cold conditions. The cable on the right operates the throttle, the vertical one below, the choke for cold weather starting.

thicken the crankshaft webs. These changes were enough to cope with up to 70 bhp from the A-series engine, which now used a bore of 62.94 mm with the same stroke as before.

Early tests with a prototype Mini resulted in an extremely high top speed (for the day) of 92 mph on the 37 bhp produced by an A-series unit in 948 cc

Right and below: These are rare pictures taken in 1958 of the 948-cc unit with which the Mini was intended to go into production, mounted in ADO 15's subframe, complete with ancilliaries. The 848-cc engine followed exactly the same layout with, when viewed from the front, in the first picture, the radiator on the right, with dynamo next to it, sharing a common belt drive to the cooling fan, concealed in the radiator's cowling. Below the dynamo is the oil filter with the starter motor next to it below the distributor, and ignition coil, which is mounted on top of the bell housing. Behind the bell housing at that point can be seen one of the suspension units, with the independent front suspension, uprights, driveshafts and brake drums to the sides of the subframe, which surrounds the lower crankcase of the power train. When viewed from the back in the second picture, the suspension units can be seen clearly with the steering arms reaching backwards when they linked up with the steering rack mounted on the bodyshell into which the power train's subframe was inserted. The gearlever, which rose at a point behind the carburettor, inlet and exhaust manifolds (with the air cleaner on top) protruded into the Mini's body so that, in effect, the car's speedometer was directly between the driver's hand on the gearlever and the carburettor. The strips of felt on the back of the subframe helped provide insulation from noise, vibration and harshness with the subframe's rubber mounting blocks which are not shown.

Left: By the time the Mini went into production the air cleaner had been reshaped to fit better into the aperture in the bulkhead behind the speedometer. The brake and clutch reservoirs are visible on the left (with the fusebox and a windscreen washer bottle on the inner wing, or flitch plate) and the windscreen wiper motor and drive in the right-hand corner. On left-hand-drive Minis, the layout was similar except that the hydraulic cylinders were moved to the right to be fitted above the brake and clutch pedals in the mounting covered by a plate which can be seen behind the engine's thermostat housing. The hose across the top of the engine was connected to the heater unit in the car at one end and to a cylinder head valve at the other. This valve could be opened to let in heat or shut to cut off the heater.

Left: Part of the gearchange mechanism can be seen clearly here, between the power train's finned sump and the exhaust pipe to the right. This pipe was firmly bolted to the engine and gear selector housing, with rubber mountings to the body, to help counteract the engine's torque. The heavy black cable to the right of the picture runs from the starter motor to its operating button on the floor inside the body.

form on one SU carburettor. This was more than the cheap concept could stand, so it was decided to reduce the size of the engine rather than to uprate components such as the brakes. It was also decided to turn the power train through 180 degrees to shelter the carburettor from potential icing in cold weather. This action exposed the ignition system to the elements, but it did not worry BMC at the time. They were confident that they could waterproof the system, such had been their success with military applications.

The decision to turn the engine round involved a choice of revising the

Above: The Mini's transmission, when viewed from the top side with the front forming the bottom face in the picture, shows the primary gears on the left. The gear selector mechanism on top protrudes into the crankcase, with the straight-cut first gear ratio in the centre. The final drive and differential are contained under the centre spar of the transmission casing.

Above right: The independent front suspension is pictured here from the front on full droop with its attendant constant velocity joint enclosed in a rubber gaiter. The top of the Armstrong tubular shock absorber would be bolted on to a bracket on the bodyshell's flitch plate upon installation, with the suspension's rubber bump stop visible behind the shock absorber's body. The pipe to the front is, of course, the flexible hose for the hydraulic fluid which operates the attendant brake.

Above right: The rear suspension's subframe followed the same principles as the front although it was outwardly of different design. Each rear wheel and brake was mounted on a massive trailing arm which compressed the rubber 'doughnut' at the back by a lever and socket. When the subframe (which carried the rear exhaust pipe bracket) was mounted in the bodyshell, above, the top of the shock absorber was bolted into a high point in the body's wheelarch.

camshaft, distributor, oil pump and some of the bearings to cope with an engine which ran clockwise—when viewed from the flywheel end—or introducing a set of transfer gears in a primary location to enable it to continue running anti-clockwise while the gearbox ran clockwise. This extra set of gears entailed a 4 per cent loss of efficiency in the transmission, but was considered preferable because it was cheaper than revising the engine, which, in any case, was producing more than enough power. The extra noise made by the new transfer gears was mitigated by the fact that at high speeds they improved the life of the crankshaft. The extra durability was a result of lengthening the crankshaft to accept the primary gears between the rear main bearing and the flywheel, which

reduced its torsional vibration frequency from 29,400 cycles per minute to 24,300. This meant that a phenomenon known as the 'fourth order critical period of vibration' (the real killer of a four-cylinder crankshaft) remained outside the normal running range of 6,000 rpm. Higher order resonances at lower speeds had amplitudes too small to be dangerous.

These factors were made all the more important because a worthwhile reduction in engine capacity meant that the unit would have to rev harder so as not to lose too much power. The best compromise resulted in reducing the stroke from 73.72 mm to 68.26 mm in an unchanged bore of 62.9 mm. Power losses were then contained to 34 bhp at 5,500 rpm rather than the higher output at 5,000 rpm. Torque suffered, too, with a reduction from 50 lb/ft at 2,500 rpm to 44 at 2,900. But these figures were quite adequate from the new capacity of

Top left: The cost of the basic Mini was pared so far that BMC (like many other manufacturers) were keen to promote the sale of accessories which offered a far higher profit as a percentage of the cost as units. Thus, pictures were taken in 1959, before this Mini (a Morris) was introduced, showing it bedecked with everything BMC were selling as accessories at the time: fog and spotlights on brackets mounted on the radiator grille, wing mirrors, windscreen rosette, windshield exterior visor, roof rack and a stick-on electrical demisting element for the rear screen. Independent manufacturers soon thought of dozens of other things to bolt, screw or stick on your Mini . . .

Top right: Just for the record, a pre-production Mini bodyshell is prepared for technical photography with a rope to hold open the driver's door, revealing the vital transverse seat mounting beam which stiffened the floor so much.

Left: A second view of the unfortunate Mini which lost half its bodyshell shows how the subframes bolted into place. The rather narrow tyres are, of course, the original Dunlop cross-plies.

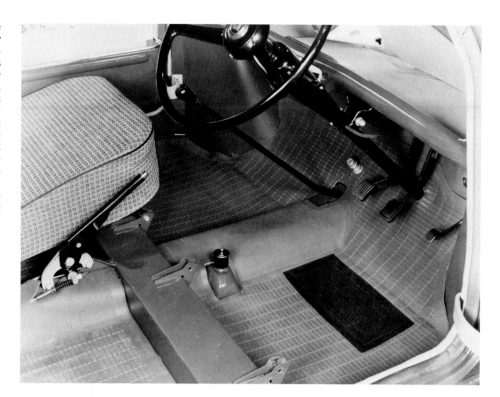

848 cc even when the Mini's body was widened 2 ins to an overall 4 ft 7 ins. Maximum speed fell to 74 mph, but it was still competitive with potential rivals, some of which—the small Fiat in particular—were lagging behind in the 60 mph range.

An additional advantage in swinging the engine round was seen in the reduction by 20 per cent of the area needed for the water radiator's core. This came about because in the original set-up, with the radiator on the left of the car when viewed from the front, the cooling fan had to suck air through the core from a partial vacuum under the wheel arch. The fan then became far more efficient on the other side as it pushed air out into the wheel arch's low-pressure area . . .

Once the decision had been taken to include the normal A-series transmission in the crankcase, rather than bolting it on behind the clutch, engine installation problems sorted themselves out. Mounting the flywheel and single dry plate clutch outboard of the transfer gears had been part of the original scheme because it distributed the driving load better and made the clutch easier to service. This unit could now be removed and replaced without disturbing the transmission.

The general layout of the engine and transmission reflected great ingenuity. The first primary drive gear was a 24-tooth helical running freely in pressure-fed plain bushes on the extended crankshaft. At the rear end of this gear (taking the radiator end of the engine as the normal front), was a toothed coupling which drove the fabric-lined clutch plate; the teeth on the coupling provided a

Left: The de luxe Mini of 1959 was still spartan by modern standards, but much better furnished than the basic model. The carpets were quite stiff and generally stayed in place. Two-tone upholstery, flecked cockpit trim, and the heater in the centre were other parts of the standard specification. Both seats were kept in position for photographs of this left-hand-drive model because BMC did not wish to draw attention to the starter button, which remained on what was now the passenger's side of the cabin.

necessary degree of end float for the plate in its released position. In its driven position, the clutch plate was trapped by spring pressure between the pressure plate and the flywheel attached to the extreme end of the crankshaft. The clutch was hydraulically operated through a lever pivoting in a lug on the clutch cover and operating a spring withdrawal plate through a ball thrust bearing. A great deal of thought went into preventing the engine and transmission oil from reaching the clutch. This problem was eventually solved by a lip-type oil seal fitted with a garter spring. The drive was taken from the primary gear on the crankshaft to a 31-tooth idler gear, which in turn meshed with a 24-tooth gear on the end of the gearbox's first motion shaft. This shaft for the four-speed and reverse gearbox, with synchromesh on the top three ratios, ran directly behind the crankshaft. Its layshaft ran in needle roller bearings forward of the input

Above: The push button 'locks' on the Mini's sliding windows saved a lot of money in production and proved a boon to sneak thieves who inserted carefully-shaped pieces of wire between the panes to push home the button, free the glass, and gain entry to the car.

Top right: Despite vigorous attempts to sell the Mini Moke as a miniature Jeep to armed forces throughout the world, it had to stay on the shelf until 1964, when it bowed in as a fun machine held in high regard by 'dedicated followers of fashion'.

shaft, with the final drive gears and differential contained in an extended casting from the deep finned magnesium sump which carried everything below the normal cylinder block. The final drive was accompanied by part of the gear selection mechanism, which followed a contorted path through the engine to layshaft.

Early prototypes had a gear lever protruding through the fascia like a horizontal umbrella handle. This was accepted practice in some European cars, but it was felt that it would not go down well in Britain. Besides, it made for a rather vague action. Ironically, once the engine was turned round and the gear selection mechanism had to run through the sump, and up to a more normal lever on the floor, it became even more vague! This was especially evident when compared with the far more direct-acting linkage on the A35 and Morris Minor.

One of the major problems which had afflicted front-wheel-drive cars before the Mini was in the universal joints that were needed to convey the power from the gearbox to the front wheels. When a normal joint is turned through as little as 15 degrees it shows a strong tendency to straighten itself under power, leading to unpleasant—and sometimes downright dangerous—consequences for the steering and general handling. The technical solution had already been worked out when the Mini was on the drawing board. It was a constant velocity joint in which the power is conveyed through ball bearings operating in a three-point cage, cluster and socket. This joint, however, is inherently larger, more costly and has a shorter working life than the simpler component.

But dedicated development by the British firm of Birfield reduced these deficiencies and their joint became more attractive when it was realised that it could operate successfully through as great an angle as 40 degrees. These vital outer joints were linked to the final drive by the cheaper Hooke-type universals with sliding-spline drive shafts to accommodate suspension movement. An equally vital degree of elasticity was retained in the drive line by rubber inserts in the Hooke joints' forged steel spiders. Without such cushioning, something would have snapped under load.

The front suspension was, not surprisingly, similar to that of the Morris Minor, with single forged links above and below the driveshaft, located by a rubber-mounted tie rod. The layout was arranged to give a roll centre about 2.5 ins above ground level. The Morris Minor's rack-and-pinion steering was adopted as the best available from the BMC parts bin—and probably anybody else's at the time. There had been some development, however. The rack was now adjustable for wear, having shims which could be removed from the mounting of a bronze plate which kept the rack and the pinion engaged, and felt bushes at the end of the rack to dampen noise. The hub carrier also differed from that of the Minor, having nylon bushes in the ball pivots at top and bottom. But inboard, each suspension link still ran in a needle roller at the top and rubber at the bottom.

The suspension medium was quite unlike that of any other BMC car, of course. Each unit—one for each wheel—had an inner and an outer cone with the rubber bonded between them. The inner cone was mounted in a strut and the suspension linkage so arranged that the weight of the car, acting along the axis of the strut, tended to force the cones together, in a combination of compression and shear. The actual shapes of the rubber cones and plates had been worked out as a result of extensive research. One of the many advantages that resulted from the use of rubber for these units was that it absorbed shocks very well and consistently. This allowed exceptionally light settings to be used on telescopic dampers specially developed for the Mini by Armstrong. In general these dampers provided very little resistance to low-speed wheel movement, but built up rapidly under high frequency vibration; the valving, however, was arranged to give more normal rebound characteristics. The same principles were used at the back, where each wheel, hub and brake drum was suspended by a sturdy trailing arm mounted in a needle bearing. The roll centre, in this case, was at ground level.

At a relatively late stage in the Mini's development it became obvious that a variety of vehicles could be built to accept the power train, steering and suspension, so they were mounted in subframes which could then be quickly bolted to whatever floorpan was deemed suitable. These were also found to be highly desirable as a result of an intensive 30,000-mile, 75 mph, test run with a prototype which nearly broke up on the rough perimeter track of the local Chalgrove airfield. Cushioning for the subframes—which also distributed the suspension loads over a wider area—helped eliminate these metal fatigue failures.

With hindsight into subsequent developments for racing, it is interesting to note that Issigonis devoted a good deal of thought to the possibility of tying the rear wheels together with a light beam axle to ensure that at all times they would stay parallel to each other and vertical to the car. This system was finally rejected when it was realised that such an axle would take up too much room—room that would otherwise be used for rear seats or luggage. There were also advantages, of course, in each wheel remaining completely independent, such as when one hit a big bump. Care was taken to ensure that the trailing link prevented the wheel displaying anything other than vertical movement. At the same time, the rear wheels were set up with a degree of toe-in (while the front wheels had toe-

Top right: Minivans were far easier to sell in large numbers to commercial users because they were more economical that their chief rivals, the heavier Morris Minor, Austin A35 and Ford 5cwt vans. The Post Office were among customers who could drive hard bargains on special equipment because they bought such large numbers. These pre-production examples were supplied to Post Office specification in 1959 to help win such an order. Money was saved on the very practical rubber back bumpers to reduce the total cost with extras such as secure door latching, Yale locks and anti-theft window grilles for the post box collection model in the first picture *(bottom right)* and the interior shelving, partitioning, and ladder rack for the engineer's van in the second illustration.

Above: In its normal commercial form, the Minivan had a second-skinned floor at the back with the spare wheel slotted in under one side behind the passenger seat, and the battery under the other part of the platform.

Top left: Commercial vans (without windows in the side, behind the driving compartment) were considerably cheaper in 1960 than the equivalent cars because they did not attract compulsory purchase tax. Thus BMC's rear seat conversion, enabling the van to carry as many passengers in comfort as the saloon, was an immediate success with the impecunious. Room was liberated for the seat's footwell by cutting away part of the raised flooring and relocating the spare wheel on the body side in front of the wheelarch.

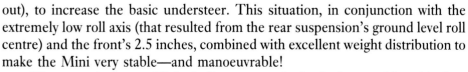

Left: When the van's back seat conversion was fitted the battery occupied a rather untidy place in the opposite side of the body to the spare wheel. But it made a very cheap new 'car' . . .

out), to increase the basic understeer. This situation, in conjunction with the extremely low roll axis (that resulted from the rear suspension's ground level roll centre) and the front's 2.5 inches, combined with excellent weight distribution to make the Mini very stable—and manoeuvrable!

The commitment to 10-inch diameter road wheels that would enable four passengers to be squeezed into the box-like body, meant that the section of the Dunlop tubeless crossply tyres had to be increased from the 4.80 ins visualised, to 5.20 ins. The only other real problem that was encountered during the running gear's development was in braking. The 7-inch by 1.25-inch drums, with leading and trailing shoes all round, proved more than adequate at the back. Their self-servo effect was so great that the rear wheels locked up under the weight transfer associated with heavy breaking. As a result it was decided to take the battery out of the engine compartment and put it in the luggage boot to help keep down the rear wheels and to fit a rear-brake pressure-limiting valve. This Lockheed device ensured that with pedal pressure up to 40 psi—which would be needed to stop the 1,288-lb car in 75 ft from 30 mph—the main line hydraulic pressure would be distributed equally front and rear; above that a plunger cut off further pressure to the back drums, rendering rear-wheel skids unlikely.

The bodyshell, with a front track of 3 ft 11.75 ins, rear of 3 ft 9.875 ins, and overall height of 4 ft 5 ins (which allowed a ground clearance of 6.375 ins), was of simple, but ingenious, design. Double-skinning was kept to a minimum to contain costs and limit the weight to 310 lb. Relatively small box-section sills gave easy access, but proved perfectly adequate (with similar seat-mounting beams) in their job of helping prevent the floorpan from twisting. Wide parcel shelves front and rear, with a deep rear seatback, plus deep pockets beside the rear seats and in the doors, stiffened up the top of the body considerably. A conventional scuttle structure and inner wheelarches did their job so well that in later years it proved practical to replace the welded-on front wings and the bonnet with a one-piece glass fibre moulding. It is interesting to note that only four years earlier it had been considered necessary to have massive screen pillars on a car of such integral construction, whereas now, such was the rigidity of the Mini's basic box (showing a torsional twist figure of 6,500 lb per degree) that it was possible to use far more slender pillars and allow a far greater area of glass. Production costs were minimised by the use of exposed seams where body pressings were spot welded together. This philosophy was carried through to the door hinges, which were bolted on the outside of the skin, rather than concealed in complex boxes. There was an additional advantage here in that the absence of any complicated window winding mechanism or remote control for the door handles meant that more elbow room could be provided in doors of a very slim section. Thus the simple wire cord to operate the door handle and sliding windows were seen as virtues.

The rest of the interior was equally spartan with standard and de luxe models of the Austin Seven or Morris Mini-Minor going into production simultanously for the launch in August 1959. Additional features on the de luxe cars included two-tone leathercloth upholstery and foam rubber cushions, screen washers, pile carpets in place of rubber, an adjuster for the passenger's seat as well as the driver's, hinged instead of fixed rear quarter lights, extra trimmings and an additional ashtray and lamp in the rear seat pockets. Extras for either model included a heater and a radio.

Development continued even as the Mini went into production at Morris's works in Cowley and Austin's at Longbridge. Before the end of 1959 the radiator cowl had been split for easier access, a pivoting quadrant fitted to the handbrake to ease the cable's operation, and the steering action had been improved by increasing the castor angle from 1.5 degrees to 3. The quality of the trim was improved, with new, more secure, window catches early in 1960. The trim was tidied further with padding around the instrument cluster and in the doors and side panels. The shock absorber action was made smoother and the fuel tank fitted with a drain plug. This was necessary because all petrol contains an element of water which tends to lay at the bottom of the tank. It was this moisture that was being blamed for a spate of misfiring.

More major developments centered on what you could hang on the back of a basic Mini engine module and driving compartment. In the spring the first Mini variant was introduced, this was a van, although the British Army had been testing prototype Mini jeeps—later to become the Moke—since October the previous year. The Mokes used a special floor pressing and had only six inches ground clearance to ensure good handling on normal roads. Naturally the Army found this something of a handicap off the road, but the theory at first was that the four soldiers who could be transported in this vehicle could easily shoulder it and carry it over rough terrain. This did not always work out well because they had to carry a lot of rations and weapons in addition to 2.5 cwt of Moke! But the trials went on for a long time, including attempts to float the Moke down from planes by parachute. This did not work out very well either because the Moke's flat floorpan displayed less than perfect aerodynamics for a well-controlled descent. Great things were expected also of the traction that would ensue from having the Moke's engine over its front wheels—but the weight of four fully-equipped squaddies in the back was so great that the wheels became too lightly loaded for a good take-off on a slippery hill.

Meanwhile the more conventional Minivan became a great success. A new extended floorpan incorporated a 4-inch longer wheelbase at 7 ft 0.15 ins, with additional room behind the rear axle line taking the overall length to 10 ft 9.875 ins from 10 ft. The van, with its flat floor swaged for strength, was to prove particularly attractive for commercial use not only through its economy of operation but because it had an exceptionally low load height of 1 ft 5.5 ins. The spare wheel, stowed in the boot of the saloon, was moved to a new position, slotted between the load platform and the main floorpan on the nearside of the vehicle, with the battery in a similar position opposite. The space under the load platform behind the rear axle line was then occupied by a new bolster-type fuel tank. Overall, the flat floor which topped off this lot measured 4 ft 7 ins long by 4 ft 5.75 ins at its widest point, giving 46 cu/ft of cargo space and another 12 cu/ft if the option of a passenger seat was not taken up. The rigidity lost by the necessary deletion of the saloon's rear bulkhead and parcel shelf was amply compensated for by the resultant box sectioning of the floor. Features which now seem odd included a flap in the roof, taken from the Austin A35 van, for ventilation as there were, of course, no side windows. The van was also fitted with a rear door divided in the middle rather than the more conventional one-piece pressing. Although the divided door cost more to make and offered few advantages, if any, in operation, it was invaluable to BMC in that it saved 2 ft on the nose-to-tail production line as vans were assembled with their doors open.

These Minivans were an instant success, not only with commercial users, but with private owners, too, as no purchase tax had to be paid. This reduced the price from £510 or more according to the trim of a saloon, to only £360 for the very austere van, which had a stamped-in grille at the front in place of the saloon's more ornate separate fitting.

The spartan appeal of the van was heightened when BMC marketed a conversion kit that made it nearly as good as a saloon. In this case the load platform was pared away at the front to provide a footwell, with a folding bench seat to take passengers in the back. The spare wheel was then bolted to the inside body panels along with the battery, which had been given a neat fibre cover. The only problem with this new, even more economical, form of transport, apart from the obvious lack of visibility in the back, was that such vehicles were restricted to 40 mph by law—leading to a spate of speeding convictions!

BMC were also very cheeseparing with their trim to keep down the price, fitting twin wing mirrors as required by law, but deleting the far more useful interior mirror to save money. The overall weight of the Minivan remained about the same as the saloon, the lack of trim making up for the extra metal. Nevertheless, the rear suspension was stiffened to cope with loads of up to 5 cwt including the driver, and the tail always rode slightly higher than that of a saloon when the van was unladen.

The estate car version of the Mini which followed in October 1960 was quite naturally based on the van and weighed about 1 cwt more, at 11.5 cwt, because it was trimmed to the higher level of the saloon. It also had a wooden frame glued on the outside of the metal panels behind the front door line. This

Right: The Mini Traveller, or Countryman, depending on whether it was a Morris or an Austin, version of the van was far more upmarket. It had side windows and saloon car furnishings, and normally came with the de luxe trim, including overriders and chromed radiator grille. It also had two wing mirrors (of legal necessity in Britain) and an interior mirror, which BMC insisted on making an extra because there was no law saying a car must have one if it had wing mirrors! BMC's sales people also insisted on it having wooden trim like the popular Morris Minor Traveller to emphasise its social desirability.

was to make it look like the Morris Minor Traveller which needed this traditional wooden framework to support its body panels. In fact, the Morris version was called the Mini Traveller, with the Austin-badged variant adopting the marque's traditional Countryman model name. BMC's salesmen had managed to convince the management that gentry would not buy a dual purpose car which looked too much like a van fitted with windows! The sliding windows of the new Mini estate made the interior much less claustrophobic, and were generally considered a good thing—so much so that the salespeople's fears were to prove groundless! Such windows could also be fitted to the Minivan, but meant that purchase tax would have to be paid, as they usually found their way into vans only when this element of the price had been reduced by a sharp decline in the secondhand value. The estate was a lot more comfortable inside than the van in keeping with its higher price of £623 including purchase tax, although it still lacked an interior mirror as standard!

Left: BMC's Sales Department reasoned that a Mini estate without the woodwork would look too much like a van, but had to accede to public demand for just such a model at a slightly lower price, and much to the amusement of the designer, Sir Alec Issigonis, who was against all forms of superficial styling . . .

The spare wheel and battery were now located under the rear floor where the fuel tank had been fitted in the van. A saloon-car-style tank was fitted, therefore, in the nearside rear flank, complete with trimming, which reduced the minimum overall width to 3 ft 5 ins. The weight distribution was also altered from 61.3 per cent front/38.7 per cent rear for the saloon to 55.4/44.6 for the estate, making the stiffer rear suspension shared with the van a necessity. The load carrying ability of the estate was much the same as that of the van, however; 18.5 cu/ft remaining in the back for nearly 1 cwt of luggage even when the seats were fully occupied by four adults. The overall effect of the estate was far more attractive than that of the van, with fully-carpeted hinged floor panels and side and roof lining. All these fittings made the estate—which shared a 0.5-inch

Above: left and right: The interior of the Mini estate was exceptionally neat featuring a carpeted platform to conceal the spare wheel and battery under the floor. The car illustrated is a partially-completed pre-production model with tape protecting its chrome bumpers and no securing frame for the battery.

higher roofline with the van—far more civilised. The way in which its padding reduced the drumming associated with the bare metal box back of the van was quite noticeable.

Meanwhile considerable problems had arisen with early Minis through water leaking into the interior through the sills because their joints had been lapped the wrong way. The official excuse for not detecting this defect before the car went into production was that the summer of 1959 had been exceptionally dry—but it didn't really hold water when you realised that such development had actually been taking place in 1958! The real reason was that Mini development had been rushed and it cost BMC a great deal to retool for a new floorpan with the sill lapping reversed to keep out the water spraying up from the road wheels. A foam filling which set rigidly was also introduced at the same time to combat the water problem.

Seat belt anchorages were fitted in anticipation of new safety legislation and to help boost profits by the sale of seat belts as extras. A distributor shield was placed behind the radiator grille as a final cure for the misfiring which occurred when a Mini's ignition system was soaked by spray from a vehicle in front or by driving rain. The shock absorber mountings were also reinforced and, oddly, years later, the 1959 and early 1960 saloon cars became in great demand from racing Mini constructors because the bodyshells were lighter! Other changes in 1960 included a change from square splines on the drive shafts to ones which curved inwards to reduce wear, a neater air cleaner, larger front wheel bearings and a cranked gear-leaver to counter complaints from some quarters that only an ape could drive a Mini in comfort . . .

The final work associated with the introduction of the initial range of Minis was completed when a pick-up version of the van went into production in April 1961. This popular little vehicle followed the pattern of the van closely with a bulkhead behind the cabin which helped restore the rigidity lost by cutting off the roof and top half of the sides from a point behind the side doors' rear pillars. Lapped and gusseted side panels completed the rear cargo area with a drop-down rear platform for loading and extra carrying capacity. A canvas tilt—the

Above left/right and opposite: The Mini range was supplemented in 1960 by a new pick-up version of the van for those who needed to transport bulky items. Apart from a truncated cabin, it was supplied with a drop-down tailgate and a tilt, so named after the rudimentary, lean-to shed-like covering on some horse-drawn trailers and typified by the hoods on Western pioneers' wagons. Happily, knowledge of aerodynamics had progressed along with cars and the framed tilt was so well designed and made that it was well able to survive the rigours of Mini pick-up work.

commercial description for a hood—with a detachable tubular frame was provided as a standard fitting with two front seats.

Finally a fine new fresh-air heater was phased in on the De Luxe that went a long way towards alleviating the eternal misting up of earlier Minis fitted with an antique 1950s heater which merely recirculated the air already inside the car.

III

The Mini-Cooper

No sooner had enthusiastic drivers realised that the Mini could be cornered far faster than anything like it before, than tuning firms began offering conversions of all descriptions to improve the performance. Sales of this equipment boomed to such an extent that the factory could hardly ignore the potential—and it took little persuasion for BMC to put a high-performance model, the Mini-Cooper, in to production in July 1961, despite the misgivings of their original designer, Alex Issigonis. This car proved so successful in competition, as well as in the marketplace, that other versions followed, culminating in the sensational Cooper S types from 1963. In turn, these homologation specials (cars produced in small

Right: Ready to go and taxed for a year, the Mini-Cooper with its distinctive wide-slatted radiator grille (in Morris form) and Super bumpers started a trend in August 1961 for small sporting saloons that was to all but extinguish the traditional open sports car. Standard colour schemes included a roof panel in white or black to contrast with the basic colour of the bodywork.

numbers primarily to circumnavigate international competition rules)—created such a demand that they, too, went into full production.

The idea was first mooted by world champion racing car constructor John Cooper, who had been running BMC A-series engines in Formula Junior—the equivalent of today's Formula Three. He suggested building 1,000 special Minis with 1,000 cc engines to take advantage of the knowledge gained in Formula

Left: The Mini-Cooper's power output was increased partly by the use of a long centre-branch exhaust manifold and twin heat-shielded SU carburettors, equipped on early examples with wire mesh air filters. The cable tucked between the carburettors ran from the gearbox to be connected to the speedometer when the unit was installed in the bodyshell. The remote control gearchange with its long alloy casing, which helped steady the engine in the shell, can be seen clearly, with the small disc brakes that replaced the drums on the front suspension.

Left: The Mini-Cooper featured a number of minor underbonnet changes not directly allied to the more powerful engine, which has been fitted with an optional chromed rocker cover in this case. The ignition coil was resited on top of the dynamo to make room for an underbonnet starting button in its former place on the bell housing. This button—a boon to mechanics working alone on the engine—had been displaced, in turn, by the trunking seen on the left of the picture for the new fresh-air heater, the on-off heater circulation valve of which was now operated by the light-coloured cable from inside the car. The windscreen washer bottle was also moved to a spot near the wiper motor.

Above: The Mini-Cooper's disc front brakes, although criticised later for inefficiency, offered a great advance in stopping power over the drums of their day. The caliper shown on the left of the disc operated from a position ahead of the axle line.

Junior and qualify the model for competition in international touring car races. Cooper pointed out that it would be a relatively simple exercise to bore out the engine, raise the compression ratio and fit twin carburettors with more radical camshaft timing. Conversions marketed to provide the Mini with a remote gearchange like the A40 and Morris Minor had been selling well, and made gearchanging easier and more precise, so Cooper was keen on that as standard. The brakes would have to be uprated, so he suggested fitting discs at the front. Obviously such a car would cost more, so once the idea had been approved by the BMC board, they went along with the suggestions for a more luxurious interior and two-tone paintwork to take the new Mini upmarket.

Cooper's car company worked out that to achieve a desirable 85 mph straightline speed in a reasonably short time, the Mini they would need 55 bhp from 1 litre—which was not over-ambitious considering they were getting 82–3 bhp at the time from Formula Junior engines. Once these engines had passed the 70 bhp mark during development, however, they had needed a new crankshaft, so the Mini-Cooper to be was built around a shaft of stronger than standard specification. The cylinder bores presented problems in production when they were bored out, so—as the engine needed a new crankshaft in any case—a longer throw unit was designed, increasing the stroke from 68.26 mm to 81.28 mm. In this form, the bore could be reduced from 62.94 mm to 62.43 mm to allow a greater safety margin and still raise the capacity to 997 cc. Highly-tuned standard-specification 848 cc engines had shown a tendency to shatter their timing gears due to the torsional vibration problems above 6,000 rpm—or at least wear out the gears very quickly—so the new engine was fitted with a damper to make such high revs safer. It also had an oilway drilled into the crank

Right: Inside the Mini-Cooper, the superior specification carpets became standard with the central speedometer surrounded by a water temperature gauge on the left and oil pressure dial on the right, the contents of the fuel tank being recorded in the slot at the bottom of the speedometer face. The radio fitted to the car illustrated shows one of the compromises needed for in-car entertainment in the early Mini. Sir Alec Issigonis did not approve of radios in a car, so he did not provide an obvious space in which to locate a receiver! The new remote control gearlever is also illustrated along with plastic extensions to bring the tips of the lighting and wiper switches within reach of a finger. These were very popular with the owners of mark I Minis.

Left: This is a 1961 studio shot of the Mini-Cooper's luggage boot, showing the new detachable estate car-style carpeted platform, but not the tip of the shock absorber mounting because the subframe had not yet been raised into place in this pre-production car! The bootlid, which had been formerly lined by the Mini's rubber boot mat, was now fitted with fibre backing.

and lead indium bearings to better withstand high revs. Domed pistons were used to raise the compression ratio from 8.3:1 to 9:1 with revised cylinder head porting to give better breathing on twin 1.25-inch SU carburettors. The exhaust system was also reworked with a larger bore and three-branch tubular manifold. A 948-coded camshaft was adopted with 0.312 ins of lift against 0.280 ins and larger inlet valves using double valve springs to extend to safe rev range to 6,000 rpm. This head and valve gear had been developed in parallel with requirements for the new mark 11 Austin-Healey Sprite and Mark 1 MG Midget. The extra 16 bhp (an overall 55) was achieved at 6,000 rpm with a rise in torque from 44 lb/ft to 55 at 3,600 rpm.

The final drive remained the same at 3.765:1, but the intermediate ratios were raised to, overall, 12.05 (against 13.657), 7.21 (8.176), 5.11 (5.317), to make better use of the increased power and torque. The top gear ratio could remain the same because of the new engine's ability to cope with higher revs. Cooper's centrally-located gear change was mounted in an aluminium extension casing with a short, stiff lever between the front seats.

Lockheed developed new small 7-inch diameter disc brakes to fit within the front wheels, which increased the effective breaking area from 55 to 157 sq ins— and was servo-boosted, the rear brake pressure-limiting valve being retained in modified form with standard drums. Later, in March 1963, these brakes were beefed up and a lower pressure rear anti-lock valve fitted from July 1964.

The body was little changed from that of the earlier Minis, a new duo-tone paint scheme, with the roof in a contrasting colour, providing immediate identification, along with a distinctive slatted grille. Inside, a new vinyl-coated material was used with a redesigned instrument panel in which a water temperature gauge was mounted on the left and an oil pressure gauge on the right. The interior lamp was moved from the instrument panel to the roof to make way. Strangely, a rev counter was not offered, even as a factory extra, suggested maximum speed change-up points being marked on the speedometer at 28 mph, 47 mph and 72 mph. Corresponding figures for the standard 848 cc car were 23, 38 and 58. A great deal of extra sound deadening material was used in the interior and around the wheel arches, with a 16-blade radiator cooling fan to help combat criticism that Minis were incredible 'buzz boxes'.

IV
Super Minis

Naturally there was a considerable demand for a more luxurious Mini than the normal De Luxe, along the lines of a Cooper, but without the modifications made purely to increase its performance. This demand was met by the introduction of the Super model with a broadly similar interior and paint scheme to that of the Cooper, in August 1961. Like the Cooper, the Super had detail improvements, such as levers to open the doors from the inside (in place of cords), carpets rather than rubber mats and a carpeted luggage boot floor. It also had the extra soundproofing and a fresh slatted grille. The 16-blade fan made such a difference to the engine's whirr that it became standard throughout the range, the basic Mini and the De Luxe being little changed otherwise apart from having a plated grille instead of a painted one. Key-start ignition was also introduced on the top models and all cars were fitted with stronger steel road wheels after a spate of breakages on hard-pressed racing versions which

Left: For a short while, from August 1961, the Super version of the Mini with slatted grille and vestigial nudge bars on the bumpers, became the most luxurious Mini. Like the Cooper, it also had a two-tone colour scheme and smart new wheel trims.

threatened to give the road cars a bad name. Less brittle cast alloy suspension trumpets were fitted from May 1961.

Two months later, in October 1961, a completely new upmarket line in Minis appeared with the Riley Elf and Wolseley Hornet. Like the Austin and Morris Minis, these variants were almost identical except for detail trim and distinctive new upright radiator grilles. The new grilles lifted up in company with their bonnet and although they represented an attractive styling exercise, they did little for engine access and frequently proved a hindrance to people working underneath. Bangs on the head became the price to pay for being fashion conscious. Stronger bumpers like those on BMC's bigger saloons were fitted front and rear with additional embellishments, such as a chromium-plated waist strip, window frames, bright wing trims, and bigger hub caps.

The big difference at the back, apart from a wraparound bumper, was that there was now a recognisable squared-off boot that made the cars 8.5 ins longer than standard. The capacity of this new boot was 6 cu ft—enough to cover a large suitcase and various odds and ends. The bootlid now lifted up, rather than dropped down to provide a similar platform area. The overall carrying capacity, therefore, remained virtually the same, except that bulky luggage culd now be made more secure. To be fair, BMC were quite justified in not encouraging owners to carry a great deal more luggage lest they upset the balance of such a small car.

The Mini-Cooper style colour schemes were adopted outside, and the interiors were much plusher with better-padded leather-faced seats. A full-width wooden dashboard contained lockers on either side of the Elf, the slightly-cheaper Hornet retaining an instrument panel more like the Super. Better

Right: Inside the Super, which had the Cooper-style instrumentation and key-start ignition, the standard door-pull cords were replaced by small chrome-plated levers. They were a mixed blessing, often catching the elbows or clothing of the unwary.

Left: Soon after the Super had been introduced, the far more upmarket Wolseley Hornet and Riley Elf arrived with restyled front and back, far superior trim and stronger bumpers. Oddly, these cars did not have overriders at first—possibly to give them a more elegant appearance. They also featured additional chrome embellishment round the waistline and an ashtray with a lid, plus, for the first time on a standard Mini, a bonnet lock. Early cars had the gutter strip removed from the front wings to present a smoother line, in keeping with the sleek new rear wings. By April 1962, however, these mark I models had reverted to the standard gutter strip at the front and were fitted with substantial overriders.

Left: The Riley Elf cost slightly more than its close cousin, the Wolseley Hornet, chiefly because it promoted more extravagant colour schemes. But, in essence, it was almost exactly the same as the Wolseley, although it was sold through a different chain of dealers.

Above left/right: In January 1963, uprated editions of the Riley Elf and Wolseley Hornet (illustrated) were announced, featuring a new 998-cc engine and twin leading shoe front brakes, the boot lid now having a counter-balancing mechanism in place of the earlier pop-in-place stay. They also carried chrome strip denoting them as mark II models.

Right: The dummy radiator grille lifted up with the bonnet of the Riley Elf and Wolseley Hornet (shown here) with a bracing stay remaining in place across the front of the engine compartment. Underbonnet accessability was certainly not for the unwary!

quality carpet was used on both new models and the doors had carpet lining to help reduce drumming. Various items, such as the gearlever—still the original Mini 'bent walking stick' rather than the Cooper's remote change—were chromium-plated.

Overall, these changes raised the weight by 190 lb to 1520 lb, with the result that, at first, the Elf and Hornet were slower than standard Minis and the braking ability more marginal when coping with the 14 per cent increase.

Meanwhile development on the standard Minis began to catch up, with larger brake cylinders being fitted to all models from January 1962, cloth upholstery replacing vyanide in March, and the De Luxe and Super being effectively combined as the Super de Luxe with a new grille and over-riders and improved trim in October. For some time, an estate without the glued-on wooden side frames had been marketed abroad. This was now introduced on the home market at the same time, at a slightly lower price than the normal estate car option. Austin versions of the Mini, which had been called the Seven, now became simply the Mini.

Warranty claims on Mini transmissions reached historic heights and cost BMC nearly all their early profits on the range. The real trouble sprang from the fact that, for economic reasons, the Mini initially had to inherit the gear sets from the Austin A35 and with them synchromesh that was not strong enough; there was also a problem with an oil seal which had not been specified at a sufficiently high quality. The synchromesh—which had proved perfectly adequate in the A35—now had to overcome the inertia of additional gearwheels in the Mini, which was its undoing. Not surprisingly, it could also be over-ridden very easily, especially in the highly-stressed second ratio. Therefore, Mini gearboxes often 'went' in second gear before the end of their warranty period, with dire consequences for BMC who had to finance rebuilds. Various solutions were tried, including improving the gearchange mechanism inside and outside the box, in the hope that a more precise action would help the synchromesh to last longer. But the fundamental weakness of having constant-load synchromesh over-rode these stopgap solutions. In the end there was nothing for it but to redesign the gearbox to a generally stronger specification, with baulk-ring synchromesh which was introduced in October 1961.

The overhanging clutch had also led indirectly to lubrication problems. It created as much as 25 psi centrifugal force against the oil seal at the end of the crankshaft, which, in time—usually between 17,000 and 22,000 miles on hard-driven Minis, and sometimes within the 12-month warranty period—could cause the seal to give way. Oil was then sprayed on the clutch linings, costing either the owner, or BMC, unnecessary expense. This well-known fault also hit the value of secondhand Minis and led to extensive heart-searching at BMC. Eventually the trouble was cured in December 1962 by spending 1 shilling (5p) on a Deva metal bush that needed no lubrication, rather than 4 pence (less than 2p) on the existing seal, which required an oil passage in the crankshaft. The Deva bush 'dry' crank saved everybody a fortune, although it must be realised that the only way the Mini's cost had been kept so low initially was by very tight

Top left/right:
The interior appointments of the Super de Luxe, which replaced the Super and the De Luxe models in October 1962, included better quality vyanide upholstery *(opposite right),* sun visors mounted on massive chrome-plated brackets, and lidded front ashtrays with substantial metal door pulls and kickplates.

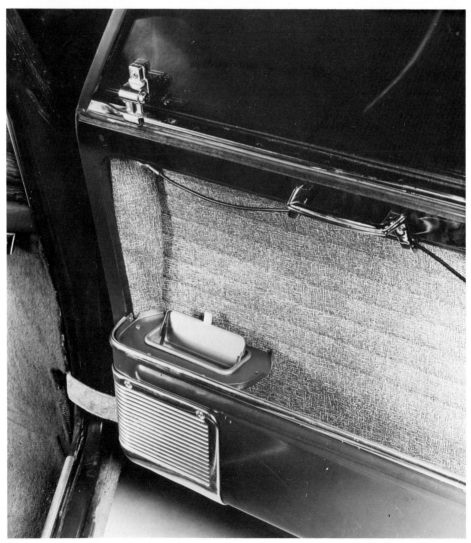

budget control. The transmission trouble on early Minis well illustrated how critical was the dividing line between cost and effectiveness.

More obvious faults, such as snapping exhaust systems, were cured by fitting stronger engine stabilising bar mounts and tougher clamps between the downpipe and the manifold that were better able to resist the engine's natural rocking movement on and off the power.

Soon after, in January 1963, complaints that the Elf and Hornet were too slow were countered by the introduction of a new 998-cc engine which was quite different in detail from the 997-cc Cooper unit. This engine had a bore and stroke of 64.58 mm by 83.72 mm—making it a much 'squarer' unit than that of the Cooper—and was resultantly better able to withstand high revs. It produced, in single-carburettor, 8.3:1 compression form, 38 bhp at 5,250 rpm with 52 lb/ft of torque at 2,700 rpm. The extra 4 bhp and 8 lb/ft of torque over the 848 cc engine restored the performance of the Elf and Hornet. It made observers wonder why, despite its revving ability, BMC had gone to so much trouble to build a different engine with virtually the same capacity as the Cooper. This was because there was ample spare production capacity for crankshafts of the new unit's 3-inch stroke and very little for the 3.2-inch stroke Cooper.

Wider front brake drums and twin leading shoes were also fitted to the Elf and Hornet at the same time to cope with their increased performance. These models were then given a Mark II designation.

Finally, in February 1964, the arc of all Mini windscreen wipers was reduced from 130 degrees to 120 to avoid fouling the windscreen's rubber seal.

Development of the Mini Moke—which had been shown in public for the first time in March 1962—was continuing in an attempt to sell it as a fighting vehicle. Generally it foundered on poor ground clearance and construction which appeared flimsy against the high-selling, but far heavier, Land-Rover. Its case received fresh impetus, however, when the experimental department at Longbridge built a twin-engined version with a 948-cc engine and transmission at the front and an 848-cc unit with steering locked in the straight-ahead position at the back. Rods and levers provided a remote gearchange beside the driver from the rear unit. The clutches and accelerators were linked, however. Thus the driver had a gear lever for each hand, separate ignition and starter switch for each engine, which could be run either together or independently, but only a single clutch and accelerator pedal. The road surface provided an adequate way of co-ordinating the individual engine's power outputs! This amazing machine proved to have a mind-boggling ability to scramble over difficult surfaces providing they were not too rough—but still they did not catch on with any of the armed forces which evaluated it, along with conventional front-engined only Mokes. The even more versatile Austrian Haflinger, which had inferior straight-line performance, but far greater ground clearance, met their requirements.

BMC then decided to cut development losses by introducing the Moke in conventional 848-cc single-engined form on the normal consumer market. It was launched as something of a flop in Britain in March 1964 and continued in

Opposite right and below: The Mini Moke that went into production in basic form in Britain between 1964 and 1968 (first picture) was to inspire all manner of glass fibre copies before continuing in production abroad and eventually in Australia with wider 12-inch diameter wheels (second picture), 'roo bar, roll cages and high-backed seats. Relatively few Mokes were made, but they achieved a fanatical following and command high prices today.

production at Longbridge only until October 1968—with 90 per cent of the 14,518 sold going for export to countries with warm climates where it could be used as an open-air taxi or a very light truck. The situation in Britain had not been encouraged by the Customs and Excise's refusal to classify the Moke as a commercial vehicle (like the van and pick-up), and thus free it from purchase tax. Once production had ceased in Britain it was transferred to Australia, and eventually Portugal, where it continued to be a low-volume option in the Mini range into the 1980s.

V

The All-Elastic Minis

Issigonis had been experimenting with a novel form of hydraulic suspension for at least seven years before the Mini came out—but he could not introduce it in the Mini at first because it needed more development to bring down the cost. It was a close-run thing, however, and eventually his new Hydrolastic suspension, developed by Alec Moulton and Dunlop, who had been responsible for the Mini's rubber doughnuts, made its appearance on the Austin and Morris 1100—larger versions of the Mini—in 1962.

It was then only a matter of time before this form of suspension found its way into the Mini, such was the power of Issigonis's authority. The eventual introduction had to be delayed until October 1964 when the new suspension units had been made small enough to fit in the Mini's existing sub-frames with hardly any modification. To have retooled the body and sub-frames for a new suspension would have been far too expensive.

Such were the apparent virtues of the Hydrolastic system that it was launched with a fanfare as 'The Suspension With The Big Car Ride'. In essence, it was intended to damp out the over-progressive action of the Mini's rubber doughnuts and dispense with shock absorbers at the same time! It still used rubber as the springing medium and linked either end of the car by transmitting a special fluid to the suspension units at each wheel through pipes. The fluid contained roughly equal proportions of water and anti-freeze with some rust inhibitor, and, at the insistence of the Customs and Excise, an additive to make it undrinkable! More seriously, the intention was to make the fluid resistant to changes in temperature, and BMC were notably successful in this sphere. The advantage here was that there had been continuing problems with conventional dampers overheating in their overworked capacity in the Mini, which was already gaining a reputation for having a rather choppy ride. The virtue of the new Hydrolastic suspension was seen as an advanced form of pitch control by means of a fluid connection between the front and rear suspension units on each side of the car.

Each Hydrolastic unit was, in essence, a cylinder with its lower end closed by a rubber diaphragm and its upper end closed by a doughnut rubber spring like that used in the original Mini. Half way up the cylinder was a partition which

Right: The new Hydrolastic suspension for the Mini—pictured here roughly assembled with Cooper components on a jig in BMC's experimental workshop—was launched with a great fanfare, but proved too expensive in the long run for a cheap economy machine such as the Mini. The piping connecting the front and rear suspension units can be seen clearly in this photograph along with the smaller-diameter brake pipes, the fuel pump in the left-hand side of the rear subframe and the back suspension's tensioning springs on top of the radius arms.

Left and below:
There were detail differences beneath the bonnets of manual and automatic Minis, with the manual Wolseley Hornet version in the first picture showing a different air cleaner and more standard ancilliary attachments than the automatic Riley Elf made in the same year (1967) which has, of course, no separate clutch hydraulics and a re-shaped bell housing.

located a damper valve. In the middle of the doughnut spring there was an orifice leading to a pipe connecting the Hydrolastic unit to its corresponding unit at the other end of the car, the links being fore-and-aft rather than diagonal. The whole system was filled with the special fluid, and the action of this

Right: The compact dimensions of the main components in the Mini's automatic transmission were emphasised by this exploded diagram.

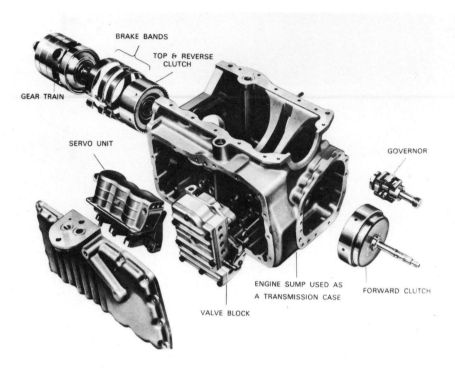

Above: The automatic transmission—in a Riley in this case—was operated from a neat quadrant on the floor which gave a change-ratio lever that allowed either fully-automatic selection or manual override.

springing medium was as follows: when a front wheel went over a bump, the wheel's linkage, acting against the lower diaphragm, forced the fluid in the lower part of the cylinder through the damper valve, which ironed out most of the shock, and forced the rubber doughnut upwards, causing it to act as a spring. A portion of the displaced fluid was then forced along the connecting pipe to enter the rear Hydrolastic unit, jacking up the back suspension slightly, and thereby levelling the car . . . and, in theory, giving it a pitch-free ride.

There had to be some compromises in the spring and damper rates, however, and the Mini was duly fitted with tension springs at the back to provide further damping. This was because of the considerable difference in weight distribution when a car was carrying only a driver, and when it had four passengers. All Minis—with the exception of the heavy load-carrying vans, estates, pick ups and Moke—then received the much-vaunted new suspension.

Nevertheless, the attitude change when the saloons were fully laden was such that the headlights pointed into the air at an unacceptable angle and the system was never allowed into Germany as a result. This tail-down attitude—which was also apparent on hard-accelerating Coopers—was reduced by as much as 50 per cent by fitting stiffer rear compensating springs in December 1964. Early Hydrolastic Minis were also more conscious of outside temperatures and wheel activity than the makers liked to admit. This made them squeak as they went over bumps vigorously, although the condition was soon alleviated by a minor design change to the Hydrolastic damper valves.

Experience with hard-pressed rally cars also led to much stronger gearboxes being fitted to Minis made after October 1964, along the lines of units

Above left and right: The Wolseley Hornet (first picture) and the Riley Elf lost their exposed door hinges in October 1966, this mark III example also featuring air inlets in the front wings (second picture) with horizontal slats operating in conjunction with the new fascia vents.

which had also made their appearance in the Coopers. The object of the changes was to reduce internal friction and consequent overheating of the lubricating oil. This was achieved by reducing the pitch diameter of the gears; in other words, the gear diameters remained the same, but the teeth were bigger and stronger, although there were fewer of them. The helix angle was also reduced to cut down end thrust. Second and third constant mesh gears now ran on needle rollers rather than bronze bushes, while the roller bearings for the idler wheel, first motion shaft and lay gear were now caged to prevent the rollers from skewing and creating friction. Better change-speed forks with an increased contact area were were adopted at the same time to cut down on crunching. Most new cars were also going over to diaphragm spring clutches, so the Mini followed suit to take advantage of the lighter operating load and greater torque capacity of these units. A superior scroll-type oil seal was also substituted on the primary gear from January 1965.

At this time, all Minis were to receive the key starter (which meant that they had to have a starter solenoid, too) and were equipped with a warning light to show when the oil filter became clogged. All standard brakes were now uprated to the 1.5-inch wide Elf and Hornet units. Minor changes also included an interior light which came on when a door was opened, crushable sun visors and a plastic-frame driving mirror—all in the interests of safety. The price went up, too, but by only 4 per cent, which was a considerable tribute to BMC in their attempts to make all Minis a good deal more sophisticated.

Further afield, BMC subsidiaries, such as that in Australia, were adapting the Mini to meet their own market. By 1966, the Australian Mini De Luxe— always a Morris—had the 998 cc Wolseley Hornet engine as standard. It also had wind-up windows and swivelling quarter lights, the Cooper's remote gearchange, a more reliable mechanical fuel pump than the normal one (which

Above left and right: Inside, the Hornet (in the first picture) continued with the standard Super de Luxe style instrument panel (in wood-veneered trim) while the Riley (fitted with a special steering wheel in the second picture) had the full-width fascia, both manual models receiving the remote Cooper-style gear lever. The revised door trim which accompanied the mark III's wind-up windows can also be seen in the second picture.

was exposed to a lot of road debris), and self-parking windscreen wipers. Their Mini 850, with the 848 cc engine, continued with the dry rubber suspension as the De Luxe went over to Hydrolastic. But the cheaper model still got the Hornet's wider brakes. Both cars had Cooper-style grilles, but the plain hub caps of the most basic British Mini and no tubular over riders like the Super de Luxe. The Australians also stuck with the rubber mats and did not bother changing to the Super de Luxe's instrument panel.

A revolutionary automatic transmission for the Mini was also announced in October 1965 although production did not go ahead for several months. Initial problems were caused by siting production in an elderly factory. The new gearbox used a delicate hydraulic system and had to be assembled in clinically-clean conditions—which the old factory was unable to provide at first. A six-month delay followed while air conditioning was installed but further teething troubles meant that production of the automatic Mini did not start in earnest until the 1967 model year. One of the first problems to arise was that oil surge on fast corners caused the drive to cut out. This was cured by moving the gearbox's oil pump to the centre of the sump. Very few early automatic Minis survived without extensive modifications.

The new transmission was to a design by Automotive Products and manufactured jointly with BMC. It was extremely sophisticated for its day, offering two-pedal motoring with a torque converter replacing the clutch and fully automatic gearchanging. It was exceptionally well suited to small car use because it had four forward ratios to compensate for the relative lack of torque in a small engine. Most automatic units needed a larger engine because they had only three forward ratios. The new unit was made even more attractive in its Mini application because it offered full manual control as well. All gearchanges were made by a single Cooper-style lever on the floor, with a Drive setting for full manual operation, neutral, reverse and the four forward ratios. AP made the hydraulics, filters and special parts, while BMC produced the gears, casing and parts shared with other cars, and assembled them. The new gearbox had to be exceptionally compact to fit in place of the normal transmission and was highly unusual in that it used the engine's lubricant rather than special oil. Instead of the normal epicyclic gear trains used on most automatic transmissions, the new AP design used beval gearing like that of a conventional differential, or, more correctly, two differentials. These operated within each other, and represented the first application of this principle. Vertical helical gearing conveyed the drive down to an input shaft of the four-speed epicyclic unit and final drive pinion. Individual ratios were engaged through brake bands and clutches by means of hydraulic pressure, controlled by a valve block, operated, in turn, by the gear lever. A governor engaged varying ratios as applicable when the lever was in the fully automatic position, with a kick-down override on the accelerator pedal to engage a lower gear instantly for extra acceleration. To make up for the inevitable power loss associated with pumping so much oil around in an automatic transmission, the engines of Minis equipped with this option had a 9:1 compression ratio cylinder head, and a larger MS4 SU carburettor on a new inlet manifold. This gave them a little extra power and torque to make up for the transmission drag.

It remained only for safety bosses to be fitted to the forward facing door handles of all models in January 1966, following a bad accident in which a child was impaled, before a Mark III version of the Elf and Hornet was introduced in October 1966. These cars were of far neater appearance outwardly, having new concealed door hinges and the seams at the back of the body ground-off for flush welding. The sliding windows were also replaced with conventional wind-up windows which did not make the doors much thicker. The additional space was needed, in any case, for the concealed hinges. The outer door handles were also changed to a conventional push-button fitting employed on bigger saloons now that there was more space for the mechanism inside. Adjustable fresh air vents—which had been introduced with great effect on Ford's Cortina—were also provided on either side of the fascia with a superior gearlever rather like that of the Mini-Cooper occupying a place between the seats.

VI

The Mini-Cooper S

Such was the success of the Mini-Cooper in competition that BMC were encouraged to develop it further, with more power, as it had been made obvious that the basically-standard chassis could cope with it. Engine conversions for racing Minis—particularly those marketed by Daniel Richmond, a friend of Issigonis, who ran Downton Engineering—provided consistent race and rally winners. The A-series engine had also been developed to produce much higher power outputs in single-seater racing cars. Most of this work had been in the 1,100 cc stock-block category of Formula Junior, and was continuing in the 1,000 cc Formula Three which replaced it in 1964. It was in this area of development that BMC looked for a more powerful engine for the Mini-Cooper. The only trouble was that the 1,100 cc capacity in which they had the most experience was not particularly beneficial for race or rally cars, which were now running to 1,000 cc and 1,300 cc classes. Care was taken, therefore, to ensure that any new engine could be changed readily to a near-1,000 cc or

Right: The Mini-Cooper S looked like the normal Mini saloon—except for discreet badging and wider, ventilated, wheels shod (in 1963) with Dunlop SP3 radial-ply tyres. It was also sprayed in similar two-tone colours to the normal Mini-Cooper, but—with the new big-bore 1071-cc engine—it was considerably faster. BMC saw its main market with well-heeled sporting enthusiasts, and promoted it as such with airfield settings to emphasise the additional power.

Left and below left: Minis, whether the 1,275-cc 1966 Tulip Rally winner (picture one), or with Gordon Spice at the wheel of one of the last works racers in 1969 (picture two), retained a very standard appearance outwardly because only minimal bodywork changes were allowed under international competition regulations. In any case, keeping the shape as near standard as possible helped promote sales of ordinary Minis.

1,300 cc capacity. The, 1,100 cc capacity had the most going for it initially, however, as that had had the most development.

The basic problem with the mass production A-series engine was that the bore sizes were too small to allow valves of adequate diameter for racing. The only way to remedy this within the external dimensions of the cylinder block was to alter the bore centres. As it happened, the normal A-series block was not machined on the production line, so it was relatively easy to move out the end cylinder centres by 0.125 ins and the inner centres in by the same amount to allow the bores to be enlarged to 70.6 mm to give 1,275 cc on a stroke of 81.33 mm—almost the same as that of the 997 cc Mini-Cooper. The 1,275 cc capacity would be popular in that it allowed a 1 mm increase in bore size for specially-built competition engines without taking out the capacity beyond 1,300 cc. This was the sort of leeway that was needed in preparing such machinery. All four bores were siamesed for production (if that expression can be allowed!). Once the 1,300 cc limitations were established, the lower limit was reached by reducing the stroke to 61.91 mm to give 970 cc—with the same amount of latitude for the preparation of special engines which needed to stay below 1,000 cc. When allied with the original 848 cc engine's stroke of 68.26 mm—which was also used on the Formula Junior engine—the capacity of 1,071 cc was arrived at on the 70.64 mm bore. This would be the first engine option introduced on the new S-for Sport Minis. The big attraction from the production point of view was that the new engines could be machined on the same equipment that was being used for BMC's mass-produced 1100 range of cars.

Right: The servo unit used to assist the more powerful brakes of the Mini-Cooper S is pictured here sited on the left-hand side of the engine compartment of this 1275S model.

Above left: With the introduction of the Mini mark II bodyshell, the Cooper S followed suit, carrying the same distinctive 'square' rear lights and bumpers devoid of nudge bars. Twin fuel tanks—one on each side of the tail—were now standard, along with a neat little badge on the right of the bootlid bearing the legend 1275. A new style of more aggressive badging was adopted front and rear for the mark II models, however.

Above right: Ventilated steel disc wheels stayed with the standard Mini-Cooper S throughout its production life, but . . .

Left: Owners frequently substituted aluminium alloy wheels, such as these bearing the brand name GB. They adopted the familiar pattern of the much more expensive Minilite magnesium wheels used on works cars, and were made by a cycle accessory firm run by former international rally star Gerry Burgess.

Apart from having crankshafts of differing throw, all five engines (the 1,100-cc Formula Junior, the 1,000-cc Formula Three, and the 970, 1071 and 1275-cc S types), were identical in design, although the 1275 needed a taller cylinder block to accommodate its long stroke, and 970-cc connecting rods (which were 0.125 ins longer) to push its pistons to the top of the 1071 cc block. All of them had a magnificent new crankshaft which was much stiffer than normal and made from high-grade EN40B steel, nitride-hardened by none other than Rolls-Royce. They were fitted with enormous 2-inch big end bearings, the same diameter as the main bearings, so that there was plenty of capacity to withstand a new 7,200-rpm limit on the long-stroke units. The short-stroke engines ran up to 7,800pm without entering dangerous vibration periods, but a torsional damper was fitted—just in case.

The mass-production A-series engines had big ends split at 45 degrees at the axis of the rod, and big end bearings which were considerably offset from the centre line of the cylinder. The S-type big ends were split straight across to give a stiffer and more stable bearing support. The width of the main bearing was narrowed from 1.063 ins on the 948-cc engine to 1 in, to reduce the offset which remained even after the cylinder centres had been moved. It had been found that with engines equipped with offset bearings, nearly all the load was carried by the portion directly below the shank and that the offset part became a passenger which acted as little more than a distance piece. The chief cause of this condition was lack of rigidity, of course, but some improvement was made by off-setting the big end bolts as well so that they fell halfway along the bearing.

Overall, these changes made room for inlet valves of 1.40 ins diameter and 1.219-inch exhaust valves—33 per cent and 52 per cent bigger than before. They were very expensive, being made of Nimonic 80, a heat-resistant nickel-based alloy originally developed for gas turbine use, with stems that had welded-on stellite tips to resist rocker wear. The cylinder head, distinguished by an extra securing nut and bolt, was designed around a revised port shape to give the best air flow. Differences in power between the five engines stemmed from camshaft design, compression ratio, manifolding and carburettors and eventually fuel injection with an eight-port head. The 1,100-cc Formula Junior engine, the prototype of the series, produced 98 bhp on a twin-choke Weber carburettor with 89 bhp from the early Formula Three engine, which had a compulsory inlet restrictor of 36 mm.

Using a fairly mild AEA630 camshaft like that of the 997-cc Cooper, the first S-type engine, the 1,071 cc, provided a good spread of torque between 3,000 rpm and 5,000 rpm peaking at 62 lb/ft at 4,500 rpm. This made the new car much more tractible than previous highly-tuned Minis and better suited to rallying as a result. The engine produced 70 bhp at 6,200 rpm on twin 1.25-inch SU carburettors to much-improved overall performance. Lubrication was also improved by enlarging the oil galleries and fitting a competition oil pump with a 75-psi pressure relief spring. An oil cooler was offered as an extra.

In standard form this 1071S Mini-Cooper, introduced in April 1963, had the normal 3.77:1 Cooper final drive with intermediate ratios of 5.1, 7.21 and

12.04. An optional 3.44:1 final drive raised these ratios to 4.67, 6.59 and 11.02, with close-ratio boxes using a 3.77 final drive giving intermediates of 4.67, 6.7 and 9.66, and a 3.44 final drive producing 4.27, 6.13 and 8.84. Detail changes were made to several gearbox components to strengthen them for competition. Needle rollers were used for the second and third mainshaft gears and an Ina bearing on the idler and first motion shaft. The standard clutch was also modified by fitting bonded linings and double springs to better withstand prolonged high-speed running and absorb the extra torque.

The brakes were much improved by increasing the disc diameter from 7 ins to 7.5 ins and the thickness of the discs from 0.25 ins to 0.375 ins. This not only increased the swept friction area from 104 sq in to 120 sq in, but meant that the greater mass of metal was able to absorb 80 per cent more heat—proving that much more resistant to face. Harder grade pads and linings were fitted in

Left: Although Mini-Cooper S competition cars remained much the same outwardly, they differed dramatically under the skin, and were far from standard inside. This 1966 works rally car, the Hopkirk Monte Carlo machine, has a radically revised dash carrying, principally, a rev counter in front of the driver, numerous extra switches for the auxilliary lighting, and—in front of the navigator—a Halda Tripmaster to help his calculations. The accelerator pedal has been enlarged to help heel and toe control and a standard-diameter steering wheel retained to cope with the considerable power put through the front wheels. The door pocket sides are padded, with the driver's door equipped with a clip in the front shut face to hold a tyre pressure gauge.

Above left and right: The interior of the standard Mini-Cooper S cars varied little from that of other Minis, however, apart from special flecked upholstery.

conjunction with a Hydrovac servo. The pressure-limiting valve for the rear brakes—which were standard—was revised in line with their relatively light loading.

Wider, 4.5-inch, ventilated steel wheels were listed as an option, but fitted as standard with 145–10 radial ply Dunlop SP tyres, which were far superior to the C41 cross-ply tyres then fitted as standard on Minis. Cornering stability was improved at the expense of a slightly harsher ride. A higher ratio, 2.3 turns from lock-to-lock, steering ratio made the new Mini-Cooper S even more manoeuvrable. Extras included an additional long-distance fuel tank fitted opposite the existing one. Otherwise, the only other distinguishing factor on a 1071-cc Mini-Cooper S were neat little S badges on the bonnet and boot lid.

The initial plan was to produce 1,000 of these cars to qualify them, for international group 11 touring car competition, four times this was passed before the 1071S was replaced by the 1275S and the 970S in March 1964, prototypes of the new cars having been used in competition the previous year. The 970S was officially produced until January 1965 to give it the maximum homologation—or qualification—life of five years without having to produce too many of these relatively expensive little engines. By reputation, these cars, which could be obtained only on special order, were the sweetest-running Minis of all. Their engines produced only 65 bhp at 6,500 rpm, but gave away little to the 1275S on the track on fast rallies because they were so much smoother and revved far faster without blowing up. The 970S had only 55 lb/ft of torque at 3,500 rpm, however, against no less than 80 lb/ft at 3,000 for the 1275S, so the bigger engine was a more versatile, and therefore better, long-term proposition. In any case, BMC were planning to upgrade most of their A-series engines to 1,275 cc in the near future. Thus the 1275S continued in production as an excellent, if rather harsh, road, race and rally car as the 970S was dropped as soon as enough had been built to compete in the 1,000 cc class until 1970. In its ultimate 999 cc

form, with a Formula Three engine, it produced nearly 100 bhp.

Various improvements, such as the diaphragm clutch, had been introduced on the Coopers at the same time as on normal Minis, and, somewhat surprisingly, the high-performance S types went over to Hydrolastic suspension in company with the other Mini saloons in 1964. Competition Coopers, particularly the more powerful ones, suffered from a too high a rate of pitch on the new suspension, and, after experiments at pumping in the fluid under higher pressure, they were frequently changed back to 'dry' rubber suspension. Some owners retained the fluid suspension, however, as there were a few rough surface events in which a skilled driver could use it to advantage when overcoming large obstacles. But even after the other Minis reverted to rubber suspension—because the Hydrolastic system was very expensive to make—the limited-production 1275S retained it, until the model was replaced in March 1971, to use up units held in stock!

Changes peculiar to the Cooper (which went out of production in November 1969) and Cooper S, included optional reclining front seats from November 1965 and twin fuel tanks and an oil cooler as standard on the 1275S from January 1966. The eventual reason that the Mini-Coopers went out of production was that tyre developments had rendered it uncompetitive in international competition and BMC were going through a period of rationalisation in which they concentrated on the higher-volume models and were especially ill-disposed towards ones on which they had to pay royalties, such as the Mini-Cooper and the Austin-Healey Sprite, which was axed at the same time.

VII

The Latter Day Minis

The Mini range had been in production for eight years before much was done to rationalise it. Demand had been such that only piecemeal alterations could be made which did not necessarily apply across the range. The myriad models were duly rearranged in October 1967 into five different types of Austin and Morris saloon with the Riley Elf, Wolseley Hornet, van, pick up and Moke continuing virtually unchanged. In essence, the new standard saloon was an 848-cc economy model with the single-carburettor 998-cc engine being fitted to a Super de Luxe bearing Mini 1000 badges. This engine—the same as that which had been used in the Riley and Wolseley—was also fitted as standard to the estate cars, with the commercial vehicles retaining the cheaper and more economical 848-cc unit. The smaller engine could be specified in a Super de Luxe bodyshell, but only if you ordered a whole fleet of them to justify the disruption to normal production. In the same way, export models were soon to be offered with the 1,275-cc A-series engine developed for the larger 1300 saloon range which replaced the best-selling 1100s. All models of Mini, except the van and pick up with their stamped-in grilles, and the Moke, Riley and Wolseley, received a restyled bodyshell with a more aggressive oblong-shaped grille and larger rear lights to comply better with foreign regulations. This meant that the rear panel had to be retooled, so the opportunity was taken to pare an inch away from each side of the rear window to make the interior lighter. The Super de Luxe's wrap-round overriders had to be abandoned because the back ones got in the way of the new rear lights in what was called the Mark II bodyshell.

All cars of 998 cc and 1,275 cc were fitted with the Cooper's remote control gearlever and the higher 3.44:1 final drive ratio. Automatic Minis continued to have the higher, 9:1, compression ratio engine with the attendant SU HS4 carburettor.

BMC—which had now become British Motor Holdings—had discovered that now seat belts were being offered as a relatively common option, people often wore them, and found, in turn, that they could not reach the switches and heater controls on the dashboard without releasing the buckles (inertia reel belts to allow them to do this without unbuckling were in their infancy then and cost

Left: By 1967 the Mini was losing its youthful appeal in the face of competition from new models by rival manufacturers which were not only new, but looked new. Rather than invest heavily in a radically-revised Mini—with other BMC cars needing more urgent attention—the Mini was given a facelift in the hope that a more aggressive appearance would attract a fresh following. The standard Mini-Cooper, badged now as a 1000, was taken into the forefront of this campaign with a typical young couple—as seen through advertising agency eyes—visiting, first, the zoo and then (as ever) an airfield to try a glider for size, their Mini-Cooper with its broad grinning grille and corporate rear end bearing mark II script to provide them with the passport to their dreams.

Above left and right: The mark II Minis sold well, but so did their rivals, so once British Leyland had established themselves they ordered another facelift for a new range of square-fronted cars which they hoped would make the Mini look much more formidable. The 1275GT, for instance, which took over from the Mini-Cooper S, proved once more to be the customiser's dream, this 1973 example carrying as many parts personal to the owner as any Mini of the 1960s.

more). The switchgear was moved forward 3 ins on the Mark II Minis to improve matters, a crushable roll being added to the parcel shelf edge for universal safety. The old fascia continued to be fitted to standard models.

But the brakes were improved on all Minis, including the commercial vehicles. Their action was made lighter by increasing the bore of the slave cylinders to 0.94 ins at the front from 0.8 ins, and 0.75 ins at the back from 0.625. When linked with the existing master cylinder the increased hydraulic pressure magnified the pedal's action. In theory, this would have meant that there would have to be more pedal travel—an undesirable quality—but, in reality, the lower line pressure that resulted decreased the expansion experienced by the brake pipes and hoses, which, in turn cancelled out any greater movement: a neat bit of practical engineering.

Such careful thought also resulted in the turning circle being reduced to 28 ft from 32 ft. This was achieved by cutting the rack with 25 teeth instead of 15, and increasing the steering arm lengths by 0.094 ins. The slight degree of offset which resulted allowed the tie rods to clear the back of the subframe. That left enough room in the outboard universal joint and the wheel arches to allow the road wheels more movement. It made people wonder why BMH—in the form of BMC—had not thought of it before.

The reason this tighter steering circle had not been adopted earlier was because a higher degree of precision in assembly was needed. BL got over this particular problem by drilling a hole in the rack housing which aligned with another in the rack itself when it was in the dead ahead position. Everything could then be bolted up precisely with no margin for error. All the extra teeth were not really needed—it just happened that they represented the number available on the next standard cutting broach.

There were a number of changes in the electrical equipment, too, bringing the Mark II Minis in line with more modern cars. The old floor-mounted dipswitch was replaced with a headlamp flasher, indicator switch and horn push on a single stalk on the right-hand side of the steering column. The winking warning light that used to be on the end of the indicator stalk was relocated in the speedometer dial with high beam and ignition warning lights, and the horn was given a louder tone. Self-parking windscreen wipers were also provided at last. The speedometer, and the oil pressure gauge, when fitted, had metric markings added and instruments were surrounded by new bezels to reduce the risk of injury in a crash. The seats on all except the standard car and commercial vehicles were reshaped to give better location.

The Riley Elf and Wolseley Hornet received all these changes except those to their rear styling and lighting, which remained the same as before, along with their distinctive radiator grilles.

At the same time, BL began to phase in a new all-synchromesh four-speed gearbox to replace the earlier one with a 'crash' first gear. The Cooper S versions of the Mini were the first to receive the new all-synchromesh transmission from October 1967, with all Minis eventually being fitted with it by September 1968. Meanwhile AP's automatic gearbox had progressed to an uprated mark II version.

Around this time, BMH began to phase in proper interior door handles in place of the cable release which remained on basic Minis—but already, as they became British Leyland in 1968, more far-reaching changes were afoot. In the interests of promoting a corporate identity, the old names Austin and Morris were being phased out from the Mini range, along with Riley and Wolseley. There was a period when 'Austin' Minis had Morris hub caps, and vice versa, and the Riley and Wolseley became more difficult to buy. By August 1969, the Elf and Hornet had been discontinued and soon after, all basic cars became BL Minis, although they often had minor items of trim bearing the old brand names until stocks had been exhausted.

A new range of Clubmen cars was introduced in October 1969 and the Countryman and Traveller went out of production. Their bodies lived on, however, but allied now only to the Clubman's dramatically restyled nose. This squared-off facelift was 4 ins longer than the Mini's old front and gave little advantage other than slightly better engine accessibility. The salesmen were convinced, however, that it was just what the Mini needed!

The basic Clubman was almost exactly the same as the Super de Luxe other than for its new nose and a revised interior which included an instrument binnacle ahead of the driver for the first time and the face level ventilation that had been featured on the Elf and Hornet, plus a new steering wheel. In company with the rest of the Mini range, apart from the commercial vehicles, it now received larger versions of the Elf and Hornet's flush-hinged, wind-up window, doors. Hydrolastic suspension was retained, with the estate keeping its dry rubber suspension and identified by plastic-covered steel trim in place of wood. An automatic variant of the Clubman was cancelled at the last moment—after it had been announced—when it was feared that demand would not be sufficient to justify changes on the production line.

A 1275GT version of the Clubman amounted to a cut-price Mini-Cooper

S, BL hoping that its reduced insurance rating would boost sales. Although the single-carburettor engine had the same bore and stroke as that of the Cooper S, it was, in fact, quite different. It came direct from the Austin and Morris 1300 saloons, and was the same as that which had normally been fitted to Minis destined for export to countries where petrol was cheap. It gave only 59 bhp against 76 for the 1275S, which continued in limited production, but had superior torque at 84 lb/ft against 79 lb/ft, on the standard 8.3:1 compression ratio. It could not readily be uprated to a 1275S engine, however, as the bottom

Opposite and below: The Clubman was essentially a Super de Luxe with the new square nose (picture one in 1974 form), and revised interior which included a new door trim (picture two), now that it had gone over to wind-up windows and concealed door hinges, plus a new instrument binnacle in front of the driver (picture three, of a 1275GT).

end was of far less exotic manufacture and the head was different, too.

BL had hoped to give the new 1275 cc engine more edge by lowering the final drive ratio to 3.65:1 from 3.44, but this was not altogether successful, particularly in view of fuel consumption, and in just over a year that had changed back to the 3.44 gearset. At the first change, however, they had closed up the gearbox ratios to 1.43:1, 2.22 and 3.52, for a more sporting performance, and they did not change back when the final drive reverted to 3.44. The Cooper S disc brakes and wheels were fitted as standard, however, closely followed by Rostyle steel wheels which had been introduced on the group's MG sports cars. The Cooper's servo was not offered at first on the 1275GT because BL had worked out that softer brake pads and linings would be a cheaper alternative on a car which was not so quick anyway. In face of constant criticism that the Cooper S did not have a rev counter, they spent the money they saved on one for the 1275GT, but still did not offer one on the faster Cooper S!

Standard cars, now known as the 850 or 1000, received the wind-up window, flush-hinge doors and went back to the dry cone suspension to pay for the changes. It was not until March 1970, though, that the Cooper S received the new doors—complete with the plush Clubman trim—but not the instruments with the rev counter. This model was known as the Mark III and never changed from Hydrolastic suspension. Production had been discontinued by the time BL rationalised the rest of the range—the 1275GT and Clubman saloon— on dry rubber in June 1971.

The export market for the 1,275 cc standard Mini (called the Mini 1300), had been pioneered in Italy. Here the Lambretta scooter manufacturers, Innocenti, were building their own variants on the Mini theme, rather like the Australians. In general, the Innocenti Minis, with more exotic trim than their British cousins, sold to younger people in a high income bracket who wanted a more fashionable alternative to the ubiquitous Fiat. Sales had been so good since Innocenti replaced their earlier Austin A40 clones with Minis in October 1965 that Italy became BL's biggest export market (supplying kits of mechanical

Top left: Innocenti, meanwhile, carried on their own sweet way, producing Minis specifically to meet the needs of their Italian market, which proved so attractive that they were even imported to Britain! This is one of the last made with a Mini-Cooper style bodyshell before they went over to a new shell more like that of the contemporary Fiat.

Top right: The fuel crisis of 1973 saved the most basic Mini, the 848-cc model now badged—once again—the 850, which continued to sell well because it cost so little to run. This 1979 model differed in essence from those made 20 years earlier only in having a mark II bodyshell, wind-up windows, concealed door hinges, radial-ply tyres, slightly better seats and the remote change all-synchromesh gearbox.

parts and some panels). So when the firm's founder, Ferdinando Innocenti, died in 1972, BL bought his car division for £3,000,000 to protect their market. At that point, the range consisted of a 998-cc Innocenti Mini 1000, a Mini Matic with the 1000-cc engine and AP's automatic transmission, a Mini T1000 estate, a Mini 1001 (a de luxe version of the Mini 1000), and the Mini-Cooper 1300 (in reality, a 1275S). BL soon began to rationalise that range after acquiring the car division, but kept the Innocenti Mini-Cooper in production until the end of 1974 because the founder had not signed a 10-year royalty agreement with John Cooper until his production started in 1965. Eventually, Innocenti, who also made their own body presses, went over to manufacturing a Fiat 126-like car with Mini mechanicals that, in 1974, pre-dated the Austin Metro by seven years.

Meanwhile, back in Britain, a financially-fraught BL could make only minor changes to their Minis. The radiator cowling was discarded in 1971 and all models went over to alternator changing, with their other cars, in December 1972. The synchromesh had been improved during that year, however, and split-type needle roller bearings fitted to the transmission's idler gears.

A new rod-change gearbox required fairly major expenditure, though, as

Below: The 1275GT remained firmly at the top of British Leyland's Mini range in 1979 (picture one), with trendy sailcloth upholstery (picture two), and a neatly tailored boot (picture three), to accept the larger fuel tank on the left, with a compartment for tools and rear washer reservoir on the right (picture four).

the floor pressing had to be altered—but it was necessary to fit in with the rest of BL's transverse-transmission cars. The new gearbox first appeared in January 1973, followed by new driveshafts with plunging constant velocity joints from May that year. Minor changes included fitting better door check brackets. Inertia-reel seatbelts had become so popular that price could be reduced sufficiently to fit them as standard across the range in February 1974, with the heater becoming officially a standard fitting on the 850 in April 1974. In reality, it had been impossible to buy an 850 on the home market without a heater for years—just in the tropics. Puzzled customers had to pay extra whether they liked it or not.

BL were having to make heavy investments in meeting American emission controls for their other cars and the benefits were carried over to the Mini range with SU HS4 carburettors, and revised manifolding and timing from May 1974. Racing Minis had frequently been run on 12-inch wheels to give more room behind them for larger brakes, so with the advent of low-profile tyres (that did not mean the wheel arches had to be changed), they were fitted to the top-of-the-range 1275GT from July 1974. It also got a two gallon-larger fuel tank rather than resorting to the earlier and more expensive, Cooper solution of fitting twin tanks.

As the world's first oil crisis bit deep, outstandingly economical cars such as the Minis rose to new heights of popularity. The 850, which at one time was available only on special order, enjoyed renewed sales and the single-carburettor 1,098-cc A-series engine, which had been used in the earlier Austin and Morris 1100 saloons, was offered as an option in the Clubman bodyshell from October 1974. This was, in fact, a 998-cc A-series unit with the stroke lengthened to 83.8 mm. Special Edition Minis with non-standard trim boosted export sales to

Top left: One of the last Clubman estate cars made, bearing the name Traveller, still proved capable in 1980 of attracting the indefatigable customiser, the type of owner who thought far more of his car than the vast majority who bought rivals in the same price range . . .

Top right: As did the Mini 1000 of 1981 which was still going strong with wide wheels, spats, nudge bars, and blackened windows . . . just like the 1960s.

Right and below: British Leyland proved capable of a bit of customising, too, producing special edition Minis such as this Sprite which took the name of their popular small sports car of the 1960s and a Riley before that. The 1983 Mini Sprite featured such details as colour-coded bumpers, wide wheels and a special grille bonnet lock (picture one), with its own badging and wheel trim (picture two), plus interior trim (picture three), similar to the Clubman and 1275GT, but also showing distinct signs of Metro 'supermini' influence.

plus chrome door mirrors and green and white paintwork with a gold coachline. The 1,098-cc engine was also made standard on the basic Clubman models.

Now that it seemed certain that Minis would stay in production for many more years, they were refined. Softer rear spring and damper settings were adopted from May 1976 on all models except the 1275GT, estate and commercial vehicles to improve the ride, and all Minis were fitted with new subframe mountings which reduced noise, vibration and harshness. They also received new twin-stalk controls, a heated rear window, radial-ply tyres, hazard lights, ignition lock, larger pedals and moulded carpets.

Europe by almost 10 per cent as people hit by a new-found austerity traded down from larger and more luxurious cars.

By October 1975, all Minis had received a new 88-degree Centigrade thermostat in the interests of fuel economy now that the engine could run hotter on modern, stronger, gaskets. The 850 was also given anti-tip seats at last! The 1275GT got reclining seats . . .

BL also decided to try the Mini Special philosophy, which had been pioneered in Italy, on the home market with a Limited Edition Mini 1000, which had orange striped trim, reclining seats, special carpets, and face level vents,

Outwardly they were unaltered, until August 1977 when they all received trendy new matt black grilles. The 850, in addition to its new look, had a steering wheel from the Austin Allegro which had replaced the 1300 range, and grip for the handbrake from the same cousin, in place of bare metal. A vanity mirror in the passenger's sun visor and a ticket pocket in the back of the driver's visor completed the package. The Mini 1000 now sported a coachline along each side of the body just below the windows and reversing lights were built into its rear light clusters. Inside, in addition to the new steering wheel, the 1000 had new front seat backs adjustable for rake, and cropped nylon upholstery with two tone stripes. A dipping rear view mirror became standard and both front doors were fitted with map pockets in belated response to a continual outcry over the loss of the front wells when the doors went over to wind-up windows.

The 1100 cc Clubman in saloon form had all these changes plus tinted glass, different wheel trims and a lockable fuel cap. The estate had flanking stripes instead of a coachline. And inside, the Clubman models received a leather-bound Allegro steering wheel, with stripeless upholstery. The 1275GT was also fitted with Denovo tyres as standard and given a second exterior mirror.

The Minis then continued substantially unaltered as BL concentrated on development of their replacement, the Metro. But sales were so strong it was decided to revamp them once more when the Metro was introduced in October 1980. The 848-cc engine was abandoned in everything except the van and pick up, with the long-nosed Clubman saloon variants. The Clubman estate continued to be sold until stocks were exhausted, using the designation of a revised Mini 1000, the 1000HL.

This was, in effect, a Mini 1000 with a Clubman interior and the new Metro's 'A-plus' engine and transmission. This 998-cc A-series engine had a stiffer block to reduce noise, nimonic exhaust valves, a crankshaft torsional damper, hydraulic timing chain tensioner, more durable spade-type oil pump and more fatigue-resistent fillet-rolled crankshaft. It ran on an 8.3:1 compression ratio with a single HS4 SU carburettor, that—with revised manifolding and twin exhaust outlets, new camshaft, advanced timing and increased valve lift—gave 39 bhp at 4,750 rpm and 52 lb/ft of torque at 2,00 rpm on two-star fuel.

The transmission was also redesigned on what was to be heralded as the new 'Quiet Mini'. The gear teeth were refined with larger needle roller bearings and closer tolerances. The 3.44:1 final drive ratio was retained, and the former 1275GT's 7.5-gallon fuel tank adopted as standard. A new steering wheel designed for the Metro was also fitted, with fresh upholstery featuring nylon inserts in a tartan fabric. New technology also improved building standards to such a degree that the quieter noise level could be maintained inside the car.

The more basic Mini 850 bodyshell with its original central speedometer was then adapted to the revised engine to be marketed as the Mini City.

These cars continued to sell well because of their diminutive size, price and fuel consumption and received a higher, 10.3:1, compression ratio cylinder head and 2.95:1 final drive for ultimate economy as the 1000HLE and City E, in April 1982—by which time there were no more estate bodyshells left. The van and the pick up were also being built only to fleet order.

But still there was a demand for a more luxurious Mini and the smart new Mayfair model replaced the HLE in September 1982. This had a Raschelle cloth trim like that of the top-line Metro Vanden Plas, head restraints and doors with cut-pile carpets, tinted glass, radio as standard, passenger door mirror, locking fuel cap and optional alloy wheels with arch extensions. The Mini City E got a heated rear window, passenger's sun visor, reversing lights and a black fuel filler cap as compensation.

Below and opposite page: The Mini 25 followed the same lines of philosophy in 1984 with a reversion to the traditional Mini parcel shelf (picture one), door pockets (picture two), but the retention of a well-upholstered back seat (picture three), special wheel trims (picture four), and a logo which celebrated the Mini's 25th anniversary.

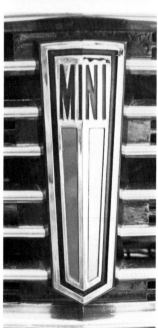

In August 1984, the 12-inch wheel diameter which had been successful on the 1275GT (but not the Denovo tyres) were adopted for the City with new 145/70 rubberware. Even more important, the new wheels allowed plenty of room for disc brakes at the front, allied to uprated rear drum brakes. The Mayfair, in similar mechanical guise, was then revamped as the 'Mini 25' to celebrate the model's 25th anniversary. Naturally the colour of this new de luxe model was silver (with grey and red stripes), for a planned home market production run of 3,500. The wheelarch extensions were colour-keyed with the bumpers, grille, door handles and other exterior hardware. Inside, the Mini 25 followed a successful theme which had been adopted for the MG version of the Metro, with reclining seats trimmed in charcoal velvet, and red piping with a 25 motif. Head restraints and zipped front pockets were integral. The carpets followed the same colour scheme with red seat belts, a three-spoked leather-rim steering wheel, radio and stereo, reversing and fog lights, face level vents and opening rear windows. Similar special edition models continued to sell well, the 1985 edition being known as the Mini Ritz.

VIII
Contemporary Road Testers' Reports

Early road tests of Austin and Morris Minis left journalists with a sense of wonder and very little in the way of criticism apart from, chiefly, the gearchange and items such as the rear window latches. They also quite consistently quoted a fuel consumption averaging around 40 mpg that was to establish a historic target

Left: The first Mini, produced in 1959, set the standard for years to come with a fuel consumption in excess of 40 mpg.

Above: Freak of the automobile world . . . *The Autocar*'s Mini provided a target for other makers such was its roadworthiness.

Above right: The seats provided good comfort and support when compared to others in the 1950s, the inclination of front squab appearing a little too far back for some contemporary tastes!

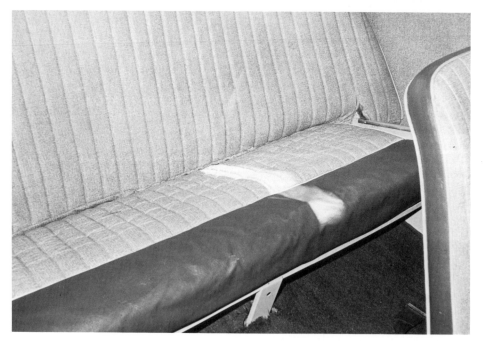

Right: The front seats might have been rather thin but they gave plenty of legroom in the back as a result.

for years to come with later models. This has since been attributed to the fact that small cars were normally driven a good deal slower in those days—Britain had only just received its first motorway when the Mini was introduced and there was not much dual carriageway—although a lot of the credit must be due to the first cars being lighter than the ones which followed.

Left: Drivers soon became accustomed to the steep rake of the steering column while the windscreen pillars appeared commendably thin against those used in earlier forms of unitary construction. The layout of the controls was not so good, however, with the speedometer and fuel gauge partly obscured by the steering wheel rim and the minor switchgear out of immediate reach.

Below left/right: Extensive testing of prototype Minis devoid of badging led to almost identical pre-production examples being used in the first road tests by magazines. This car was pictured at Little Chalgrove and in the Oxfordshire lanes in 1958.

By far the most comprehensive reaction was conveyed in the world's oldest motoring magazine, *The Autocar*, in August 1959, which commented on a Morris de luxe model, registered 383 GFC:

> 'Throwing convention to the winds often produces freaks in the automobile world, but when done by a clever and imaginative designer the result may be outstanding. This is certainly the case with the Mini-Minor, which . . . was found to set new standards of comfort and road worthiness in the very small family car class.'

The Autocar noted that the Mini looked low and small on its 10-inch wheels but found that inside it had as much space, or more, than in many larger cars. Head and elbow room was adequate and the rear seat wide enough for two adults, plus a small child on short journeys. They also said that legroom in the rear compartment was sufficient for passengers even when the front seats were fully back. The seats were a little on the small side, but they provided good comfort and support for all but the very large, although the front squab angle might be inclined a little too far back for some tastes. Drivers soon became accustomed to the steeper-than-average rake of the steering column. The screen pillars were commendably thin, and although only a very tall driver could see the whole of the bonnet, there was no difficulty in judging the car's width quite accurately. The speedometer and fuel gauge were partly obscured by the steering wheel rim, however, and the minor controls along the edge of the parcel shelf were not within easy reach. *The Autocar* thought that the pedal footpads were rather small, but decided that this was acceptable because little effort was needed to operate them. 'In fact, the whole transmission feels as smooth as in a good conventional rear-drive car,' they reported happily.

Below left: Very early Minis featured sliding window catches fixed permanently in place on the door rail to engage moulded projections in the side glass. These catches caught the elbows of the occupants and were soon replaced by the more conventional catch on the window itself.

Below right: The Mini had a rear window which was notably large for 1959.

Rapid starts on a wet road or on a loose uphill surface produced some wheelspin, but the steering remained easy to control. Gear noise was not considered to be excessively high, although it was audible at all times, especially at first. With light loadings, second gear starts could be made. But *The Autocar* added: 'Being very long, the central gear lever needs considerable movement between gears and the action was rather stiff on the test car, particularly for the engagement of third. The fact that the lever had to be moved in an upward arc with outstretched arm made this action worse. Occasionally first and reverse were difficult to engage with the car at rest. Synchromesh on the upper three gears was easily beaten during fast changes both up and down.'

So far as the performance was concerned, *The Autocar* commented:

'Having a dry weight of only 11.25 cwt and a maximum power output almost as high as that of the 948 cc Morris Minor 1000 engine, the Mini-Minor's performance is more lively than that of the larger model. The smaller engine peaks at higher revs, namely 5,500 rpm, and it is smooth throughout the range. It is also quiet up to 55 mph in top but noisier at the natural cruising gait of 60 mph, when the fan can be heard also. Throttle response is so immediate, and the engine so willing to rev freely, that it is

Below: The Mini was so small and manoeuvrable that you could almost park it on the sidewalk, said *Sports Cars Illustrated.*

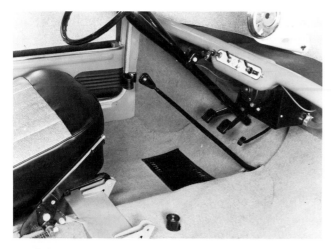

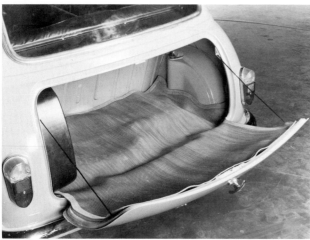

Top left: Sports Cars Illustrated noted that the Mini's steering column was angled like that of an Indianapolis racing car and wondered why the starter button was located on the passenger's side of their cars.

Top right: Simplicity was the keynote of the earliest Minis—the lightest of all production models—with the engine compartment notably devoid of all but essential equipment.

Lower left and right: Another reason for the early Mini's relatively low weight was the simple trim, luggage boots being provided only with a moulded rubber mat rather than any more comprehensive covering.

often necessary to restrain it from exceeding the chosen speed. Yet this is a very flexible unit, the car pulling away smoothly from 14 mph in top. At full throttle and a maximum speed of a little over 70 mph (actually 72.7 mph), the engine remained smooth and showed no sign of distress.

'Third gear ratio is sufficiently close to top to be useful for open road acceleration and gives an absolute maximum of 61 mph, though 55 mph would be the normal peak speed. On leaving a built-up area at 30 mph, in this gear, 50 mph is reached in 10 secs. With two up and some luggage, a re-start was made easily on a 1-in-4 test gradient, but 1-in-3, on dry concrete, proved just too much for adhesion and power.

'With a very light car such as the Mini-Minor, passenger weight is a substantial proportion of the total, yet some additional acceleration figures from 0 to 30 mph and 50 mph with both three up and one up showed very small differences compared with those given in the performance table, with the usual load of 3 cwt.'

The precise performance figures worked out at 16.9 seconds from 0–

50 mph, 26.5 from 0–60, and 23.3 seconds for the standing-start quarter-mile, with an average of 40.1 mpg, which coincided with the steady-speed average at 60 mph.

Some of the reservations with which front-wheel-drive was being received were revealed in the comments:

'It is believed that any person, unaware of its front-wheel-drive layout, could drive this car—in the fairly unhurried manner that most small family cars are driven—without noticing any difference on this score in its handling compared with that of conventional models.

'Steering is light and accurate with adequate self-centering action, and its rack and pinion does not exhibit the "stickiness" found in some models so equipped. Although at 70 mph a little vibration is felt at the wheel, below this speed road wheel movements are not noticed at all, yet the steering has a positive feel.

'When fast cornering is indulged in, the behaviour is clear-cut and predictable and the car plays no tricks. As with any front-drive car, corners are best taken with the engine driving the car, the front wheels pulling it round in the direction which it is steered. In this condition, the Mini-Minor understeers, but not excessively, and tight or open corners can be taken very fast with complete confidence. Wet or dry, one never feels any doubt that the car will get round. Cornering on the overrun cancels out the understeer, and tyre squeal is more easily produced. Suddenly closing the throttle in a corner causes the turn to be tightened, though not violently, and with a small correction it completes the turn at a slightly changed angle.'

Above: Instrumentation was kept to a minimum with a speedometer dial enclosing a mileage recorder in the middle, a fuel gauge below, and warning lights—for low oil pressure on the left, a lack of electrical charge on the right, and high-beam warning on top.

Left: Export Minis were badged as the 850 (this example being a Morris, equipped with not only a roof rack and heated rear window element, but an optional lockable fuel cap, chrome exhaust pipe extension, and reversing light).

The Autocar found that roll was negligible with just the driver aboard, slightly increased with four people in the car, and steering characteristics were about neutral when cornering fast with power on. Oversteer could be produced by too-fast cornering with a full load of passengers and luggage—and 'some caution in these circumstances would be natural enough with any family car as small as this.'

The ride was considered excellent with average irregularities in the road surface readily absorbed and damped at any speed. Cat's eye reflectors in the road produced a pronounced thump and there was a roaring noise from 'coarse-surfaced' roads, however. Stones thrown up into the wheelarches made an alarming noise for testers used to more comprehensively-insulated cars. 'All the wheels remained firmly on the ground,' over poor surfaces with little pitching except when the suspension was caught out on occasion. After 1,442 miles of testing the front suspension stiffened up and the splined shafts had to be greased as recommended after 1,000 miles.

The brakes proved adequate and *The Autocar* failed to induce fade or rear-wheel lock-up. On more minor matters they said:

Below: Minis were also sold in large numbers to be used by the British Army abroad, this early example carrying a fog light, twin wing mirrors and overriders despite its otherwise basic specification.

'The push button catches on the sliding windows are somewhat difficult to engage, as the release button is being pressed when the windows are moved forwards. The windows open at both ends and the gap obtainable at the rear of the door is just sufficient for the driver to put his head through; ample for hand signals. With the rear sliding windows open it is draughty for front-seat occupants, but this provides maximum air entry in hot weather.'

This was pointed out with some feeling as the test took place in some of the most glorious summer weather that had been experienced in Britain for years. *The Autocar* added:

> 'Normally, air circulation in the body is obtained by opening the front sliding windows and one of the hinged windows behind the doors. If both of the latter are open a draught is produced. The catches of these hinged windows rattled badly and after a few miles the windows would partly close. Wind noise was notably low and conversation was not difficult even at maximum speed . . .
>
> 'For a car with such a large rear window it is a pity that the mirror is not ideally shaped to make full use of it. However, the view directly astern is very good. The spindles of the twin screenwipers are evidently placed to suit a left-hand-drive model, since there is an unnecessarily large area left unswept in the top corner of the screen. The blades are not self-parking, but the positive tumbler switch for the motor makes it an easy matter to stop the blades at the base of the screen . . . the flashing tell-tale lamp at the end of the turn indicator arm is unnecessarily bright at night but is easily masked by the hand which operates it.'

On this happy note *The Autocar* congratulated BMC for producing such an outstanding car with their rival British weekly, *The Motor*, making similar

This and facing page: The Mini Traveller as it was more commonly seen with full equipment (picture one), lengthened body featuring wooden side trim (picture two), non-adjustable rear door hinges with lighting set in the wooden trim (picture four), fold-forward rear seat squab with finger-pull loop (picture five), rear seat which clipped back into position (picture six) and luggage compartment with fuel tank at the right which could be extended by folding forward the rear seat squab (picture seven) and rear doors which were divided in the centre for ease of assembly (picture eight).

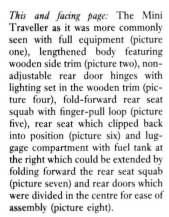

comments at the same time. They added of an Austin Seven 850 de luxe, registered YON 953:

> 'The unconventional all-independent springing of this car by means of rubber cones produces a somewhat "continental" effect, the springing being fairly firm, but immune from bottoming and with low unsprung weight to eliminate shock on rough roads. Standing by the little Austin, it is impossible to bounce it on its springs as most other modern cars can be bounced . . . the ride is naturally livelier when no passengers are being carried than with the car laden, and there are very rare occasions when, on a wavy road, the tendency of a short-wheelbase car with firm springs to follow the road undulations is not very comfortable. On the other hand, experience of the back-seat ride in very varied conditions emphasised that passengers enjoy far smoother riding in this car than in the back seats of most models costing twice as much.'

The Mini's precise steering was still something of a novelty, and *The Motor* went as far as to say: 'Some people are at first rather shy of the unwontedly light and responsive steering, but in fact this is an immensely controllable little car and physically quite untiring to drive for long distances. Many people could drive this car without ever realising that front wheel drive is included amongst its unorthodoxies, there being for example no trace of the transmission "snatch" on full lock which has afflicted several low-priced front-wheel-drive cars.'

The Motor's performance figures were almost exactly the same as those of *The Autocar* although they reckoned their car could have benefited considerably from running in.

The Autocar's next test Mini, registered 667 GFC, certainly did not suffer from any lack of use, covering more than 8,000 miles in a lap of Mediterranean countries in the hands of Ronald Barker and Peter Riviere during the month of September, with results published throughout October. Despite a variety of adventures, the Mini suffered only from intermittent thermostat problems and the occasional broken damper mounting, a piece of iron puncturing one wheel arch in Algeria as an indication of the roads covered. With similar encouragement from BMC, *Motor Sport* editor Bill Boddy had a Mini, registered 634 GWL, on test for a year, reporting in his issue of August 1960:

> 'It did not take long to become accustomed to being transported in this tiny tin can and today I never give a thought to the insignificant size of the car. You can be dazzled even by dipped headlights of approaching cars because you sit so low, puddles can be splashed over the screen because the bonnet is so abbreviated and in a fog the sidelights are so bright that the best thing to do is to stop and put up for the night. Otherwise, there isn't any suggestion of being in one of the world's smallest automobiles, nor is there any adverse indication that this is a front-wheel-drive vehicle.'

Boddy, who had just forsaken a Volkswagen Beetle, decided that the outstanding feature of his 'Minibric' was its excellent top gear performance and

Top left/right: With a full load on board—of, perhaps, two occupants, one roll of chainlink fencing, a bow saw, small stepladder, toilet bowl, eleven assorted tins of paint, three spades, sledgehammer, two broom handles with heads, four pails (of the galvanised, pre-plastic, variety), a watering can (literally, again non-plastic), coal skuttle, mop, bolt cutters and kitchen sink (picture one), the Mini Traveller's handling was actually improved, according to *The Autocar.* But exactly how it would have fared with two piglets and a bale of hay (picture two) or *Left:* the seven selected dogs a landowner might have been expected to carry (picture three for which the photographer must have had the patience of Job and amazing powers of persuasion) were not recorded.

genuinely high level of speed and acceleration which enabled him to compete with other cars, plus its already acclaimed cornering ability. He was quite happy with the brakes despite a tendency for the rear ones to lock occasionally.

He did not like the gearchange, however, and found that he had to adopt a 'very brutal' action when changing down into second and he didn't like the underhand action needed to change from second to third either. In addition, he disliked the sliding windows and considered the interior crude, but appreciated its stowage space. He also found the heater quite incapable of demisting the windows on a wet day and likened the noise of the fan to that of a dentist's drill. Later the car was fitted with a new multiblade fan and Interior Silent Travel kit—a popular selection of felt lining pieces—which was markedly successful. His rear windows blew shut at anything above 20 mph until BMC got one to stay open. Boddy found the steering 'light and extremely good but the tiny wheels cause sudden minor deviations from the chosen path when they encounter longitudinal ridges or camber in the road'.

'Tyre life is not impressive—tread is now nearly gone from the front tyres (after 11,627 miles) although quite a lot remains on the back ones. I would think front tyre life is at most 14,000 miles, which is a very long way behind the minimum I got from the late-lamented editorial VW.'

However, the Mini's reliability record was impressive and Boddy said: 'For a car which has been driven hard, the speedometer needle usually between 60 mph and 70, and neglected, I think it has an excellent record, especially for a full four-seater which sells for the equivalent of less than £100 in pre-war terms, and yet is so amusing to drive the leading Grand Prix drivers enthuse over it.'

But so far as its styling was concerned, he said: 'Nothing will make me

Right: The Motor Industry Research Association's proving site near Nuneaton was widely used by road testers to gain data, this Mini-Cooper pictured in 1961 undergoing trials to check the maximum gradient on which it could restart and the security of its handbrake. Tractability, *The Motor* discovered, was one of the 997-cc Mini-Cooper's greatest virtues . . .

enthuse over the minibric's appearance—walk round it and it seems uglier and uglier, the size of the steering wheel being the last straw!'

But an equally sporting driver, John Bolster, of the monthly *Motor Sport*'s new weekly rival, *Autosport*, liked his test Mini so much that he ordered a new one! Bolster said of his test example, registered XOV 811, in August 1959:

'I knew at once that this would be by far the best machine that BMC has ever produced. Timed tests have convinced me that for most of the journeys which I carry out, it is small physical dimensions which count. Here is a car which has all the Continental features, such as independent rear suspension . . . at first sight the car is not beautiful to look upon, yet one soon grows used to it, and the sheer good sense of the design appeals enormously.

'Quite the most outstanding feature is the suspension. In spite of the small wheels, the ride over atrocious road surfaces is superb, and the cornering power is phenomenally high for a saloon. Really bumpy corners may be slid under full control in a manner that no car with a rigid rear axle could emulate.'

BMC had high hopes of selling large numbers of Minis in America, where the Volkswagen Beetle had established a good market as a result, initially, of being sold on discount by BMC's importers. Ten thousand Minis were allocated for the 1960 model in America, with the monthly *Sports Cars Illustrated* magazine enthusiastically analysing one in June 1960. They reported:

'The Austin 850 is 25 per cent shorter than a VW, which probably makes it the smallest "full-sized" car ever. That's full-sized by European standards, of course, for it's for four passengers. On one occasion we did stuff six adults into the test car, including a hapless General Motors executive, but fortunately we were only going halfway round the block. Another time, travelling four-up on the Long Island expressway, we all agreed that we had more room for ourselves than four people in a large domestic that stayed alongside for a while. The 850 is incredibly large inside, yet equally small outside. It's in some ways an adult's toy—the kind of car you feel you can park on the sidewalk. Yet for all its fun it's a very real automobile, full of purpose and ability. Its metier is urban driving, yet it's quite capable of cruising in the sixties, or even faster.

'The 850 is delightful to drive. Its steering is quick, light and precise. There is no stickiness whatsoever, and despite the extraordinarily low figure of 1.16 turns to full lock, the 850 may easily be steered with one hand grasping the hub. And this with the front wheels carrying 65 per cent of the load. The rack and pinion mechanism does not transmit road reactions, yet always presents an accurate "feel" of the road . . .

'We did all our cornering and acceleration testing with the 6 extra psi in the tyres recommended in the handbook for "fast driving". Normal pressures are 24 and 22 psi, front and rear. With 30/28, we found the ride virtually unchanged while the cornering must be described as incredible. The 850 is low-powered, but even deliberate efforts failed to provoke a side-slip. On wet blacktop, our courage gave out before the tyres lost their grip, as we had no intention whatsoever of inverting the machine . . .

'There are two common objections to small tyres such as these on the 850. One is that they wear out quickly since they turn faster; the other is that they get lost inside big chuck-holes. Considering how they look, their figure of about 1,070 revs per mile is not vastly higher than, for example, a 5.20 × 13's figure of 905. Besides, small tyres cost less, so on a miles-per-dollar basis the disadvantage isn't so marked. On this subject, our contributing editor in Coventry, Edward Eves, reports an estimated life of some 8,000 miles. This sounds excruciatingly low but to grasp its significance one must understand how enthusiasts drive in England. For normal driving, he predicts 15,000 miles. American roads have smoother, less abrasive, surfaces, so still higher mileages no doubt can easily be achieved.

'As to getting lost in big holes, we can only report that the suspension more than makes up in this respect. Rushing down cobblestone paving and hurtling across just-filled construction ditches on New York City's miserable streets never caught the 850 unprepared. The irregular surfaces could and did make the body rumble but between the rubber suspension and the superb seats, the ride was much more comfortable than most cars of any size.'

Right: The vertical, remote-control, gearlever, although some distance from the steering wheel rim, was found to be ideally located for quick changes.

Sports Cars Illustrated shared BMC's hopes of overcoming American prejudice against small cars, pointing out:

'Most "mini-cars" seriously short change the people who ride in them. They are usually hard to get in and out of, and there is rarely anything like enough room for husky, corn-fed Americans. For this reason they've never made a permanent dent in the market, not in Europe where storage and operating space is more at a premium than here. Just as Volkswagen surprised a lot of people with its unexpected success, so, we think, will the Austin and Morris 850s.'

The American magazine was, of course, referring to the mid-1950s spate of bubble cars when they noted that 'mini-cars' had never made a dent in any market . . . After noting that the angle of the steering wheel was much like that of an Indy car (an Indianapolis roadster as used in their premier track race), they wondered why the starter button was not on their driver's side of the floor, and passed comment on the excitingly-low advertised price of $1295 (at a time when the US dollar was fixed at 2.8 to the £). They estimated that with essentials such as a heater, Minis would cost up to $1444 for coastal cities, which was still considerably less than any other full-sized import.

With these factors in mind, they summed up:

'Ever since the first post-war Austin landed on American shores, each new small car design has been welcomed with "It won't sell here." Some have overcome the experts' pronouncements but many have not. Europe's rose is sometimes America's dandelion, for our requirements differ. The 850 may bloom and it may wither—which will tell us more about our fellow countrymen and their needs than about the 850 itself.'

Left: The early 997-cc Mini-Cooper had a lot of extra sound-deadening material under the bonnet and in the engine compartment, with the interior heater's fan mounted on the left-hand flitch plate as viewed from the front. The brake and clutch master cylinders were fitted on the right, with the windscreen washer reservoir on the left, of this left-hand-drive model.

Despite the continuing success of BMC's small sports cars, using Mini components and featuring far less interior space, the saloon did not catch on. It would take the oil crisis fifteen years later for American ideas of what was a proper saloon car to be downgraded, by which time the Mini had been overtaken by many competitors.

The Mini Estate

But the estate car certainly caught on in Europe as soon as it was introduced in 1960, with *The Autocar* once more providing the most comprehensive assessment in September that year. They pointed out that the lengthened body of their test car, registered 240 KFC weighed 1.3 cwt more than that of the equivalent saloon and meant that an extra 5 per cent of the overall weight was concentrated on the rear wheels. This affected the balance only slightly but had other noticeable effects:

'Not surprisingly, these changes, particularly the weight increase and possibly the not-so-clean body shape, have had their effect in bringing about a drop in performance. Allowing for the fact that the performance

Right: The Mini-Cooper's new disc front brakes were considered one of its best features in 1961.

figures were taken in rather poor conditions, none of them match those obtained with the saloon. In usual road test trim—with two occupants and test equipment aboard—it took the Mini-Traveller almost a second longer to cover the standing quarter mile. With a full load—two occupants and 400 lb of ballast—nearly another three seconds was required to cover the same distance.

'As expected, a head wind was found to have a very severe effect in the upper regions of performance; on the test track, turning from a cross-wind leg with a slight tail-wind factor full into the wind resulted in a drop of 10 mph. There is little doubt that the wooden styling pieces caused a considerable amount of drag.'

So far as the stiffened rear suspension and increased ride height at the back was concerned, *The Autocar* said:

'One result of this is a slightly greater roll resistance, bringing about a slightly higher degree of roll on the front end, so that the outside front wing on entering a corner dips more noticeably than with the saloon version. This gives the impression that some roll oversteer is about to replace the initial slight understeer—in fact, this was found not to happen.

Top left: 'Lady drivers need never know about the 50 per cent power increase,' said Bill Boddy, editor of *Motor Sport*, only the slatted radiator grille and Cooper badges showing much difference from the normal Mini detail features outside. *Top right:* Mini-Coopers built from October 1961 to October 1962 had the Super-style bumpers with plain over-riders (picture one) with Coopers built after that having the Super de Luxe trim including bumpers with nudge bars (picture two).

Below left: Minis modified slightly to the general specification of this works car, driven by David Siegle-Morris into sixth place in the 1960 RAC Rally, proved capable of more than 100 mph in road tests.

Below right: The Minis modified in the manner of these Cooper works racers in 1962 with Dunlop D7 tyres and lowered suspension provided a startling performance.

Top left: De Luxe editions of the Mini were often sent out to test, laden with BMC's dealer-fitted options, such as auxiliary lights and wing mirrors (picture one), whereas journalists queueing to test the first editions of the Super (in Austin guise) in 1961 had cars devoid of any excess weight (picture two) *top right,* before the Super de Luxe (pictured here in Morris form), replaced the De Luxe and the Super in October 1962 with a new grille and the Super's nudge bars (pictures three and four) *middle:* Radio sets still proved something of an embarrassment with new obvious mounting point (picture five) *opposite left,* while reversing lights hung in a rather exposed position under the back bumper (picture six) *opposite right.* Stronger American-style nerf bars took a long time to catch on as optional extras, however, this works example having been photographed as long ago as 1961 (picture seven) *opposite centre,* but imitation wicker-work sides, sunroof, headlamp 'eyebrows' and ornate wheeltrims on this Harold Radford version—as seen at Cowley in 1963—were an immediate success (picture eight) *opposite bottom.*

'A significant characteristic of the handling is that, under power, there is a slight understeer effect; if the power is removed while a corner is being taken the car turns more sharply into the bend. This change from understeer to oversteer is not at all disturbing, being very gentle when cruising and easily controllable at faster speeds. With a full load on board, the handling is improved—if that is possible. Any tendency to roll at the front disappears, and if the throttle is closed while cornering, transition from under to oversteer is even more gentle. It is necessary to follow the recommendation of increasing the pressures of the rear tyres when a heavy weight is carried in the back of the car; failure to do this resulted in marked directional instability when braking or on the over-run. The change in weight distribution in comparison with the saloon has not noticeably affected front-wheel traction.'

With due allowance for high winds, *The Autocar*'s performance figures were certainly down, at 67 mph flat out, with a 35.8-second 0–60 mph time, a 24.3-second standing-start quarter mile and average of 38 mpg—which still amounted to only a penny a mile for petrol on pre-metric standards. The turning circle had been increased only slightly to 34 ft 3 ins left, 34 ft 3.5 ins right. In less severe conditions, however, *The Motor* recorded similar figures in their test of a Traveller registered 454 AVP published at the same time. Their comments also fell largely in line with those of *The Autocar*, apart from adding that 'the possibility of an extra passenger sitting in the luggage compartment when all the normal seats are occupied will interest some people.' They also noted that the extra inches in the wheelbase seemed to make the front-seat ride better, whereas rear-seat passengers placed directly over the stiffer rear springs suffered a jerkier ride than in the saloon. Headroom in the back 'just sufficed for an average tall man, although his head was too far up in the roof for him to enjoy a really good view of distant scenery.'

In their opinion, also, the 'half-timbered' body had a very British air of being truly fully furnished. John Bolster agreed and went some way towards explaining the philosophy behind adopting wooden battens in his test of a Mini Traveller for *Autosport* in December 1960. He said:

'The shooting brake, station wagon, utility, call it what you will, is an extremely popular type of dual-purpose vehicle. When I was a boy, a certain aura surrounded these machines, and I don't mean just the scent of the varnished timber of which they were constructed. Chauffeur-driven, they whispered down the long gravel drives of the big houses, taking beaters to the shoot or collecting guests from the train. One kept the chassis of last year's Rolls and sent it to the coachbuilders for such a conversion, after which it became the most useful form of transport that any family could possess. There has been a revolution and the spacious days are no more.

'The Traveller which I took over was resplendent in white paint and varnished wood, and I had to admit that it was monstrously handsome. I purposely drove to fetch it in my own Mini, so that the comparison (between an early saloon and the estate car) would be immediate, and I at once admired the better quality of the carpets, upholstery and interior trim. I found that the little brake had a slightly better gearchange with rather more effective synchromesh.'

Subsequently Bolster had a most enjoyable trip to Paris in the Traveller, with the luggage compartment occupied by friends on occasions for quick trips to local bars, during which he received one citation for 'abusive stationing and paralysing the circulation . . .' in other words a parking ticket.

Early Modified Minis

All manner of firms tried their hands at improving the performance of standard Minis, chiefly by modifying the well-tried A-series engine, in the early days—many with a noted lack of success. But one of the firms which achieved an excellent name was Arden, of Tamworth-in-Arden, Warwicks. Their normal conversion, costing £38 5s (£38.25) consisted of an exchange gas-flowed cylinder head with its compression ratio raised to 9.5:1, uprated valve springs, a special inlet manifold to accept a second SU carburettor—the original being retuned to work in conjunction with it—the additional carburettor, a three-branch exhaust manifold and wire flame traps to replace the air filter, plus a straight-through silencer. Arden pointed out, however, that the performance would be just as good on two 1.125-inch SU carburettors and fuel consumption could be improved if the extra money was spent on replacing the existing 1.25-inch carburettor. *The Autocar* approached an Arden Mini with interest and reported in February 1960:

'These small BMC cars have set such a high standard of roadholding in their production form that they are able to deal quite happily with the additional speed resulting from the Arden conversion. Tyre pressures were increased by 6 psi all round for test purposes. There was no tendency to slide on wet surfaces and the little car appeared very happy when flat out at 85 mph. As with all conversions to standard production engines, one cannot expect something for nothing but fuel consumption is no great significance when speed is the object. When the car was driven hard on the road and full use made of the acceleration, 30.1 mpg was recorded for 256 miles, which included circuit testing. On the other hand, driving the car more normally on local domestic journeys, and not exceeding 50 mph in top gear or 4,000 rpm in the intermediate gears, the Arden conversion produced a fuel consumption of 51.2 mpg. From above 70 mph, all-square stops were made, but more braking power was needed.'

Apart from the considerable increase in top speed, the acceleration of the Arden Mini showed a consistent improvement throughout the range, culminating in a 0–60 time of 20 seconds, 6.5 seconds faster than normal.

Right: The Super de Luxe Mini, still acclaimed for the large amount of interior space it offered, now featured plastic trim with more adventurous designs.

Top left: No sooner had the Riley Elf and Wolseley Hornet been introduced (picture one) than BMC began marketing extras such as this attractive all-leather radiator muff for cold conditions (picture two) *bottom left*.

The Mini-Cooper

In view of the popularity of conversions such as that offered by Arden, the introduction of the Mini-Cooper aroused great interest, as did road tests of early examples. *The Autocar*'s example, registered 319 EOE, achieved a maximum average of 84.7 mph with a 0–60 mph acceleration time of 18 seconds, the standing-start quarter mile being covered in 20.9 seconds with a fuel consumption figure of 27 mpg. These statistics, for a car costing nearly £150 more than an Arden-converted Mini, may not have sounded very impressive, but it was the way in which the Cooper achieved them which endeared it to the testers. *The Autocar* reported in September 1961:

'Tractability was the immediate virtue noted with the car. Although it is said that lessons learned in Formula Junior racing have been incorporated in the power unit, this has not been done at the expense of slow-speed running or middle-range performance. The best recorded speed on the road was 87 mph, yet it was possible to pull away from as little as 14 mph in top gear without snatch. Indeed, once the novelty of the higher maximum speed has worn off, most owners will find that the main attraction of the car is its brisk performance in the important 40 to 70 mph range. The standing quarter mile time was covered without recourse to top gear. With such a performance up its sleeve, the Austin Cooper becomes an astonishingly fast means of reaching B from A . . .

'The vertical, remote-control gearlever, although some distance from the steering wheel rim, is located ideally for quick changes; its action on the test car was slightly stiff, but precise.

'From the viewpoints of both traffic driving and performance, the choice of gearbox ratios could hardly be bettered. The larger engine, giving 50 per cent more torque, has made higher indirect ratios practical; 46 mph is now the second gear maximum and almost 70 mph is possible in third. Since the engine will pull down to walking pace in second and almost that in third, most traffic driving is done in those ratios. Quick changes, made easier by the new remote lever, revealed shortcomings in the synchromesh when taking acceleration figures, but in normal use the slight delay essential to quiet engagement of the gears would not be irksome.

'The 16-blade fan, now fitted to all ADO15s (BMC's code name for the Mini) is a tremendous improvement on the previous four-blader in respect of noise.

'Because of the Cooper's considerable extra power as compared with the standard Minis, the slip angle of its front tyres is greater through "full-throttle" corners; in other words, it understeers more. Consequently, the sudden reduction in front tyre slip, if one closes the throttle in the middle of a corner, is much more abrupt and noticeable; in the same way one can "straighten out a corner" by opening the throttle wide in the middle of it. Given time and experience, the art of driving this vehicle to its safe limits is soon acquired, because it is a vehicle which holds its driver's attention and interest through the sheer pleasure of driving it.

'One of the main reasons for the extremely good road holding of this model is that there is very much more tyre tread contact with the road than on most modern cars. Slight changes in tyre pressure will alter the handling to a surprising degree.

'Quite one of the best features of the car is the Lockheed disc and drum brake system. Moderately high pressures are required for small reductions in speed, but thereafter the action is progressive, with a reassuring feel.'

Subsequent experience has shown that the brakes could be much improved, and it is some indication of how much lower braking standards were in the early 1960s to learn of such a good reception to the first Mini-Cooper's brakes! *The Motor*, however, commented in their test of a car registered 434 MFC, in September 1961:

'Application of disc brakes to the front wheels has certainly achieved the desired result of eliminating fade in severe conditions. Several stops from 60 mph or more, made in a quick series, can produce a smell of hot brakes as large amounts of energy are dissipated, but instead of their effectiveness fading, the brakes then become rather more responsive to moderate pedal pressures. In utter contrast to what has been normal, the one circumstance which can require an embarrassingly large pedal effort to bring the wheels to locking is the need to make an emergency stop when the brakes are completely cold.

'This is the fastest production saloon of its size ever to figure in our road test reports. So much performance, combined with a lot of practical

Left and below: The testers were most impressed with the performance offered by the Mini-Cooper 1071S despite a phenomenal thirst for oil in early examples (picture one), the 70-section Dunlop SP tyres on its ventilated steel disc wheels being considered to be of low profile in 1963.

merit and quite a high standard of refinement will obviously make many people decide that a sum of about £680 is better spent on this model than on something bigger but no better.'

Bill Boddy then took over *The Autocar*'s test Cooper for *Motor Sport* in October 1961, commenting:

'First impressions are of less "punch" than anticipated and lack of "through the windscreen" retardation, but it didn't take long to appreciate that a very sensible balance between docility and urge has been struck in what, after all, is a production model, and that the extremely powerful and impeccable disc braking has been cleverly applied to permit maximum application, even on slippery roads, without disastrous loss of control. The splendid brakes are supplemented by a fine continental-note horn. Lady drivers need never know about the 50 per cent power increase, except in terms of top-gear pulling . . .'

British correspondent Dennis May then took over *The Motor*'s road test Cooper to report for *Car and Driver* (the American successor to *Sports Cars Illustrated*) in November 1961:

'These GT miniatures have outgrown the 850 label and are being marketed internationally through established BMC channels as the Morris Mini-Cooper and the Austin Seven Cooper. ADO50 is their factory symbol.

'Comparison between the performance of the Mini and the closely-related Austin-Healey Sprite Mark II puts the writing on the wall for owners of BMC's alike-in-all-but-name A-H Sprite and MG Midget. To out-speed and out-accelerate Sprites and Midgets at minimal expense, the tool you're going to need is a dinky sedan with the Cooper suffix.'

It was more than a year before John Bolster could report on the Mini-Cooper in *Autosport* (in December 1962), but he had the benefit of having seen many in action before writing:

'The Mini-Cooper can be used for any purpose for which the standard model is suitable. It is just as good a shopping car and not noticeably noisier than its bread-and-butter sister. In this connection, one must criticise the remote control gearlever, for it does "telephone" a lot of noise in to the interior of the vehicle. The actual changes are quite quick, and the closer ratios greatly improve the car . . .

'The ride is fairly hard, with some pitching, but many sports car enthusiasts are by no means averse to such suspension characteristics. The standard of comfort is acceptable, and in the case of the test car it was greatly enhanced by the optional fresh air heater, a tremendous improvement.

'The speed of the Mini-Cooper is held down to a little below 90 mph by the rather unstreamlined shape. Tuned Minis have certainly gone

Left: The flecked upholstery and trim were more suitable for a lady's boudoir than the inside of a rally car, according to Bill Boddy of *Motor Sport*!

Left: No sooner had Paddy Hopkirk won the Monte Carlo Rally in 1964 with a Mini-Cooper 1071S, registered 33 EJB, than it was transferred to more publicity-gathering as a test car, surviving all manner of adventures to be retained first by BMC, then British Leyland, and now Austin-Rover as a display car in delightfully-original condition.

Above left and right: The interior of road test Mini-Cooper S cars was largely standard, but that of 33 EJB far from normal.

faster, but the extra power needed to increase the speed appreciably could only be supplied by a rather "hot" and not very economical engine. The acceleration is in a different world from that of the standard Mini, and cars which habitually overtake that worthy little machine are themselves overwhelmed by the Cooper version.

'The average speeds which can be achieved, particularly over difficult terrain, can only be described as incredible. The engine is very willing and the gear ratios are so right that even very fast sports cars cannot shake off this Mini. The disc brakes, which initially left something to be desired, are now perfectly adequate and really pin the little projectile down . . .

'What is so remarkable, though, is the phenomenal "dicing margin" that is available. Most cars with high cornering power tend to be unforgiving. In the hands of an expert, they are most impressive, but the novice who tries to drive on the limit will eventually spin off ignominiously. The Mini-Cooper can be driven up to and past the limit of adhesion by quite a moderate driver. When he appears to be about to enter the *decor* he simply eases his foot momentarily. The tail comes round, the sliding car loses speed, and another burst of throttle sends him on his way.

'Fundamentally, this type of stability renders it possible to travel fast in safety when the road is not well known to the driver. He will find that he can beat pilots of his own calibre who have faster cars, simply because his Mini-Cooper will look after him when he is indiscreet. The extra power available makes the Cooper version even safer than the standard car. The only danger is that the Mini driver may later try to handle something else with similar carefree abandon. Frankly, it can't be done!'

Bolster's car, registered 769 MFC, possibly with the advantage of more prolonged running-in, returned better performance figures than those of *The Autocar* and *The Motor*, which were virtually the same. Bolster's figures were 88 mph flat out, 17 seconds for the 0–60 mpg, 20.8 for the standing quarter mile, and between 27 and 31 mpg.

More Modified Minis

A series of tests followed chiefly in *Autosport*, of modified Minis, many of which were capable of more than 100 mph. The first was a well-known 850 cc example, registered JRA 85, which had been raced all over Europe by John Aley. The car doubled as the Aley family transport and had minimal modifications. They consisted chiefly of a higher compression cylinder head by Don Moore, of Cambridge, with gas-flowed ports and manifolds, a BMC 948-pattern camshaft, with lightened rocker gear and a balanced bottom end. Little had been done to the suspension apart from fitting Koni shock absorbers adjusted to their stiffest setting, with Ferodo AM4 competition brake pads and Dunlop D7 racing tyres moulded to a road-going pattern. Patrick McNally reported in *Autosport* in November 1961:

'The suspension gave a perfectly comfortable ride although it was set harder than a standard car. But the D7 tyres gave the car some exhilarating handling characteristics in the wet, for in the upper speed ranges the car slides beautifully through corners unlike any other Mini I have tried.'

The quality of Moore's work also showed in a 0–60 mph acceleration time

Right top left: The Mini-Cooper 1275S, whether in standard (picture one) or works guise (picture two) typically presented a slightly tail-up attitude at rest, the brake servo, where fitted (pictures three and four) *bottom left right:* occupying a place on the left-hand side of the engine compartment.

of 14.5 seconds, a 19.5-second standing-start quarter mile and a top speed of 89.5 mph with 32 mpg.

McNally then went on to test two special Mini-Coopers, the first bored out to 1,122 cc by Alexander's of Haddenham, Bucks. In addition to special lightweight pistons, it had a gas-flowed 9.5:1 compression ratio big-valve cylinder head with twin 1.5-inch SU carburettors. Wheelspin was the chief problem with a balanced engine which could reach 8,000 rpm. In addition, the suspension had been lowered by reducing the rate at which the rubber compressed. McNally reported in July 1962:

> 'On the road, the car proved something of a sensation, being able to out-accelerate nearly everything in sight. What it couldn't out-accelerate, Mini suspension made up for, and it left behind many completely disillusioned, once proud sports car owners.
>
> 'However, it did have one shortcoming. As with nearly every Cooper-Mini I have driven the brakes were appalling, and definitely not up to the job of stopping even a standard car let alone this projectile. Again, Mini suspension and the inherent understeering characteristics of the car saved any embarrassing situations from becoming acute.'

McNally recorded a top speed of 106.2 mph with an 8.5-second 0–60, and 17.2-second standing-start quarter mile, fuel consumption averaging 25 mpg. Either the car had suffered, or his figures were flattering, for when *The Autocar* tested the same vehicle in September, they could only reach 100.5 mph, with 10.7 seconds for the 0–60, and 18.2 for the standing-start quarter mile, fuel consumption remaining at 25 mpg.

McNally then went on to another ton-up Mini, a Cooper bored out to 1,088 cc by Downton Engineering, of Salisbury, Wilts, who were to be responsible for much of the work on the subsequent Mini-Cooper S. Daniel Richmond, of Downton, would not reveal exactly what had been done to the engine—apart from that it was largely along the lines of the Alexander conversion—but it was sufficient for McNally to record a 108.2 mph maximum, 8-second 0–60, and 16.8-second standing quarter mile, but with 26.5 mpg, later in July.

The following month he tested an 850 cc Mini, modified by Arden, which had a Formula Junior cylinder head and a single Weber DCLD carburettor from a Ferrari 250GT, with full-race camshaft, close-ratio gearbox and competition brake linings operated by an extra-large servo. This extraordinary vehicle was reported to have hit 102.3 mph flat out with an 11.5-second 0–60 time and 18-second standing quarter mile, while returning an amazing 30 mpg.

Seven days later, McNally reported on another 850-cc Mini, tuned by Vic Derrington of Kingston upon Thames. This had a high-compression gas-flowed cylinder head and Mini-Cooper camshaft, with a Weber carburettor, and straight-through exhaust system. Monroe front shock absorbers had been fitted with a rear anti-roll bar which reduced a tendency to lift wheels under hard cornering. McNally also found an SPQR remote control gearchange useful on the way to recording a 90 mph maximum speed, with a 0–60 time of 14 seconds and standing quarter mile of 19.5, fuel consumption increasing to 32 mpg.

John Bolster then tested a rare supercharged Mini fitted with a Shorrock 'blower' by the Allard Motor Company of South London. He reported enthusiastically for *Autosport* in August 1962 of a conversion that invariably raised objections by insurance companies, because of lurid examples in the past:

'Blowing is considered by many people to be the best way of increasing the performance of an engine. This is because no dismantling or alteration of parts is necessary and the low-speed flexibility is always greatly improved. It was thus most interesting to put a supercharged Austin Seven through a long and arduous test.

'All the advantages of the supercharger are at once apparent. The car accelerated cleanly from less than 15 mph in top gear. Further up the scale, as a positive pressure is built up in the induction tract, a delicious sound is heard, reminiscent of the days of real motor racing. This characteristic supercharger whine is more prominent inside the Mini because the compressor is situated right against the bulkhead. Nevertheless, it only becomes really inspiring at peak revolutions, below which the unit is singularly unobtrusive.

'The supercharged Austin Seven has many of the attributes of a tuned example, for it is considerably faster than standard and has a very useful improvement in acceleration. Yet it also boasts a flexibility in top gear that is entirely foreign to a raised-compression, twin-carburettor job. During normal driving, a standing start in third gear is perfectly natural with no clutch slipping or judder.'

For the record, Bolster achieved a maximum speed in this 850-cc model of 82 mpg, with a 15.5-second 0–60, 20.6-second standing quarter mile and 27 mpg. McNally then tried a Mini-Cooper tuned by Taurus of West London in September for *Autosport*. This had a very low-priced £27 conversion consisting of a 10.5:1 compression ratio gas-flowed cylinder head similar to that used on Group II racing Minis, with rejetted carburettors. The results were astounding, a top speed of 95 mph being recorded, with an 11.2-second 0–60 time and 18.1 seconds for the standing quarter mile. Fuel consumption however, fell to 25 mpg.

The Autocar were equally impressed with the Taurus tuning gear when they tried both a modified 850-cc Mini and converted a Cooper in March 1963. They reported after a long hard winter:

'Originally it was intended to carry out a simple test on a Mini fitted with a stage one cylinder head and straight-through silencer. However, a combination of circumstances (and the weather) caused this to be modified into a double test.

'The truth of the matter was that, very early on, the tuned Mini was found to outperform a new Mini-Cooper that was being used by a member of our staff. As a result, it was decided to have similar modifications carried out on this car and then report on them both. It is seldom possible with these tests to compare a particular car before and after conversion, and as most owners are naturally interested in the difference tuning will make to their car, it was thought that this would be a valuable point.

'With the Mini-Cooper, which had clocked a mileage of under 1,800 before the work was carried out, a log had been kept from new and the petrol consumption was averaging about 30 mpg. After conversion, this fell to 25.9 mpg over 1,179 miles, which included all the performance testing and much traffic driving.

'Before the cylinder head was modified there had been a very marked vibration period in the engine at 3,000 rpm with a recurring harmonic at 6,000 rpm. After the combustion chambers had been equalised this was much reduced and barely noticeable in the gears, although at a sustained 6,000 rpm in top (not possible before) it could be felt, and heard as a chatter in the gearlever.

'Perhaps the most satisfying aspect of the conversion is the big increase in low-speed torque. On the standard car, clean pick-up from low engine speeds is not a strong point, and frequent use must be made of the gears. After being modified, the car will pull strongly from under 20 mph in top with no trace of hesitation or pinking on super premium fuel, despite a compression ratio of 10.4:1.

'The performance figures—91 mph maximum against 84.7, a 14-second 0–60 against 18, and 19.4-second standing quarter mile against 20.9—for an outlay of only £28, including fitting and tuning, are quite remarkable . . .

Right: Heinz gave away 57 Wolseley Hornet convertibles as prizes in a competition in 1966, the cars pictured here at the works of Crayford, who cut off their tops and fitted them with special fold-down hoods.

'The Mini that was tested at the same time was an early example that had been rallied hard for many thousands of miles. Considering its previous life, the engine felt surprisingly sweet, and was in fact smoother than the Cooper right up to its maximum speed.'

For only an extra £18.50, this car was capable of 80 mph with a 19-second 0–60, a 21-second standing quarter mile, and an average of 33 mpg. A slightly higher top speed of 83 mph, with a 19.5-second 0–60, was obtained for a £19.80 cylinder head conversion by the new firm of Janspeed—started by former Downton employees Jan Odor and David Bowns—when McNally tested their 850 cc Mini for *Autosport* in May 1963.

Better fuel consumption (37.3 mpg) and acceleration (18.8 seconds for the 0–60, 20.8 seconds for the standing quarter mile), were achieved by a £26.75 exchange gas-flowed big-valve cylinder head by Nerus, of Rye, Sussex, at the expense of ultimate speed (81 mph) when tested by *The Autocar* in July 1962. Similar figures were recorded by *Motor Sport* when they tried a Mini from Nerus, a firm run by Frank Webb, who had specialised in cylinder head design at Lagonda, HWM and with gas-flow expert Harry Weslake.

Two Minis which had won the British Racing and Sports Car Club's national saloon racing championship were also tested by the club's monthly magazine, *Motor Racing*. Editor Alan Brinton was highly impressed by John Whitmore's Don Moore-tuned example, running in similar trim to Aley's car, in December 1961. He found this car, registered TMO 840, capable of more than 100 mph, but still perfectly suitable for road use, even standard seats being retained. But when associate editor John Blunsden came to try the next year's title winner, in December 1962, he found it far from ideal for road use. It was a works Mini-Cooper which had been driven by John Love, and featured far more extensive modifications. The 77 bhp engine revved freely up to 7,500 rpm, but hardly pulled below 4,000 and needed rebuilding after every third race. The suspension had been lowered by 1.75 ins—the maximum practical—and the brakes fitted with Ferodo DS11 competition linings. Blunsden reported from his special racing seat after lapping Brands Hatch:

'It really is an amazing car to drive. You think to start with that you are right on the ragged edge, until you realise that you have been through that bend faster in other cars that you know cannot lap as fast as a hot Mini. So you try a bit harder, and you find that you go round easier next time, and then you go a bit faster still, and it is still just as easy. Then, almost without realising it, everything seems to click into place, and you feel you've been driving it all your life. If anything I would say that there was just a little less understeer than is apparent on a standard production Mini, and in view of the much higher cornering speeds involved, this means that there has been a considerable reduction. This is a big help in driving through a corner, as there is not too much scrub from the front tyres, and therefore more "feel" at the steering wheel.

'The important thing when pushing it hard, is not to go into a corner too wide, and consequently with not quite as much power on. If this happens, the inevitable understeer becomes a nuisance and you have to ease back to kill it.'

But the advent of a new monthly magazine aimed at Mini enthusiasts (and ladies in particular), which gloried under the title *small car and Mini owner, incorporating Sporting Driver*, sounded a warning note for tuners who exaggerated performances figures. In one of their first tests for the *Sporting Driver* part of the magazine, in December 1962, they demolished claims that a Mini-Cooper with a £105 Alexander Motortune conversion (consisting of a 1078-cc rebore, 1.5-inch SU carburettors, bigger valves, stronger valve springs, 9.2:1 compression, and straight-through exhaust) would also do 105 mph. Their maximum figures were 92 mph, with an 11.4-second 0–60 mph time. The unfortunate Mini also boiled merrily after performance figures had been taken, partly due to the fact that its special bolt-on electric fan—intended to force air through the radiator from inside the wing—failed to cope with an inadequate radiator pressure cap. Not all tests of early modified cars went well.

The American Minis
Meanwhile the Americans had had time to assess the Mini according to their own needs, and the leading U.S. monthly magazine dealing with imports, *Road & Track*, reported in December 1961 of a standard 850 model:

'Many people are inclined to judge something new by its first impact on them, and if the new object, whether a functional piece of consumer goods or an *objet d'art*, isn't somewhat conventional, it is likely to receive harsh criticism before its true value, or appeal, is discovered. And the 850 certainly doesn't conform to anybody's preconceived notion of the ultimate vehicle. After getting over the initial shock of the unusual body configuration and the unorthodox engine placement, the automobile buying public has, generally, accepted the 850's strictly functional design.

'In the U.S. where space is not (always) at a premium, this extra compactness is not looked upon with the enthusiasm it receives in most European cities. In crowded London, Paris or Rome, the narrow, winding, streets and crowded conditions make driving and parking problems more acute than in New York, Chicago or Los Angeles—although residents of those areas may find this hard to believe . . .

'We have long been advocates of larger wheels on cars—not the smaller wheels that seem to be so popular with automobile designers today. In all fairness, we must admit that the tiny wheels of the Austin posed no problem during our two-week test of the car. In view of the primary purpose of the 850—as a second car, or even an only car if no long trips are proposed—designer Issigonis's point about smaller wheels to allow more interior space is well taken. In all, we believe the best use for the 850 will be in short hauls and city traffic, where it is ideal.'

Road & Track's contemporary, *Car and Driver*, compared a Mini-Cooper with a similarly-priced, but bigger-bodied, Saab 850GT (a Swedish front-wheel-drive two-stroke saloon), in July 1963, and found the Mini wanting for comfort, but certainly not performance. They said:

'Driving both cars is pure joy. The Mini is madness, and we tended to laugh a lot while zipping around New York and New England. The Saab is serious, more like driving a proper GT machine. The Mini is much more responsive, and can be hurled about with complete ease and security. The Saab is more deliberate in the manner of its going, and requires higher effort and much practice to be driven as fast as the Mini on any kind of tricky road. Where the Saab wins, in this connection, is in the interior comfort; the seats are so perfect, and the driving position so natural that one never tires of fast driving. The charm of the Mini, on the other hand, begins to pale when one's knees start to ache, and the feet are going to sleep for want of any place to put them.'

Car and Driver rated the Mini-Cooper as more of a sports car than most sports cars. They said:

'If it's being driven simply for a lark on an afternoon when you have nothing to do, or if your spirits need a lift on the way home from work, the Mini-Cooper is the car for you. It is not, in our estimation, particularly *au point* for long trips under any circumstances, or even moderate trips when somone has to occupy the back seat . . .
'Even though we feel that we should be against the minute 10-inch wheels of the Mini-Cooper on principle, we can find nothing wrong with them in practice, except for a proclivity for disappearing down an occasional gopher hole. From the standpoint of the sports car enthusiast, it's a lovely car that will put many more expensive jazzier-looking, machines to shame with its handling and performance. However, as a practical combination car for the sports car enthusiast-family man, it has some limitations. The front seats simply are not comfortable enough for the long distances travelled by a typical American driver.'

Car and Driver also gave a warning of problems ahead for the British car industry in America that were to last into the 1980s when they said, with the beautifully-built Swedish Saab in mind:

'The Cooper Mini, partially because of near insurmountable labour troubles of the British car manufacturers, and attendant quality control problems, comes off as a little less car.'

The Riley Elf

The Riley Elf was reasonably well received by the British motoring press, even in its early 848 cc form. George Bishop, editor of the new *small car* (for short) magazine, pointed out in September 1962:

'Heads turn when you drive the Elf. People recognise it as some rich relation of the BMC twins, but are puzzled by the boot at the back, the chrome waistband, and the cloud of cigar smoke around it.

'Outside, the Elf has a differently-shaped bonnet and the traditional Riley radiator shell that lifts up with the bonnet, all ready to bang your head on.

'At the rear it has a boot with six cubic feet capacity which will take many odds and ends or one large suitcase and fewer odds and ends.

'The Elf, a creature which surely should be light and airy, is in fact 190 lb heavier than a standard Mini . . . the boot lid is decidedly heavy to lift and, by the way, ready to snap down like a Zambesi crocodile on the unwary. Some counterbalancing would be a good thing here.

'Seats are definitely Pullman class in comparison with the third-class tourist of the ordinary Mini, having cloth to sit on and lean against, with what looks like real cow leather where the wear comes. Unfortunately the deeper seats reduce headroom slightly, and presumably to give an illusion of more room in the rear seats, the front seats do not travel back as far as in the standard Mini, thus reducing the driver's legroom. No doubt the stop could be moved.'

Criticisms aside, Bishop went on to explain:

'Even in these days of mechanical marvels, a road-testing machine had not yet been devised. So no matter how many stopwatches, fifth wheel check speedometers, Tapley brake meters, and other tester's aids are used, it is still the impression the car makes on the man which comes out in the test report.

'If the man and the car do not get on, no matter how good the figures, he will still convey to you that he just didn't like it. So let us say from the start that I liked the Riley, and had a great deal of fun driving it.

'The finish is better than on the cheaper Mini versions, and the interior, with better seats, carpets and all that wood and leather-like stuff, is cosier. Getting in and out of Minis, like finding vacant parking meters [which were just being introduced in Britain] is an acquired art, but you don't think about it once you have learned it.'

Bishop must have been lucky with his 848 cc Elf, registered 410 TLU, because it proved faster than a normal Mini at 75 mph, although the 0–60 time was as high as 32 seconds. Fuel consumption, however, worked out at 42 mpg! *The Motor* endorsed Bishop's comments in their test of the similar Wolseley Hornet in the same month, although their example, registered 991 NWL, could attain only 71 mph, although it had a 0–60 time of 28 seconds with the 23.8-second standing quarter mile time. Fuel consumption was 36 mpg. A Mark II, 948 cc, Riley Elf—registered 814 RFC—tested by *The Motor* in July 1963 achieved 75 mph with the 0–60 time much reduced to 22.6 sec (although the standing quarter mile time was, oddly, only 22.9 sec), fuel consumption falling to 35 mpg. Britain was going through a credit squeeze at the time, and *The Motor* commented on the Riley, which, at £574, cost £127 more than a basic Mini:

> 'Whether the extra items of equipment, performance and the prestige of owning a Riley are worth the extra outlay in these days of hardening economy, depends on your approach to motoring; if you want Mini virtues coupled with superior comfort, trim, equipment and finish, you should consider the Elf seriously.'

Left: Numerous special-bodied Minis have been built over the years, including this Riley Elf styled after a number of courtesy cars built by BMC.

The Super de Luxe

They were also able to sum up in a test of the new Mini Super de Luxe in August 1963:

> 'Experience gained during the four-year span of production has eliminated several shortcomings of the earlier models, and brought about a number of important refinements. As exemplified by the Austin Super de Luxe, the most important change is probably the provision of baulk-ring synchromesh, making gearchanging much easier, though still spoilt by the position and angle of the gearlever. The distributor, coil and sparking plugs all have plastic damp-proof covers to exorcise the former bogey of drowned electrics in torrential rain or wet mist, while a self-lubricating clutch bearing, 16-blade fan, improved instruments, additional sound dampening, a new fresh-air heater, fewer lubrication points and an extended inter-service period are other changes for the better.
> 'Without any startling maximum speed or acceleration figures, the

Above: Alternators became popular in rally Minis from around 1964, proving capable of providing enough power to operate a considerable battery of auxiliary lights. It was no longer possible to mount the coil on top, however, and it was usually moved to the left-hand side of the engine bay.

Above right: This Mini has been fitted with a 1,293-cc lightened and balanced Special Tuning large valve cylinder head, 731-cam engine with 45DCOE Weber carburettors—among the most potent and tractable road conversions.

performance of the Mini on give-and-take roads is surprisingly good thanks to its exceptional roadholding and cornering qualities. However, the upright seating position and steeply-angled steering are not conducive to driver comfort on long journeys, and the firm suspension gives a rather lively ride on indifferent roads. The remarkable amount of stowage space on shelves and in side boxes has always been a strong point on the Mini, but there is still room for improvement in the standard of trim, while the interior finish—gold brocade with powder blue striping, pale blue carpets and pale grey headlining—on the fiesta yellow test car, registered 615 JOB, was garish.

'The Mini's ability to cover long distances on a small amount of petrol is important to small car buyers. This virtue is enhanced by a willingness to run satisfactorily on regular grade petrol, costing about 4s 4d [22p] per gallon, so that although its overall consumption figures show a deterioration since our last test, the cost per mile remains unusually low.'

Maximum speed was slightly higher, however, at 73 mph, with a 25.4-second 0–60 and a standing start quarter mile figure of 23.4 seconds being traded for 37.6 mpg. Only the newly-introduced Hillman Imp proved superior on statistics when compared with the Mini. The Imp achieved 78 mph, with 44 mpg and a 0–50 mph time of 15 seconds (against the Mini's 16.5 seconds). The Mini was more flexible, however, recording a 20–40 mph acceleration time of 12.5 seconds against the Imp's 14.5 seconds. Ford's Anglia and the NSU Prinz 4 had broadly the same performance as the Mini, with the Fiat 600D lagging in everything except fuel consumption, which was only 38 mpg. What these figures did not show, of course, was that the Mini had far superior handling to any of its competitors.

The 1071 cc Mini-Cooper S

Autocar, having dropped the *The* from their title for trendy reasons, were first off the mark with a test of the Mini-Cooper S, announced only a week before their report in April 1963. The test was more hurried than they would have liked and they felt that they would have been able to extract more than the 91 mph maximum speed recorded had the weather been better and the car had a longer running-in period. They were most impressed, however, by the acceleration of this pre-production example, registered 731 HOP. The figures of 13.5 seconds for the 0–60 and 19.2 seconds for the standing quarter mile were good enough on their own—but it was the way in which the 1071S would pull cleanly from as little as 10 mph in third gear which most pleased *Autocar*. The new Dunlop SP Sport tyres were also found to grip 'in a remarkable way' to help acceleration. It is interesting to note, with hindsight, that the 70-section of the tyres was thought to be a low profile in those days, whereas in the 1980s it is considered to be quite the reverse. The wider track and larger area of rubber on the road also improved the car's stability and adhesion, said *Autocar*. The uprated brakes aroused favourable comment and the testers pointed out that although the overall fuel

Top: Early works Minis were fitted with SU carburettors fed from ram pipes, the plug leads identified by one, two, three or four spots (picture one), later cars, still with spotted sparking plug leads, having a single 45DCOE Weber carburettor (picture two) *centre*, and ultimate examples with an eight-port crossflow cylinder head and fuel injection (picture three) *bottom*. There seemed little point in 'spotting' the plug leads in this case because they were very hard to find quickly beneath the injection system's serpentine air intakes. The alternator also had to be resited at the back of the engine bay with a special belt drive.

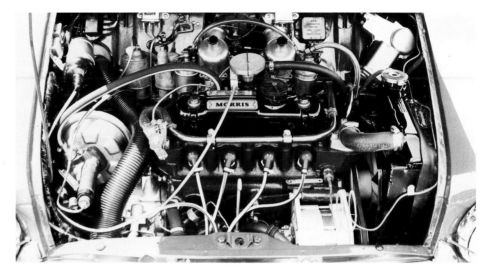

consumption of 29.4 mpg gave a range of only about 150 miles, the optional second tank was readily available. They were not alarmed at an oil pressure drop to 45 psi from 70–75 psi during motorway cruising, but suggested that an oil cooler might be necessary for competition work. The test car also gobbled oil at the rate of 130 miles per pint.

The Motor's 1071S, tested two weeks later, used oil at the same rate, but went quicker at 94.5 mph, with a 12.9-second 0–60 and 18.9-second standing quarter mile. Its fuel consumption rose, however, to 26.8 mpg. The tyres gave 'extremely high cornering power and a rapidity of response to the steering which can make cornering rather jerky until a driver strange to the car acquires the necessary lightness of touch. When he does he finds that the cornering limits are so high, both in the wet and dry, that they are difficult to explore; there is no tyre squeal and these special tyres, used for some time on BMC rally cars, reduce considerably the drift angles on bends and, in consequence, reduce also the usual change in handling between 'throttle on' and 'throttle off' conditions which becomes almost imperceptible when one is trying extremely hard.'

'The braking powers of the S are formidable, and in complete harmony with its performance. The disc-front, drum-rear, combination, allied to Hydrovac servo assistance gives extremely effective braking with only gentle pedal pressure, while repeated use brought no evidence of brake fade. The "velvet touch" proved particularly necessary in the wet when overhard application brought considerable initial pull until the discs dried off. An emergency stop from about 70 mph on dry roads, however, pulled the car up virtually all-square, with the slightest hint of wheel lock on the nearside . . .

'In all the Mini-Cooper S is a car of delightful Jekyll and Hyde character, with astonishing performance concealed within its unpretentious Mini skin.'

Bill Boddy made his 1071S go marginally quicker still for *Motor Sport* in August 1963 with 11.9 seconds for the 0–60 and 18.7 for the standing quarter mile. Top speed was 92 mph, however, and Boddy commented:

'One of the surprises I got when I first drove a Mini-Cooper was the unexpected docility—the excellent balance between good acceleration and civilised step-off, between ultra-powerful brakes and sensitive, wet-road retardation. The quality upheld in the S-series, is even emphasised by the almost luxurious Mini-Cooper interior and a flecked upholstery and trim more suitable to a lady's boudoir than the inside of a rally car!'

McNally had his 1071S, registered 732 HOP, up to 95 mph for *Autosport* in the same month with the same standing quarter mile time as Boddy, but only 12.3 seconds for the 0–60. He said:

'First impressions of the car are quite surprising, for the increased power has not affected the flexibility in any way. Driving through London is an absolute delight, the smallest gap can be taken advantage of and the gearbox permits lightning quick gear changes, which enables one to be permanently ready for every situation. In fact, you have all the advantages of the Mini coupled with really rapid acceleration and extremely potent brakes.

'Driving up to London from the country in the morning, when the pace is usually at its hottest, the S-type proved king of the road and showed itself to be the ideal car for this type of journey. Within a little while, the motoring public will realise that the little S they see in their mirror deserves the utmost courtesy.'

The British monthly, *Cars Illustrated*, descended from a UK edition of *Sports Cars Illustrated*, recorded largely the same performance figures for their 1071S, registered 63 FOL, and liked almost every aspect, apart from the clutch which editor Martyn Watkins said 'requires a strong left leg under crowded conditions. Once the road has opened up, however, and the full performance of this very lively little car can be used, the firm bite of the clutch is appreciated, and assists greatly in effecting fast clean gearchanges.'

On the other side of the Atlantic, *Car and Driver*, the American equivalent of *Cars Illustrated*, published a road test in July 1964 comparing the works Mini-Cooper S driven by Paddy Hopkirk and Henry Liddon to victory in the 1964 Monte Carlo Rally with its chief adversary, a 285-bhp lightweight Ford Falcon. British journalist David Phipps, who conducted the test in the Midlands, said:

'After the Falcon, the Mini-Cooper S didn't seem to go at all. We rowed it along with the gear lever, checked several times to see whether the handbrake was still on, and then discovered that we were doing around 80 mph after all and had gone around several quite distinct corners without really noticing them. The secret of the Falcon is torque—you just get in there with your right foot, press gently, and it responds instantly in any gear by thumping you in the back and departing onto the next county. The Mini gets similar results by the use of 7,000 rpm in the gears and 7,000 rpm round most of the turns. It handles like a precision instrument, in which x degrees of lock and y degrees of throttle opening equal cornering speeds far higher than most people would imagine physically possible.

'On really tight corners, or on narrow roads where there is a likelihood of traffic from the opposite direction, the Mini is potentially faster than the Falcon because of its diminutive size. But on reasonable roads, highways, and racing circuits, the Ford is faster (as indeed it should be) using power as a function of roadholding; the Mini may well be faster into a turn, but the Ford will invariably be quicker out of it . . .

'From the manner in which it was built and prepared—and above all, driven—Hopkirk's car deserved to win the 1964 Monte Carlo Rally. In a year when luck, the weather, and the whims of the organisers had a minimal effect, Hopkirk's victory can be described as a triumph of science. Had the rally been a race, Bo Ljungfeldt would have won easily in the

Top left: Wheels varied widely over the years, with Minilites shod by Dunlop SP41 radial tyres carrying hundreds of studs in early works Cooper S rally form (picture one) *top left*, Goodyear tyres of similar pattern often favoured on later machines (picture two) *top right*, with many other manufacturers' alloy wheels, such as these by Carmonia, following the Minilite mould (picture three) *middle left*, although Goodyear have marketed their own wheels for the Mini (picture four) *Middle right*. But Cosmic aluminium wheels remain favourites on early cars (picture five) *bottom left* with Revolution four-spokers adopted for many later Minis (picture six) *bottom right*.

Falcon—but then a 4.7-litre car should be faster than a 1.1-litre car. It's a special tribute to Hopkirk and the Mini that they equalled Ljungfeldt's time on one of the special sections.'

Autocar and *Motor Sport* were among many publications which tried these cars, *Autocar* reporting in February 1964 that the Mini (which had a lower-than-standard 4.14:1 final drive) had 80 bhp at the flywheel and 60 at the road wheels. This gave it a top speed of 93 mph at 7,500 rpm, with a 0–60 time of around 12 seconds. Mike Twite, of *Motor Sport*, was amazed to discover how standard the car was, pointing out in the issue of March 1964 that the Falcon was far from standard and it seemed doubtful that 1,000 such cars had been sold to qualify it for Group 1 competition with the Mini. He also said that all the world seemed to want a drive in the Mini which had won the Monte, including an inebriated soldier who stole it from its temporary parking place outside a club in London one night and led the police a merry chase until he was stopped by a road block in Knightsbridge!

The 1275-cc Mini-Cooper S

Three magazines managed to test an early dry suspension Mini-Cooper 1275S, registered 97 LOK, in 1964. And the first test, by John Bolster in *Autosport* in July, was the most successful. Bolster, an accomplished sprint driver, managed to get its acceleration times down to 9 seconds for the 0–60 and 17.6 seconds for the standing quarter mile, with a top speed of 100 mph. He explained:

'The figures depend largely on the skill of the driver, for a "racing" getaway merely produces clouds of rubber smoke! I made my best time by starting with the engine almost ticking over and then stepping on the accelerator. Rough driving will even promote a further bout of wheelspin on the change into second. Smooth handling pays when one has this sort of torque at one's disposal. Up to 60 or 70 mph, the acceleration is tremendous, but then the unstreamlined shape of the saloon body takes its toll . . . it cannot be too strongly emphasised that this model bears no resemblance to the typical modified Mini, many of which are rough and noisy to an extent which becomes wearisome for everyday motoring.'

By the time *Autocar* got 974 LOK in the next month, it was using oil at the rate of 120 miles per pint and the quarter mile time had been extended to 18.4 seconds with the 0–60 in 11.2 seconds. Top speed was 96 mph with 28.5 mpg overall. This was despite having fitted an electric rev counter to make performance testing easier. *Autocar* pointed out:

'Using this instrument, we tried a number of varying techniques, making changes above the power peak at 6,300 rpm, on the peak at 5,900 rpm, and below it at 5,700 and 5,500 rpm. Because of the gearbox spacing, the best times were recorded by going no higher than 5,900 in first and second, and only 5,700 rpm in third. These revs correspond to road speeds of 30 mph, 50 mph and 66 mph and are all substantially below the little yellow markings on the car's speedometer. It is possible to rev the engine to the mark at 33 mph in first and to 54 mph in second, but we never reached the mark at 78 mph in third because the engine became too rough and we feared it might suffer. Our maximum of 74 in this gear corresponds to 6,200 rpm, whereas we were able to reach 6,500 in the lower gears.

'This top-end roughness could be felt as quite a violent vibration through the gearlever, which did not, however, chatter to anything like the extent of the other Coopers we have driven. One reason for this is that a new pattern gearlever is now fitted, with a bonded rubber coupling at its base to dampen its movement and reduce resonances. There is another engine vibration, corresponding with the idling speed just below 1,000 rpm, which causes the steering column to shake, and the wiper blades to flutter on the windscreen.'

Although the 1275 engine was not noted for its smooth running, further evidence that this car had been hard-used could be seen in the comments:

'During sustained high-speed running on motorways the oil pressure dropped from its customary 60 psi to about 45 psi, indicating the need for an oil cooler under these conditions. The water temperature also approached the danger zone unless the speed was kept below 85 mph.'

Motor, which had by now also dropped *The* from its title, recorded similar times with 974 LOK a month later although the oil consumption had risen to 75 miles per pint. Their testers commented:

'Minis set their own performance standards and it is by these that we tend to judge each new specimen of the breed. In a way this is a pity because the 1275S, though probably the best Mini to date, is not the fastest of its kind we have tried. Yet judged by other production cars of comparable price, it is a truly remarkable vehicle.

'Even if some of the novelty has worn off, our enthusiasm for Mini motoring reached new peaks after only 1,500 miles in this car. With a maximum speed of 96.8 mph, vivid acceleration and still further improved handling, it is enormous fun to drive and just about the most practical toy that £750 will buy. It has most of the failings of other Minis— uncomfortable seats, an awkward driving position, bumpy ride—plus some of its own like very heavy oil consumption, but the sheer delight of driving was adequate compensation for us. Two thousand pounds will not buy a sports car that makes shorter work of cross-country journeys on indifferent roads, and even on a motorway, this Mini can average over 90 mph without apparent strain.'

Early Special-Bodied Minis

Much speculation went on as soon as the Mini was introduced as to what could be done with its basic floorpan—but few coachbuilders rose to the bait because

once all the body panels had been removed the entire structure was liable to collapse. There was also the challenge of the relatively high line of the engine so far to the front, making an elegant, down-swept, nose almost impossible to achieve. The general feeling was that if you were going to the trouble of building a special frame to get round these basic problems, you might as well fit a more powerful engine in any case. But some customers would not take no for an answer, including an Italian engineering consultant called Sergio Piatti, who commissioned competition body builders Zagato to work to what was essentially his own design. Their speciality was building very light alloy bodies over rigid tubular steel frames, which proved to be ideal in this case as the result was quite like some of their most successful work on Alfa Romeo platforms. The floorpan used was that from a Minivan to give them more scope for better lines because it had a longer wheelbase. Once this Alfa-like device had been built, it was subsequently fitted with a Downton Mini-Cooper unit of 1,080 cc running on a higher, 3.44:1, final drive. It was in this form that *The Motor* tested the Zagato

Top left: For city driving, the automatic Mini has it every time, said John Bolster of *Autosport,* a fervant fan of the two-pedal car.

Above: The Mini was on to its mark II bodyshell before production of the automatic variety really got into its swing. Badging on the standard Mini (an Austin in picture one) took the form of a chrome strip above the new Mark II boot logo with an 850 in the bottom right hand corner. The Riley and Wolseley badges were not so wide as the Mark II logo, however, so—to avoid an unbalanced appearance—their automatic script was moved down to the left-hand side of the bootlid, opposite the model name and type.

Mini in March 1962 and returned the extraordinary performance figures of 114.7 mph with an 11-second 0–60 time and 18.4 seconds for the standing quarter mile—plus a fuel consumption as low as 32 mpg overall. Technical writer Charles Bulmer reported:

'The nearest comparison is with the single-carburettor Lotus Elite. Both cars took 18.4 seconds for the standing quarter mile and had virtually the same performance up to 80 mph. Above this the Mini actually draws away, reaching 100 mph in 35.8 seconds (against 41.1) and recording a mean maximum speed 3 mph higher.

'Since the Zagato has about the same frontal area as the 75-bhp Elite and weighs 28 lb more (at 13.5 cwt), some extremely impressive conclusions can be drawn about the efficiency of the streamlining and the power output of the engine.'

The British equivalent was nothing near like so fast despite weighing about the same, although it was far more civilised inside. It was during 1961 and 1962 that the Ogle design company of Letchworth, Herts, which also made glass fibre bodies, had begun converting Minis into pretty little two-seater grand touring cars. In this case, the short wheelbase saloon car floorpan was used with much strengthening, especially around the scuttle. Ogle's glass fibre body was then bonded on at a cost of £550—effectively doubling the price of a basic Mini—and eventually limiting the production run to 80. People who could afford such a car, not surprisingly, usually went for the higher-performance Mini as a base. In the 997cc Ogle Mini-Cooper which *Autocar* tested in June 1962 had an Alexander conversion that gave it 55 bhp at the wheels—about the same claim as that of the Zagato's Downton unit. *Autocar* reported of a car that recorded 99 mph flat out with a 16.2-second 0–60, a 19.7-second standing quarter mile, and returned 29 mpg:

'With an overall length of 11 ft 2 ins, it is 14 ins longer than the ordinary Mini, whose wheelbase and track are retained. It is also 3 ins wider and 6.5 ins lower. The two doors are wide, and clear normal kerbs, so it is not as difficult to climb in and out as might be imagined. The two seats, tailored to individual drivers, are carefully shaped to give comfortable support and adequate location, and the rearward adjustment allows for the over six-footers. Head clearance is just sufficient. A dished steering wheel is fitted and the rake of the standard Mini column increased by some 10 degrees towards the horizontal. This gives a satisfactory driving position, although the pedals are offset considerably towards the centre of the car.

'Despite the proportionately small window area, the view out is good, and even the oblique back window of plastic material allows a fair field of vision for the rear view mirror. Curved and raked back, the screen is wide with narrow pillars. The front quarter lights are fixed, while those at the rear hinge outwards as extractors. Because the doors are thick, it has been possible to provide wind-down windows and also cutaways inside to increase elbow room. The door windows are properly framed and the sealing is good.'

small car were not so impressed with the far simpler Viking Hornet Sport marketed by Wolseley dealers W.J. Last, of Woodbridge, Suffolk, at £757. They rated the Wolseley Hornet, on which it was based, as 'among the ugliest, most uncomfortable, and least desirable cars ever offered to the great British public.' In their opinion, the Viking, with its soft-top conversion by the Kent body firm of Crayford, go-faster stripes, and Taurus engine modifications which gave it an extra 10 bhp, looked 'even worse than the Wolseley'.

They added, however, that 'the basic attraction of such a package is undeniable, and at only £200 more than an ordinary Hornet it offers some startling improvements in driveability.'

'Most noticeable is the low haircut which literally causes BMC's

Above: The Wolseley Hornet gained an implacable foe in *CAR* magazine editor Doug Blain, particularly because he just could not stand the radiator grille . . .

Above: The mark III Riley Elf seemed to escape the testers' brickbats, that privilege being reserved for the almost identical Hornet.

Above right: The Cooper is the car for every enthusiast who cares above all for low-cost performance, said *CAR*, muttering at the same time about a certain lack of styling, emphasised by Paddy Hopkirk's 1967 Alpine Rally-winning works example.

Right: Broadspeed produced some extraordinary Mini-Cooper S road racers, including this 1275-cc example driven by John Handley which provided many of the thrills at Mallory Park in May 1964 in a desperate duel with works driver John Fitzpatrick's Downton car. Fitzpatrick won, but Broadspeed had really arrived . . .

handiwork, apart from windscreen and doors, to stop at the waistline. The substitute hood is almost exactly like the one you'll find on grandma's vintage Clyno except that it has a couple of modern overcentre clips to clamp it to the top of the screen in front. Material is vinyl fabric on a strip steel frame and the whole thing is a fixture; you can fold it up in a vaguely unwieldy bundle over the rear backrest, but in the normal run of things you can't take it right off . . .

'With the hood up, the Viking is about as snug as any four-seat convertible we've tried. Special Perspex sidescreens keep the wind out of the rear quarters and clever little flaps with lift-the-dot fasteners take care of sundry draughts from around the tops of the door windows—which keep their rigid frames, as on the drophead Morris Minors . . .

'The Crayford conversion involves quite a lot of strengthening with

*Above and left:*Driving a Mini Moke was rather like World War One flying, said *Cars and Car Conversions*(pictures one and two), the hood having little influence without its sidescreens on keeping out the weather. Passengers, however, had to be prepared for an exciting time (picture three).

patches of sheet steel welded in under the door sills and below the back seat, plus special tongue-type door location fittings to stop flexing on bad roads. The test Viking waggled quite noticeably on wavy surfaces and we found a lot of scuttleshake when the tarmac was anything but first rate. The only consolation is that the same thing happens with almost all modern convertibles, home-made or not.

'Inside, new seat mountings make the standard seats far more comfortable and allow you to fiddle around with literally dozens of different settings. A neatly-cowled column-mounted rev counter offers essential engine information sensibly close to the driver's line of sight. An SPQR Major-change gearshift conversion successfully banishes the familiar Mini feeling of poking about with a walking stick among a boxful of loose gears. Another SPQR precision extra, a cast-aluminium organ throttle pedal and replacement nipple-lubricated linkage, helps to cut down the notorious ADO stickiness . . .

'If you're looking for a four-seat open car with plenty of driver amenities, then look no further. It may be ugly, but it's fun. And there's no second choice.'

small car found the £1,300 demonstration saloon run by coachbuilder Harold Radford far more agreeable in October 1964. Its super-quality off-white paintwork with white vinyl Webasto sunroof, and white wall Dunlop tyres attracted a lot of attention—but it was the interior which left the most lasting impression. Editor Doug Blain reported:

'Instead of the usual pesky sliding windows in the doors our car had proper swivelling quarter panels and full-width wind-up panes. But you had to look hard to notice that there weren't any corresponding winding handles on the inside. Instead, twin pushbuttons in each flank controlled electric motors buried in the fully-trimmed door panels which raised and lowered the windows precisely to order . . .'

Electric windows were still a great novelty in the mid-1960s, especially among Mini-owners. Blain went on:

'Inside the quality's laid on so thick you can actually smell the thick cowhide covering the seats, trim panels, even the upholstered box for oddments between the two front seats. The seats themselves are strictly non-standard with deep foam upholstery, wrap-round backrests, bolstered sides and under-thigh supports and Microcell lever-type adjuster mechanisms which give a full range of rake positions. At the back, a completely new matching bench replaces the original Mini item and its back rest is split to allow either or both sides to fold, revealing a carpeted platform for heavy luggage behind . . .'

We would have to wait seventeen years for the Metro to become the first 'Mini' with that facility as standard. Blain added: 'The other obvious change is Radford's substitution of a normal dash panel for BMC's instrumented luggage shelf . . .'

Amazingly, this instrument binnacle used wood-grained Formica as its trimming rather than the walnut you would have expected from such a coachbuilder. But at least Mini-lovers would not have to wait so long to get it as standard—it was very similar to that which would appear on the Clubman, except that it had a rev counter tucked away near the door, totally out of sight while driving!

Radford's interior furnishings included an expensive Motorola radio with several speakers to give a stereo effect (nobody had thought of adapting a tape recorder for a car then), cigar lighters, leather-covered arm rests, thick nylon-pile carpeting, wood-rimmed steering wheel, dipping mirror, twin vanity mirrors in the sun visors, and a demister panel for the back window because heated elements had not yet been introduced. These fittings added considerably to the weight of the vehicle, so performance was restored by a 1200-cc Downton engine. Blain commented:

> 'The first thing you notice when you open the door, apart from its weight, is the almost overpowering smell of leather from inside. It does a lot for a man, that smell; in fact, we've always thought there must be a market for a pressurepack Essence of Leather for spraying inside your vinyl-upholstered go-to-work banger.'

The back seats turned out to be more for show, or children, because the upholstery was so thick that a normal-sized adult was too restricted to get comfortable. The extra weight affected the handling, too. Blain said:

> 'Even with 30 psi in the front and 28 in the back tyres, at which pressures the ride was still completely free from bounce, we got a startling amount of tyre scrub and far more understeer than normal.'

In more modest climes, the London tuners Speedwell removed the 848 cc engine from a Mini estate, registered AMH 98A and substituted their own 1,152-cc version using an early Cooper crank and a 67.1-mm bore. Special connecting rods and pistons were needed, and Speedwell used their own alloy gas-flowed head which gave a compression ratio of 11:1. The power output with two 1.5-inch SU carburettors was quoted at 91 bhp, and *Autocar* recorded performance figures of 11.3 seconds for the 0–60, 17.9 for the standing quarter mile and 101.6 mph maximum with a very good 32.6 mpg in August 1964. They found also that the longer wheelbase improved stability of this model, christened the Speedwell Courier, over that of a normal saloon.

Motor agreed when they tested a standard Mini estate, registered 73 MOA, in the same month, adding:

> 'Increasing the wheelbase by four inches reduces the effect of the transition from understeer to oversteer should you take your foot off the throttle suddenly in a corner. Cornering quickly over bumpy roads can lift the inside front wheel (the steering goes light when it happens) but the handling remains safe and predictable at most times, with the same characteristics in the wet.'

Top left: The mark II Mini, which in standard form (picture one) or Cooper (picture two) *top right* specification, received a lukewarm response from the road testers, with criticism centring on items such as the by-now old-fashioned door pulls and lack of anything more sophisticated than a strap to retain the door when open (picture three) *bottom left*. In fact, they pleaded for wind-up windows and a little more civilisation, having experienced it in foreign cars and the Riley Elf (picture four) *bottom right*.

The estate's performance figures were well up to those of the saloon at 73 mph maximum, a 25.8 second 0–60 mph time, and a 23.3-second standing quarter mile with 38 mpg. The rival Austin A40 was slightly faster at 77 mph, but a little slower on acceleration and used more fuel at 37 mpg, whereas Ford's Anglia had a similar top speed and could do only 30 mpg while lagging marginally on acceleration. The nearest foreign opposition, Fiat's Giardiniera could not quite manage 60 mph and scored only in having 46 mpg fuel figures. *Motor* commented on the estate's conception:

'Some 15 years ago, these cars were far from common on our roads. As conversions of standard saloons, they were more the prerogative of landowners, used in the country for carrying shooting parties, fishing gear or the occasional hay bale. Such distinctions have now gone and the estate car is as much part of the road scene as, say, the Mini itself.

'Having long put up with the difficulty of wedging articles on the back seat, the shopping housewife will find the low-loading ease of the Countryman a big attraction, for the Mini is the lowest of all; dog and carrycot are both so much more easily catered for. Just as comfortable and acceptable as the Jones's four-door saloon, estate cars no longer carry the stigma of a "trade" vehicle.'

More Dry-Suspension Modified Minis

Four other tests of Minis fitted with Speedwell alloy cylinder heads were equally impressive. The head came in two forms, a GT for less-powerful BMC A-series engines and a Clubman, which was virtually the same as that used in Formula Junior units, for more powerful applications. Three carburettor kits were available for use with the head: twin SUs, a single twin-choke Weber, or the twin Amals more normally found on motor cycles. The Amals were cheaper than the Weber and more difficult to tune than the still cheaper SUs; but they gave more power than the SUs and held their tune longer. *Motor Sport* reported on a Mini de luxe fitted with Amals and the Speedwell GT head in July, 1964:

'The only unusual control is a motor cycle-type choke lever attached to the parcel shelf. The starting procedure can be tricky but once the technique is learned, first-time starts can be made without trouble. With the engine cold it is necessary to have the mixture control at fully rich and then depress the accelerator when the starter is operated. The engine usually fires first time and then the mixture control must be closed fairly quickly to prevent stalling. In extreme cold weather it may be necessary to flood the carburettors by "tickling" the button on the float chambers, but the engine always started well with us without resorting to this technique. To start the engine when warm it is necessary to "catch" the engine by depressing the throttle just after the starter begins to turn.'

The 848-cc Speedwell Mini's performance was well up to that of a Mini-Cooper because, although it was slightly slower up to 50 mph, it was quicker to 60 at 15 seconds, with a better 20-second standing quarter mile and a top speed that was faster, 86 mph. Fuel consumption with the more efficient head and carburettor combination—which could run on an octane-rating as low as 94—was an excellent 34 mpg. A Mini-Cooper with the Clubman head and 1150-cc engine on SU carburettors gave Patrick McNally the ride of his life for *Autosport* in December 1963. The car clocked 114 mph with a strong following wind for a 109-mph two-way average, and returned acceleration figures of 8.4 seconds for the 0–60 and a 16.9 standing quarter mile despite pulling a high 3.44:1 axle ratio for smoother cruising at 100 mph. This car was also fitted with a rear anti-roll bar which reduced its understeer a little. *The Motor* managed only 104 mph with the same car in the same month, with slightly inferior acceleration, but recorded a fuel consumption of 21.5 mpg. They were most impressed with its special Restall seats, of which their tallest, 6 ft 4-inch, tester commented: 'This is the first Mini I have been really comfortable in'. The only problem with the seats was that they hindered access to the handbrake and to the second gear slot if they were adjusted too far forward.

Speedwell also provided a Riley Elf with the same conversion for *Motor Sport* in the same month which achieved 107 mph, with a 12.4-second 0–60 and an 18.8-second standing quarter mile. Taking off could be quite a problem, however, as *Motor Sport* pointed out:

Top left: The long-nosed Minis, such as the Clubman (picture one), with revised interior (picture two) *top right*, more space under the bonnet (picture three) *above*, wind-up windows and improved trim (pictures four and five) *centre and below*, proved far more appealing to testers.

'The car was fitted with the standard Dunlop C41 tyres and violent wheelspin occurred all the time in first gear. By letting in the clutch at 3,000 rpm in first gear the car just stood still while the rev counter whistled round the dial, and it was only by dropping to 2,000 rpm that we were able to get the car moving at all. In dry conditions with Dunlop SP tyres it should be possible to knock two seconds off figures above 50 mph.'

The Hydrolastic Minis

Opinions differed as to the merits—or otherwise—of Hydrolastic suspension on the Mini, despite the success of the system on the longer wheelbase 1100 saloons and the recently-introduced big car, the 1800. *Autocar* were much in favour when they first tested a fluid-sprung Mini in January 1965, saying:

'The unanimous opinion after some 600 miles in varying conditions is that the new suspension only improves the Mini. Those who climb in and expect the car to feel transformed, with a silky smooth level ride over come-what-may, will be disappointed. It is still very much a Mini in the way it behaves, and although the limitations of a short wheelbase and small wheels are still apparent, they are not nearly so obvious as on the cars with solid rubber cone springs. Comparatively speaking, pitching is now eliminated and the new car rides bumps and undulations on a level fore-and-aft keel which is well matched to the even way it corners without roll. Gone is the sharp vertical jogging which disturbs the passengers and is a characteristic unique to the previous type of Mini. Gone, too, is the jerking caused by reversals of engine torque (especially on the higher-powered variants) which has caused a boom in the accessory sales of anti-friction throttle cables.

'During fast cornering, only the very edge of the precision feels missing and one can still hurl the car about to almost crazy extremes without getting into serious trouble, and with the same degree of confidence.'

Autocar also found the 1965 Mini's improved brakes, gearbox and clutch to their liking. Henry Manney was not so sure when he reported on a brief drive in a Hydrolastic Mini-Cooper S at Britain's Goodwood race circuit for *Road & Track* in January 1965:

'The increased suspension movement necessary for carrying Auntie Dollie and her parcels doesn't seem to agree with it at speed. There was more lean and the customary Mini on rails feeling was slightly lessened, even if you could stuff it through tight corners on full understeer as before.'

Autocar, possibly, had more time to assess a Hydrolastic Mini-Cooper, registered DOB 393C, when tested in September 1965, commenting after repeating their previous assertions:

'Hydrolastic systems are not yet offered with self-levelling devices, so

Above: By the time *Motor* reacquainted itself with the basic Mini in 1973 they have grown to like it a good deal more than when the mark II was introduced in 1967!

one major problem remains. A full load of passengers together with luggage in the boot causes the little car to assume a very tail-down attitude, so that the front wheels barely seem to touch the ground at all and the headlamp beams scan the horizon.

'The Mini's Hydrolastic system cannot really cope well with exceptionally rough roads such as Belgian-type pave, or with deep corrugations. It liked even less test sections of regular long-weave pitches.'

Autocar were greatly impressed with the new short-stroke engine, however, reporting:

'Despite its unchanged listed power output, it is noticeably livelier than those we have driven previously, the improvements being more obvious at higher speeds. Rest to 60 mph was achieved in 16.8 seconds (18 seconds for the 997-cc car) and there was a 12.4-second improvement in the time taken to reach 80 mph (38.2 seconds). The standing quarter mile time was also shaved from 20.9 seconds to 20.1 and the maximum speed is 5.3 mph higher at exactly 90 mph.'

Fuel consumption was 32.5 mpg.

Motor got the 0–60 time of the same car down to 14.8 seconds in November 1965, but could manage only 88.7 mph flat out. Whereas *Autocar* had said that the Mini-Cooper was now really just a faster version of the de luxe (with the advent of the higher-performance S), *Motor* were still thoroughly enjoying themselves. They enthused:

'It can be said without too much exaggeration that if you haven't driven a Mini-Cooper, you haven't lived. Even if you are a most reluctant and unenthusiastic driver and your vehicle is as mundane as a milkfloat, you would be certain to succumb eventually to its charm. In such a car, staid potterers regain their lost youth, knocking minutes or even hours off their journey times and enjoying themselves throughly into the bargain. What's more it can all be done in perfect safety . . .

'The engine has a considerably shorter stroke than the earlier 997-cc engine, so that easier motorway cruising with less wear should now be available. And readers who have heard tales about oil-gulping Coopers can be reassured: our test car returned a consumption of better than 600 miles to the pint.'

But on the Hydrolastic suspension, they said:

'Here we are less sure that an all-round improvement has been effected. Certainly, Hydrolastic has improved the ride—mainly by converting pitch into bounce—but it also gives the impression that there is a good deal more roll than occurred in earlier Minis, although to be fair we must say that this does not seem to affect its ability to go round corners at high speeds nor its feeling of safety when doing so. Another result of the

Hydrolastic suspension is to allow marked power-controlled changes in pitch attitude: quite mild application of the throttle makes the car sit up on its haunches, while equally mild deceleration—due to lifting off at high speeds, say—produces a nosedive.'

Motor also produced a cautionary note over the brakes:

'They are heavier than most, but in conjunction with the reluctance of the SP41 tyres to allow the wheels to lock, the extra effort proves more of an advantage than otherwise, making smooth braking easier and skidding less likely. Completely free of fade in our test, the brakes faded alarmingly if the standard one minute intervals [between applications] were reduced to around 45 seconds, suggesting that the heat capacity of the disc brakes is marginal.'

But John Bolster was fully in favour of Hydrolastic suspension when he tried a Mini-Cooper 1275S, registered AOE 855B, for *Autosport* in February 1965. He said:

'On the road, the Hydrolastic Mini feels almost soggy at parking speeds but the suspension seems to become progressively harder as the velocity increases. The improvement in riding comfort is very great, the Hydrolastic car giving a much more level motion, both when the driver is alone and when all the seats are occupied. At racing speeds on a circuit, the new car is just as marvellously controllable as last year's model was. Indeed, I felt even more at home in it. No doubt we shall soon see, in saloon car racing, whether the Hydrolastic system can be made to give increased cornering power or not. For use on the road, though, I am completely sold on it, from every point of view.'

Below left: The 1275GT's adoption of larger wheels proved controversial at first.

Below: The Clubman was essentially an ultra-compact yet roomy, people package which seemed to go on and on, said *Autocar* in 1975.

The Automatic Mini

Bolster then went on to test an automatic Mini for *Autosport* in May 1966, pointing out:

'Most enthusiastic drivers enjoy changing gear—it adds to the interest of a cross-country journey. Yet, nobody can obtain any pleasure from holding out or slipping the clutch for hours in the traffic of London or Paris. For city driving, the automatic has it every time, and by its nature it stands up much better to this sort of abuse.

'American-type automatic transmissions work admirably with big engines, but they soak up too much power and have too few ratios for use with really small power units. Yet the lively small car is the ideal traffic car, and there is a tremendous demand for automatic drive in something very much more compact than a V8.

'Obviously the physical dimensions of the Mini-Minor make it an excellent vehicle for town use, and BMC were extremely wise to take a clean sheet of paper and start right from the beginning when designing an automatic version . . .

'There is no clutch pedal and the car will move away from a standstill on any of the four gears, though obviously a top-gear start is a fairly leisurely proceeding. The maxima on the four speeds are similar to those of a standard Mini, but first gear contains a freewheel. This is a sensible safety feature, for it would be easy for a careless driver to engage first by mistake and lock the front wheels at speed . . .

'By far the most impressive feature of the new box is its mechanical efficiency. Except that one cannot spin the wheels at the getaway by brutal clutch work, the automatic Mini feels just as lively as a standard one. Indeed, with its instantaneous upchanges on full throttle, it would probably leave the other car in typical town driving.'

Bolster then went on to record a maximum speed of 73 mph with a standing quarter mile in 23.3 seconds, although he emphasises that his figures were obtained one-up whereas those of many other magazines included a passenger and heavy test equipment. His fuel consumption was an impressive 37 mpg. *Autocar*'s two-up plus test equipment figures were slightly inferior when they tested an automatic Mini, registered DOK 445C, in October 1965, and the fuel consumption rose to 33 mpg. They said:

'Only when one is driving hard and keeping the accelerator to the floor is there sometimes a bit of a lurch during upward changes, whereas in the ordinary way—particularly when pottering in busy built-up areas—they can be practically imperceptible. Downward changes on the overrun, as occur when one is dropping speed to a crawl or standstill, are likewise scarcely noticed . . .

'One is apt to overlook the fact that the automatic shift points are graded to suit the engine's torque curve, and that not much time is saved by taking it up to higher revs by "using the stick". While one has the impression that much better progress is being made when shifting manually, in fact we found this saved only 0.3 seconds in a quarter mile from a standing start . . .

'If one chooses to spend most of the time in automatic drive, the manual holds are still useful—for instance, when one wants to hold third a few mph above the automatic change-point while overtaking other vehicles or tackling a long climb, again, in hilly country they are invaluable to increase engine braking during lengthy descents.'

The Wolseley Hornet Revisited

By August 1965, *small car* had grown up to become *CAR* magazine with a brief to cover all kinds of cars, including those beyond the former 1,600-cc limit. But editor Doug Blain's opinions changed little about the Wolseley Hornet as he reported:

'Road test Minis *mit* Moulton plumbing are elusive beasties, for reasons best known to BMC. We thought we would be clever and book up a whole string of Coopers and such for the last couple of months of last year, when we knew Hydrolastic was due to become standard equipment. We got the cars all right—but they were the old rubber-sprung kind, and the only amusement to be derived from them lay in trying to persuade knowledgeable passengers that they were what they were not.

'Actually it can be surprisingly hard to tell. A very new Min with the old rubber suspension feels uncannily "different", certainly from an older one which has had time to settle (ever noticed how Mini wheelarches seem to creep closer to the wheels after a year or so?) and grow firm. But the real giveaways are the nose-up jerk on takeoff and, as a week with a Hydrolastic Wolseley Hornet has just demonstrated, a great deal more understeer than with non-interconnected springing . . .

'Pitch-free ride on wavy and bumpy surfaces is supposed to be Hydrolastic's forte, and certainly in the BMC 1100 range—and even more in the 1800—there's an astonishing freedom from vertical movement even on the most frightful farm tracks. The Hornet's short wheelbase doesn't really make such an ideal platform, and at the fairly high cruising speeds of which the car is capable a sensitive driver gets the feeling that there isn't really time for the front end to warn the tail accurately about what's coming . . .

'As for cornering, that super understeer we spoke about is definitely there. Extra body roll—unexpected in a Mini-derivative but definitely present in our Hornet—could well account for it, and if so a plain old-fashioned anti-roll bar is the obvious answer.

'The less said about the Wolseley part of the specification the better; the hideous grille on the front is a mere mockery (it is more than two feet away from the radiator proper anyway) and the ungainly bustle at the back makes just enough difference to the overall length to keep the car out of the special little parking spaces which so often seem to open up for an ordinary Mini.'

Motor were less scathing about their Hydrolastic Hornet, registered BFC 943C, in September 1965, but said of the suspension:

'Its main disadvantage is that a load can make the tail dip appreciably—there are limits to the amount of luggage the car will take before the headlights need readjustment, a factor which needs more consideration on the short wheelbase Minis than the longer 1100 and 1800s. At £579 the Hornet costs over £100 more than a basic Mini and about the same as the more sporting Mini-Cooper or the more family-sized Vauxhall Viva. But the trappings of luxury inside, with thick carpets, reasonable sound deadening and wooden facia, put it in a small but useful market of its own.'

The performance figures of 76 mph maximum, 21 seconds 0–60, and 34.7 mpg put it on a par with the similarly-priced Viva, Singer Chamois derivant of the Hillman Imp, Ford Anglia Super and Fiat 850. *Motor* confined their comparisons to figures, but *CAR* went further with more comprehensive comparison tests. One—in which a Wolseley Hornet was compared with a Hillman Super Imp—appeared in June 1966. The Super Imp came out in front on styling and the fact that it had synchromesh on first gear, but fell behind on acceleration to the tune of 2 seconds up to 60 mph, and suffered from a typical rear-engined lack of stability in a side wind. It also exhibited more pitch than the Hornet and a tendency to lift a front wheel under cornering. Nevertheless, *CAR* said:

'Perhaps the thing to establish is that both the Wolseley and the Hillman are wrong insofar as they pretend to be luxury cars. They are too small to be truly luxurious and still hold four people. With this in mind, we prefer the Hillman because it is much less false: it lacks the Hornet's silly associations with a long-dead marque, and it offers a few more genuine features such as sound-deadening. The other things are valuable only when they help to disguise any economy car's bargain basement origins. In fact the only luxury to which either aspire is psychological.'

Autocar also indulged in a comparison test between a 1071-cc Cooper S and a Ford Cortina GT in August 1965. The format was novel, being based on the first year's driving by two owners of these cars, which retailed at around £750. Geoffrey Howard experienced little trouble with the Cooper, registered BLA 80B, returning as much as 2,000 miles per pint of oil. He attributed this to careful running-in and the fact that it was one of the first fitted with positive crankcase ventilation using a Smith's non-return valve which fed direct into the inlet manifold. The oil pressure held 70 psi easily even when habitually cruised at around 82 mph (5,500 rpm) on motorways, with 30 mpg being attained on average once the engine had loosened up. Like Jack Chisholm, who bought the Cortina GT, Howard fitted special front seats for more comfort. Chisholm had fancied a Cooper S, but bought the Cortina GT because of his size—6 ft in height—and the fact that he needed a decently-large back seat and luggage boot. His car also proved reliable on the whole, returning 27 mpg with negligible oil consumption; all told, he liked the feeling of space inside the car, the larger luggage boot and the fact that other drivers did not react badly to the sight of the car.

Later, in December 1966, *CAR* compared a Sunbeam Imp Sport with the ten per cent cheaper Mini-Cooper. The Imp had a far superior interior, with the addition of self-cancelling indicators and wind-up windows, and they preferred the styling with its higher roof line, but the Cooper was much better on performance, with superior acceleration and more consistent handling. *CAR* concluded:

'So which do you buy? On the figures, the Cooper is the car for every enthusiast who cares above all for low-cost performance. In the showroom, the Imp Sport scores hands down for looks, finish and above all, comfort. A combination of these two would be the finest small car the world has ever known.'

A New Wave of Modified Minis

Mini tuners continued to have a field day despite the advent of the Cooper S cars which frequently outperformed the original modified Minis. One magazine in particular, *Cars and Car Conversions*—a revised version of *Cars Illustrated*—allied itself closely to the movement to make your Mini-go-faster-no-matter-how-highly-tuned-it-was-for-a-start. Using a standard Cooper 1275S (the Bolster road test car registered AOE 855B), as a baseline in July 1965, *Cars and Car Conversions* recorded performance figures of 100 mph maximum, an 11.6-second 0–60 mph time and an 18.25-second standing quarter mile with 27 mpg, before testing a 1275S, registered CMO 859B, with a Taurus stage one conversion. This consisted of a gas-flowed cylinder head for an extra £53.50. The Taurus car in this comparison test returned 103.3 mph, with much better acceleration figures of 8.8 seconds for the 0–60 and 17.2 seconds for the standing quarter mile, fuel consumption improving to nearly 30 mpg—showing that the tuners really were learning the art well. *Cars and Car Conversions* were also particularly impressed by the much-improved flexibility offered by the new cylinder head.

Bolster then replied for *Autosport* by testing a truly exceptional 1275S Cooper equipped with no less than £284-worth of tuning gear by Downton. This car, registered 777 MCG, had its Hydrolastic suspension lowered, with the interconnecting pipes disconnected, and was fitted with adjustable Koni dampers. The result, said Bolster in December 1965, was a remarkably flat ride without loss of controllability. The engine, with a £45 gas-flowed cylinder head,

Above: Mini sales were shooting up again by the time this basic 850 model was tested in 1979, reminding *Autocar* that it still had few true competitors. 'If you really want the minimum of car there isn't much other than the Mini,' they said.

oil cooler, special manifolds and camshaft, and larger than normal SU carburettors, was also fully balanced and had a lightened flywheel. It was quoted as producing 99 bhp between 6,000 and 7,000 rpm with an 8,000 rpm maximum, 86 lb/ft of torque being attainable at 5,000 rpm. A close-ratio straight-cut competition gearbox made up the ensemble. Road wheels and tyres were retained 'for comfort'. Nevertheless, the Downton Cooper S remained completely stable at all times, said Bolster, but suffered badly from wheelspin. Once this had been subdued, the performance figures were startling, a maximum speed of 110 mph being recorded, allied to a 7.8-seconds 0–60 mph time and 16.6 seconds for the standing quarter mile; plus the most extraordinary statistic of all, a fuel consumption of 27.3 mpg overall, 40 mpg being easily attained at fast cruising speeds!

Such was the boom in sales of tuning gear that *Motor Sport* were driven to comment in May 1966, as they tested a Speedwell '1300TC,' the TC standing for Town Carriage:

'Mini tuning does not stop at competitions. Improving the breed has become almost a fetish among all Mini owners, and an absolutely standard version is a relative rarity on the roads.'

This engine was bored out to 1,293 cc and fitted with a special, fully-balanced, crankshaft, pistons and connecting rods, plus Speedwell's own camshaft—but not their alloy cylinder head. Instead, the standard cylinder head was machined to a similar pattern and fitted with lightened valve gear. In this form, with matched and polished manifolds and 1.5-inch SU carburettors, plus a lightened flywheel and standard gearbox, the Speedwell 1300TC recorded 109 mph, a 9.5-second 0–60 mph time and a 17-second standing quarter mile, fuel consumption remaining fully competitive on 27 mpg. Suspension modifications were confined to a rear anti-roll bar, but more money spent on the interior—with a woodrim steering wheel and special dashboard—so that the price was similar to that of a Downton 1275S at £1,000.

No price was quoted for the Broadspeed Cooper S tested on the road by *Autocar* in December 1965, but this was hardly surprising as it was the car registered BOP 243C used by John Fitzpatrick to great effect in group two touring car races. The engine was bored out to 1,293 cc, with a special Broadspeed 12.2:1 compression ratio cylinder head, BMC AEA649 camshaft, modified twin 1.5-inch SU carburettors, BMC competition exhaust with Broadspeed silencer, steel flywheel and BMC competition valve springs, four-bladed fan and Broadspeed oil cooler; the BMC close-ratio straight-cut gearset was used with 3.77, 3.94, or 4.13:1 final drive ratios. Dunlop R7 tyres were fitted on 4.5-inch rim Cooper alloy wheels, the lowered suspension using red competition Hydrolastic units linked to a rear anti-roll bar. Mr Fitzpatrick had the benefit of a high-hipped seat and woodrim steering wheel in an interior otherwise unchanged except for the fitting of a rev counter. *Autocar* was set an 8,500-rpm limit and noted:

'This car was particularly interesting as being the first Mini we have tried fitted with the competition limited-slip differential, and a Hydrolastic suspension modified for racing. The differential is available in very limited quantities at a high price—£59.50—and has only a brief life under racing conditions; indeed the last Broadspeed retirement was caused by the failure of this BMC-Cooper component. Strange clonks and jerks took a lot of getting used to, and it was only on a closed circuit that we really learned to drive the car fast.

'Performance, aided a little by the low 3.94:1 axle ratio (suitable, we are told, for racing at Silverstone), was quite phenomenal; this is easily the fastest Mini we have ever tested . . .

'In acceleration the Broadspeed Mini is comfortably faster than a Sunbeam Tiger throughout the speed range, and is not far behind a 4.2-litre E type up to 60 mph. The maximum speed of 121 mph is governed by the rev limit of 8,500 rpm. A more suitable final drive ratio would probably allow 130 mph, a speed shown by John Fitzpatrick at Spa this year. Although 118 bhp from 1293 cc is very high indeed for a car with mass-produced components and SU carburettors, the car shows no temperament at low engine speeds. At least 4,000 rpm, with brutal use of the clutch to promote wheelspin, is needed to get off the mark fast, but the little car can be trundled through traffic at a placid 2,000 rpm without fuss or lumpiness . . . it is not a car for rough roads for the combination of firm suspension, hairline steering and the differential make the car jump from crag to crag. The difference with this Mini is that there seems to be no understeer at all. Power-on in mid-corner merely pulls the front wheels further into the apex. The limited-slip axle is responsible for this, helping to steer the car around sharp corners at speeds impossible with the normal model. One of our testers remarked that this was the most "non-Mini" handling of any Mini he had driven. Fitzpatrick reckons the differential improved lap times at Silverstone by 2 seconds.

'On rough roads and when the wheels are spinning in the wet the whole car darts from side to side instead of the more usual snaking. Brakes are unmodified apart from hard linings back and front, and are too small to match the tremendous performance. We are told this is no handicap in a race as they are rarely used; but it could lead to trouble on the road.'

For the record, the 0–60 time was 8.2 seconds, standing quarter mile time 16.3 seconds, fuel consumption 25 mpg and oil 75 miles per pint.

Cars and Car Conversions then tested Broadspeed's '£100' conversion on a Mini 1275S, registered 5 NOB, that consisted of a 10.5:1 compression ratio version of the racing cylinder head, with a special camshaft and Broadspeed seals for the valve guides to reduce the oil consumption to 200 miles per pint. The seals also reduced the oil pressure, but not to a point unacceptable for road use with an engine which still revved to 8,000. The rest of the car's modifications, which were similar to those of the Fitzpatrick Mini, fell outside the £100 price tag. *Cars and Car Conversions* recorded 112.5 mph flat out, with a creditable 8.5-second 0–60 time and 24 mpg, before commenting:

Flexibility was extremely good: driving in traffic could be approached without the need for lower gears or clutch slipping, and if the mood took you, you could potter along at under 30 mph in top gear—below 2,000 revs—and accelerate up to a more appropriate lick without judder, snatch or any of the other road-test words which mean unpleasantness. The power really starts to arrive at about 3,000 rpm and from there on up it just keeps on coming. The standard car has markings on its speedometer to remind you to change gear at about 6,000 rpm and one of the nasty features is the way everything roughens up for the last 5 mph or so in every case. But with the Broadspeed version this just wasn't so . . . you can go up to 8,000 rpm without fuss. This is one of those cars where one is impressed less by what it does than in the way it does it. Top gear performance is all you could expect of a much larger engine, and the acceleration—in top— from around 70 up to three-figure speeds is pretty startling the first time you try it.'

By the time the Mini was approaching 25 years old, its praises were again being sung by road testers.

Cars and Car Conversions then went on to a sensational test of a Broadspeed GT 2 plus 2—based on a Mini, registered EOP 89D—in which a Cooper

1275S, modified in the manner of 5 NOB, had the roof lowered and was fitted with a glassfibre 'fastback' reminiscent of that on an Aston Martin DB6, to reduce drag. The new bodywork alone cost £600, but *Cars and Car Conversions* went a long way to justify the cost by extracting 124 mph from the car—at least 10 mph more than any other magazine—with a 9 second 0–60 time, before commenting on the new 70 mph speed limit which had been introduced as an experiment:

> 'Cruising speed? Well, the dreaded legal seventy is only about three-five on the clock, so the engine is hardly doing any work at all, relatively speaking. At this speed it is dead smooth, acceptably quiet and really very pleasant. Except that with this much power under the trotter it is damn difficult to keep it down to seventy, and the day we were followed up the M1 by a gentleman in a blue uniform will stick in our memory as being the time we used up all our self-control.'

Mini racer Neville Trickett also found the idea of lowering the roofline attractive, even if it did mean that his car would have to race against lightweight glass fibre creations in the GT class once the profile had been altered from that of the standard touring car. Both road and race versions were marketed first by Rob Walker garages and then by BMC main agents Stewart and Ardern as the Minisprint, with a basic 1.5-inch cut from the body panels above and below the waistline. In the case of the racing—or GT—version, another 1.25 ins was removed from above the waistline, which, with lowered suspension, gave an overall height of only 42 ins against the normal 53 ins. The front and rear screens were re-angled to as much as 45 degrees from the horizontal and on the GT version, the seams which normally protruded were flush welded to further reduce drag. The overall weight was also reduced still more with the competition version by using glassfibre doors, bonnet and boot lid and Perspex windows. It was in this form that John Blunsden tested the first Minisprint GT for *Motor Racing* in March 1966. It was Trickett's own car, with a 1,098-cc full-race engine producing 100 bhp at the front wheels, with the track increased by 3 ins at the front and 5 ins at the back. A five-speed dog-clutch motor-cycle-style straight cut gearbox, designed by Alf Francis and built by the Italian firm, Colotti, ran with ratios from 1.0–2.7:1 on a 4.78:1 final drive. Blunsden estimated that this car had the potential for a 58-second lap of the Brands Hatch short circuit and added:

> 'The advantage of a low body line in reduced wind resistance is obvious, but the psychological advantage of such a low centre of gravity must also be worth something—it felt as though you would need the assistance of a crane to roll this one!'

Meanwhile, far more modest tuning kits continued to sell well, with one example made by Alexander for £26 being designed so that it could be fitted in a car park during an extended lunch break—which is just what *Motor* did, reporting in July 1965 that the replacement manifold and twin Stromberg carburettors increased the speed of their otherwise standard 848-cc Mini by 4 mph to 76 mph, reduced the 0–60 time by 6 seconds to 22.8, and gave better fuel consumption at cruising speeds over 50 mph.

In a similar manner, the Essex Speed Centre offered to increase the performance of your standard 848-cc Mini to that of a Cooper 1275S for just £100. This entailed them rebuilding the engine as a 1,200 cc unit with a long-throw crankshaft and 10.5:1 compression ratio cylinder head, high-lift camshaft, twin-choke Weber carburettor and special manifolds; Spax adjustable shock absorbers were fitted with Minifin alloy brake drums to cope with the additional performance. *Autocar* found in March 1966 that an Essex-converted Mini did, in fact, match a 1275S in many respects, returning a 12.2-second 0–60 time (1 second down), with a standing quarter mile in 18.4 seconds (identical) and top speed of 96 mph (the same) with 27.5 mpg (against 28.5). They doubted, however, that it would last long . . .

Cars and Car Conversions then assessed a Mini fitted with most of the typical go-faster goodies other than engine modifications, using an 848-cc car, registered JLX 310D, provided by Taurus. Apart from having a special dashboard and door fillets, woodrim steering wheel and gearlever knob, rev counter, quick-release window catches, remote control gearchange, steering column lowering bracket, retractable seat belts and special exhaust with a central outlet, it had Taurus wheel spacers and Pirelli Cinturato radial ply tyres. *Cars and Car Conversions* said, in October 1966, that these made it 'whip round corners as if on rails,' attributing half of this ability to the wheel spacers and half to the new tyres.

Later, in December 1966, they evaluated a Ridgway Sports Conversion, in which a droopsnoot glass fibre nose, costing £24, was tacked on to the existing bodywork with eight screws, the original grille and bonnet being discarded. The chief advantage, apart from changing the car's appearance, was felt to be in a reduction in wind noise above 50 mph—but there was no extra performance.

In more serious climes, contributor Clive Trickey, an ardent Mini racer, tested a Weberised Janspeed 1293 Cooper S at Castle Combe in the same month. The car, registered JAN 4, used an early, and therefore lighter, bodyshell, with running gear similar to that of the Broadspeed group two machine. The front roof gulleys and body seams were removed to reduce drag, along with the bumpers, their mountings and the grille surround. All the glass was replaced with Perspex and the doors, bonnet and bootlid were made from glassfibre to reduce weight—although nobody had thought of making the front wings from the same material at that time. Minilite 5.5-inch rims were used with Dunlop R7 tyres on what was to be one of the first wide-tyred Minis. The suspension was set to give negative camber all round, and after lapping in 1 minute 17.9 seconds, this car went on to win numerous club races in the rollowing season.

A road-going Mini built to a similar specification by Coburn Improvements of North London, but with an 850-cc engine producing 82 bhp was tried next by *Cars and Car Conversions* in February 1967, proving capable of 103 mph flat out with a 0–60 time estimated at less than 7 seconds. This car, registered YXN 554, with completely gutted interior, was raced and driven to work—and on holiday!—by Julian Vereker, impressing *Cars and Car Conversions* by 'visibly shuddering with the racket of the engine, exhaust, road noise and the howl of straight-cut gears.'

Much the same effect so far as performance was concerned, but with fewer sound effects, was achieved by Oselli Engineering, of North Oxfordshire, who provided *Cars and Car Conversions* with an 1198-cc Mini, fully trimmed, in July 1967. The engine, based on a 998-cc Cooper unit, cost £176.50 on exchange and endowed the car with a top speed of 103 mph and a 0–60 time of 8.8 seconds—faster than a Cooper S, for less money.

After that, tests of tuned Minis became less frequent as a credit squeeze bit hard at Britain. BMC, however, continued to market equipment under the Special Tuning banner, which was aimed chiefly at competition users. Despite the credit squeeze, these items sold well and the bill for parts alone on the rally Mini (registered OBL 47F), tested by *Motor* in January 1968 came to £565—more than two-thirds of the original cost of the Cooper 1275S on which they had been fitted. This car had a 12:1 compression ratio cylinder head by Downton, with twin 1.5-inch SU carburettors, Downton inlet manifold, BMC competition exhaust and manifold, Borg and Beck 7.25-inch competition clutch, straight-cut gears, 3.76:1 final drive, lightened steel flywheel, oil cooler, alternator, four-bladed fan, Minilite 4.5-inch rim magnesium wheels, competition brake pads, linings and Hydrolastic units, progressive rear bump stops, twin fuel pumps under the rear seat, and reclining front seats. *Motor* reported:

'What astonished us in the circumstances was the flexibility. It was possible, and indeed in some circumstances preferable, to drive the car round towns at less than 4,000 rpm. Beneath that limit the car was relatively quiet: there was some whine from the intermediate gears (although not from top) and the intake and exhaust sounds were quite tolerable and, if the performance was not world-shattering, it was at least sufficient to make a respectable getaway.

'The melodramatics started above 4,000. As soon as the tachometer needle was set swinging above that point a great roar came from the curburettors (they had no air cleaners) and the exhaust noise became, to say the least, obtrusive. We used wheelspin to take our acceleration figures, but, in practice, if any sort of serious right-footing was indulged in on anything other than a bone-dry surface it was almost impossible to avoid taking off in spectacular fashion.'

The performance figures of this car, laden with navigational aids and weighing far more than a normal Cooper S, were equal to the noise: 9.6 seconds for the 0–60, 17 seconds for the standing quarter mile, there being no opportunity to drive it flat out. Fuel consumption fell to 20 mpg. John Bolster, however, just managed to hit 100 mph in a car, registered JBL 494D, to identical specification that had been driven by Harry Kallstrom in the RAC Rally, during a quick spin for *Autosport* in December 1966.

The Mini-Moke

Few magazines tested a Mini-Moke and judging by the comments in *Cars and Car Conversions* in February 1967, it was easy to see why BMC did not encourage such exercises. They reported:

'You adjust your sights when a Moke arrives. For a start, it's rather like World War One flying—there is no way of keeping either warm or dry except by virtue of the clothes you put on. So you put on a kit which makes you look like a cross between an intrepid aviator and a motor-cycling fly fisherman, climb up onto the driver's perch and wind up feeling like Nanook of the North without his kayak. The Moke has a hood, but it doesn't matter much whether you put it up or not. The thing is made to be manoeuvred by agricultural persons and so it closely resembles the cheaper sort of tractor when it comes to creature comforts. With the hood up, no rain gets inside unless it is horizontal-type driving rain, or unless the Moke is moving. With the hood down, no rain gets inside if the Moke is moving, unless it stops.

'The next thing that strikes you is that every time you are passed, the wipers fail to cope. This is less a matter for mechanical attention than an expression of the simple fact that the spray from the chap that has just past has put as much water on the inside of the screen as there is on the outside.

'The Mini-Moke is very light, so that although, once you get off the road, really soft mud stops you like a brick wall, there is no real reason why an average sort of chap in good health shouldn't hump it on to the next firm ground. Its hill-climbing ability is pretty good, but if the track is deeply rutted you need to be careful that the thing doesn't ski along on its sump shield, which also means that as soon as it takes all the weight you will lose all motive power from the front wheels.

'OK? There is something more exciting than driving the Moke—it's being a passenger in one. There comes a point, on all corners which leave the left-hand side of the car on the outside, when you realise that there is nothing between you and the ground (whistling past underneath at up to 60 mph) except God's good fresh air. Which may have excellent remedial qualities, but we never heard it was much good for a broken neck.

'We haven't mentioned, of course, that the Mini-Moke is darned good fun. So long as you don't try and make it behave like a tractor, it is reasonably practical, too, for off-the-road motoring—it won't tackle the really rough stuff, lacking the power, traction and ground clearance for the job, which is why they aren't too popular with the agricultural community.'

No performance figures were taken.

The Mark II Mini

The face-lifted Mini 1000 Mark II sold well from its introduction despite a reserved reception from the road testers. *Autocar* described it in October 1967 as being a landmark in Mini history because of the increase in engine capacity and hastened to add that it would be a reliable unit, having seen service in the Elf, Hornet and Cooper for the past four years. They welcomed the fact that the Mini could now be cruised (on its Cooper S 3.77:1 final drive ratio) at 70 mph 'in all but the strongest head winds'—and appreciated the remote control gear change. They added, however, that it had come 'at long last!' *Autocar* found that it helped make up for the lack of synchromesh on first gear. So far as handling was concerned, they were still impressed by the 'enormous margin of genuine safety', adding that 'it is hard to imagine how anyone could ever lose control of a standard Mini'. The reduced turning circle made practical even tighter parking spaces. For the first time, also, the handbrake held a Mini on a 1-in-3 hill and, with some wheelspin, the car managed to scrabble away again—another first. *Autocar* considered the Dunlop C41 cross-ply tyres very noisy, however, and decided it was 'a great pity' nothing had been done to improve heating and ventilation. The new seats were better than the old ones but still needed to offer more support under the thighs. Visibility was even better now, although the rear view mirror was still much too small. The windscreen wiper arc came in for criticism with its left-hand-drive bias, but at least 'the old game of park the wipers,' was no longer necessary, said *Autocar*. Long experience with Minis showed in their comment that there was still no door keeps, which meant that children had to watch their fingers when the doors were restrained only by their check straps. *Autocar* then pointed out:

> 'We were expecting the new Mini to be announced with winding windows, like certain versions built in Australia. This must now be the only car without them, and they are sadly missed. It is also time such economies as cable-release interior door handles were brought up to date; and some of the standards of fit and finish were disappointing. Carpets still do not lie snugly on the floor—a criticism we made in 1959.'

A higher top speed of 75 mph was recorded (against 72), with a 22.6-second 0–60 time and 22.7 seconds for the standing quarter mile. Fuel consumption increased on the test car (registered MOV 247F), to 34 mpg. *Motor* could manage only 32 mpg in March 1968, but achieved 77 mph.

CAR compared the Mini 1000 chiefly with the new Honda 'Mini'—the N600—when they tested it, also alongside a Hillman Imp and Reliant Rebel 700 three-wheeler in September 1968. They commented that the Honda, with an 80 mph top speed and 38 mpg had been represented as the greatest single threat to the British motor industry but 'reckoned that we wouldn't put it as strongly as that'.

After an extensive test, *CAR* concluded that the Honda was faster than the Mini 1000, more economical, and—at £589—cost £46 less, 'but is at the same time noiser and less comfortable with inferior handling. In so many ways it is so close to the Mini that as long as it holds its price at its present level it is bound to present a very considerable challenge. Of the Mini itself, one is bound to say that some of the room for improvement which we have always said existed is still there. Rather than the restyled grille and rear lights with which we were regaled last year, we would have liked to see a lot more attention paid to driver comfort by way of supplement to vast improvements in ride and silence.'

The Clubman and 1275GT

By comparison with the Mark II, the Clubman and 1275GT received an enthusiastic reception from the motoring Press. *Motor* managed to try both cars and an estate for their test in October 1969, and commented:

'Many of our criticisms have been answered in one go with the introduction of the long-nosed variants which are a lot more civilised and habitable than any previous Mini. The much improved seats point to a growing awareness within the Austin-Morris division of British Leyland that seating comfort really matters. Add to this the significant changes in the ventilation, furnishings and instrument layout, not to mention the all-synchromesh gearbox introduced earlier and a gearchange that feels much better than before, and the result is a dramatic overall improvement in both creature comforts and driveability. No longer is a long Mini journey something of an endurance test, even though the noise level is still high (particularly so in the 1275GT) when the engine is extended and the ride on poor roads as bouncy as ever.

'The adoption of a new straight-ahead instrument pod, fresh air vents—something which few other small rivals can boast—and winding windows that eliminate the need to juggle with the old sliding ones, has inevitably meant a reduction in interior stowage space, though what remains is still quite generous. Significantly more comfort for slightly less stowage space seems to us a fair swap.'

The Clubman saloon and the estate had virtually the same performance figures as their Mini 1000 equivalents, but, said *Motor*:

'The GT is a different story. It has a fairly unstressed engine giving about the same output as the 998 cc Cooper; so the performance is on a par with that through the gears. However, its extra torque makes it exceptionally lively in top gear, 40–60 mph taking less than half the time of the present one-litre cars, and considerably less than the old Cooper, too. It compares well against its competitors, with a 0–60 time of 14.2 seconds.'

The lower, 3.65:1 final drive ratio—from the original Mini—made fast cruising 'buzzy' said *Motor* and the 29.2 mpg fuel consumption made stops 'infuriatingly frequent with the meagre 5.5-gallon tank.'

Plate One Minimum of fuss ... the first Mini.

Plate Two Maximum sporting appeal . . . the early Mini-Cooper.

Plate Three Off-road Mini . . . the Moke.

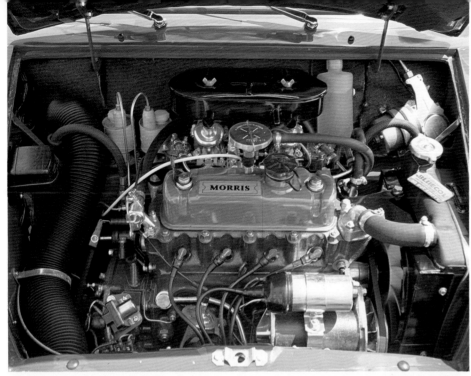

Plate Four Heart of a Mini . . . the A-series engine.

Plate Five Battle Box . . . the Mini-Cooper sees rally action.

Plate Six Birth of a legend . . . the Mini-Cooper 1071S.

Plate Seven Mini Magician ... Timo Makinen on the Monte Carlo Rally.

Plate Eight Endurance Mini .. Chris Montague in the Nurburgring Six-Hour.

Plate Nine Ultimate Mini . . . the 1275S.

Plate Ten Luxury Mini . . . the Wolseley Hornet.

Plate Eleven Nostalgic Mini . . . the Riley Elf.

Plate Twelve Working man's Mini . . . the pick-up.

Plate Thirteen Practical Mini . . . the electricity van.

Plate Fourteen Just the car for the Japanese, and any other Mini fan . . . the new Cooper S as tested by *Performance Car.*

Plate Fifteen Modern Mini . . . the Clubman saloon.

Plate Sixteen Racing Mini . . . the 1275GT in the TT.

Plate Seventeen Special Mini . . . Maguire's racer.

Plate Eighteen Upper class Mini, the latest Mayfair, aimed at the 1990s.

Plate Nineteen Back to basics . . . the Mini 850.

Plate Twenty Stately home for an estate . . . the Mini Clubman.

Plate Twenty-one Big wheels a rollin' . . . the later 1275GT.

Plate Twenty-Two The first edition . . . of a special line in Minis.

Plate Twenty-Three Ever lively
Mini . . . the first edition of the
Sprite.

Plate Twenty-Four Silver anniversary Mini . . . the 25.

Plate Twenty-Five Econo-Mini . . . the E type.

Plate Twenty-Six Step into a modern Mini . . .

Of the three cars, the GT had the best roadholding on its 4.5-inch rims and radial-ply tyres, although the Hydrolastic saloons could 'actually jerk you into the air, more easily than on the rubber cone springs.' Top speed of the GT was 87.5 mph with a standing quarter mile in 19.5 seconds. *Autocar* endorsed these comments, and test figures—except for an 86 mph top speed—in the following month.

Mature Minis

Even before the world's first oil crisis struck in the winter of 1973, the Mini was establishing itself as an economy model that was hard to beat. *Autocar* felt obliged to re-test an 848-cc model, registered EOX 548L in April 1973, to reacquaint themselves with a car which was rapidly becoming a legend. They said:

> 'One of the Mini's greatest charms is the way in which top gear may often be used for trickling along in city traffic or meandering through country lanes—this without any sign of roughness or snatch. Less pleasing is the high noise level and feeling of harshness which results from the use of medium-to-high revs. Without doubt, this is one area in which the model shows its age. On the credit side, the transmission proved to be relatively quiet. But unlike the remainder of the Mini range, the 850 retains the original-type gearchange. As a consequence, the lever is awkwardly placed and has an unpleasantly stiff and notchy action. Despite effective synchromesh on all four ratios, this is another aspect where the Mini falls short of modern standards.'

The handling remained unimpeachable and even though the ride was still 'decidedly bouncy,' *Autocar* said: 'Strangely, most people find it not as uncomfortable as at first it seems; equally oddly, it is not an unduly tiring car to drive or to ride in.

> 'With its minimal column rake and offset pedals and wheel, the Mini has a somewhat unconventional driving position. One soon gets used to this and finds that it is uncannily adaptable for people of differing build and tastes. Many a six-footer has found himself to be more comfortable in a Mini than in much larger cars . . .
>
> 'Its comparatively large glass area and minimal overhang enable one to place it with uncanny accuracy. Small wonder that most people regard it as an ideal city car!'

The performance figures remained equally unchanged, but there were considerable differences apparent in the 1275GT, registered TOF 503N, tested by *Autocar* in October 1974. It had 12-inch wheels and bigger front brakes, with higher gearing and the larger fuel tank. *Autocar* reported:

> 'The higher gearing might be expected to carry a performance penalty, and it does. All the acceleration times, both from a standing start,

and in the gears, are inferior to those of the earlier car. Since the mean maximum speed of 86 mph corresponds closely to peak power, it seems there has been a genuine loss of power with the introduction of modifications to meet the European pollution regulations. One of the advantages of throttling the engine's top-end performance is that it can pay dividends in fuel consumption at moderate speeds. This, plus the higher gearing, promised a substantial advantage for the test car, but the results were disappointing. The overall consumption emerged as 30.8 mpg, marginally better than that obtained by the earlier car.'

Autocar went on to add of the 1275GT's reversion to dry suspension:

'Our impression is that the suspension is softer than it used to be, though this makes little difference as far as the handling is concerned.'

The new low-profile tyres—Dunlop SP Sports—gave no advantage in the dry, but, said *Autocar*: 'In the wet they do rather better and certainly the Mini is less prone to aquaplane on standing water than it was with its smaller wheels.'

Despite the deletion of the brake servo, the pedal pressures remained well within bounds and 'the brakes had a very good "feel". It was possible to hold the wheels on the point of locking without actually making them slide. There is no doubt that the fade resistance of the new brakes is much improved: they also react well to water-soaking, as we discovered during a period of torrential rain.'

Otherwise, *Autocar* felt that items like the single-speed dashboard switch-operated wipers were altogether too dated for a small GT car of the 1970s. Their additional performance figures included a 14.6-second 0–60 time and 19.7 seconds for the standing quarter mile.

John Bolster returned similar figures with his 1275GT, registered TOF 514N, for *Autosport* next month, but was far from pleased with the car's appearance. He wrote:

'Oh my poor Mini! What have they done to you? First of all they have ruined the appearance, which is a great pity because the original car was completely functional and well-proportioned. That awful Clubman bonnet would look very well on a Japanese car, but it clashes hopelessly with the shape of the rest of the body. In any case, it's less efficient aerodynamically than the original bonnet and probably takes a mile or two off the top speed. They have also stuck boy racer stripes along the sides: just the thing to attract the attention of the police.

'I thought the bigger wheels would give a better ride, but this they emphatically do not. The car jiggles and hops over the bumps and every so often it suddenly jumps so violently that one feels that one's spine is broken. I can only assume that the Denovo tyres, which were fitted to the test car as an expensive extra, had something to do with this deterioration, for the larger diameter could do nothing but good. At maximum speed, a shimmy was beginning to develop in the steering, and this I have experienced before on a Denovo-equipped car.

'The tyres do away with the necessity to carry a spare wheel, but if they were the cause of the appalling ride I would rather risk a puncture any day. Perhaps it is just a matter of re-tuning the suspension to accept different characteristics, but if so this should have been done. Another bad point is that the mudguards have no proper valences and the wheels are set too wide, as a result of which the dirt from the road is flung over the sides of the car, which is charming in the country when they've been driving cows!'

The energy crisis was biting deep as *CAR* wrote in February 1975: 'With the price of petrol rapidly rising to the £1 a gallon mark, the only hope of individual freedom of movement is going to be with vehicles that can give something in the region of 40 mpg, as distinct from the common feeling of 18 months ago that 29 mpg was really not too bad.' They promptly tested a Mini 1000 (at £1184), and Fiat 127 (at £1159) and a Toyota 1000 (at £1158), before concluding:

'The elaborate fittings of the Toyota are attractive, and so is its smooth, happy engine, but it falls down by being short on interior space and having only mediocre handling and roadholding when compared with the other two.

'The Mini is an embarrassment. It's painfully out of date in just about every respect except price, but will continue to find adherants regardless; it may not be a good car any more, but it is a convenient one that the vast majority of people understand.

'Of course the Fiat is by far the best value. The very fact that its interior can be converted into a sort of estate car is a tremendous point in its favour.'

Autocar still found their Mini 1000, registered TOF 509N, most endearing, however, when tested in May 1975, despite displaying many of the faults mentioned earlier. The magazine was particularly appreciative of the improved performance—82 mph, an 18.7-second 0–60 time, a 21-second standing quarter mile—endowed by its more powerful 39-bhp engine which still managed to return 34 mpg, and the remote control gear change similar to that of the Allegro derivative of the earlier 1100/1300 range. When *Autocar* tested a Clubman, registered MOC 222P, fitted with the 1098 cc engine from the smallest Allegro, in November 1976, they were most impressed. It returned similar performance figures to the 1000—82 mph maximum speed, with a 17.9-second 0–60 time and a 20.7-second standing quarter mile—but achieved 37 mpg, which was considered very good. New subframe mountings were also appreciated in that they dramatically reduced the earlier noise and harshness, and improved the ride. They were also credited with helping to improve the gear change. Leyland Cars' corporate steering column wash/wipe stick was applauded, as were the facia vents which produced 'an absolute torrent of fresh air.' *Autocar* concluded:

'By any standard, 17 years is a long time for a single model to continue, although with many, many improvements. In some ways the Clubman falls behind its competitors in having no third-door hatchback. Yet it still retains all its original charm, plus much improved performance and amazing fuel economy. Its handling still leaves its competitors out in the cold. It is essentially an ultra-compact yet roomy people package which seems to go on and on.'

The chief point to recommend on the Clubman—considered the best of the Mini range—when *Motor* tested the car (registered MOC 221P), in March 1977 was its engine. It produced an exceptional amount of torque and returned excellent fuel economy when compared with its late-1970s rivals, the Fiat 127, Ford Fiesta, Honda Civic, Vauxhall Chevette and Volkswagen Polo. The superb handling also made it great fun to drive, although the rivals were catching up fast in this department. *CAR* added the Peugeot 104 to this list in the same month and said the main thing going for the Mini against its latest rival, the Fiesta, was that it was a lot cheaper—and still handled better.

Autocar hit back in defence of the Mini when it was twenty years old, pointing out in a road test of an 848-cc model, registered ADA 939T, in August 1979. They said:

'It is not in the least surprising to hear recently that Mini sales were shooting up again. A car like this which offers a near-certain 40 mpg to the normal owner—provided he or she does not drive it flat out all the time—is vital to many pockets these days . . . On the open road, the limitations of the performance become more obvious of course, but there is still enough to go for all normal purposes. Cruising at Britain's retrograde legal maximum is comfortably within the 850's spectrum although one does wish even more today that something had been done to quieten the car . . . Most people, especially those who appreciate the cardinal virtues of driving— good steering and roadholding, responsiveness, stability are the ones that apply here—have confessed at one time or another to an unavoidable affection for the Mini . . . The immediate, unthinking reaction today on some people's part is that the Mini has been overtaken by the competition. This is only half true—for the simple reason which torpedoes most of the argument right at the start, that the Mini still has few competitors. Such critics are thinking of Fiat's 127, Renault's 5, Volkswagen's Polo, Ford's Fiesta—but these are all very much bigger cars. Of the ten breeds of under one-litre car which in any way compete with the Mini, none are just a quarter inch over ten feet long—the Fiat 126 is nearest at 10 ft 3 ins—and the rest are none less than a foot longer; and of those only four have appreciably better overall inside space. If you really want the minimum of car there isn't much other than the Mini.'

Motor then investigated the return of the Mini to popularity during a road test of a 1000HL, registered HOK 660W, in July 1981. They concluded of this much-improved model:

'The best things about a Mini are still, in 1981, at least as good as they ever were. Its combination of diminutive dimensions, panoramic visibility, eager engine, snappy gearchange and scampering manoeuvrability still make it a cheekily effective town car which is great fun to drive. And even those who have traditionally been unmoved by the Mini's charms had to admit that its ride and refinement have been improved to acceptable standards, even if they still don't count as virtues. On the debit side, the driving position still takes some getting used to, and the heater is crude . . . but when all is said and done a Mini is a Mini is a Mini, and in its latest form we see no reason it shouldn't continue to feature in the best-sellers list for years to come.'

And when *Autocar* tested a Mini City E in July 1982 they found that it had at last got its economy back with an overall fuel consumption figure of 40.6 mpg. It was also the fastest normal Mini they had tested with a top speed of 86 mph, a 17.5-second 0–60 time and a 20.8-second standing quarter mile. After praising especially the economy in running costs they said:

'Smallness is attractive, for many good reasons, and the Mini is without doubt the smallest truly practical four-seater passenger car made anywhere. It is also correspondingly light, which is the most important requirement for better economy—more so for the majority of drivers than better aerodynamics. Couple these two points with its ease of driving, straightforward convenience, price, nimbleness and—for many people— great entertainment value, and you have a car which is difficult to kill, even if one wanted to.'

And when compared with the Citroen 2CV Charleston, Fiat Panda 45CL, Lada Riva 1200L, Yugo 45 and Skoda Estelle 105S in the same price bracket, *Motor* said in September 1985:

'Twenty-five years after its launch, the Mini is selling 23,000 cars a year—comfortably ahead of any others in its class. Why? Probably because today the Mini's virtues of compactness and economy are as relevant as they ever were. The Mini is to the small car what Hoover is to the vacuum cleaner and Kodak is to cameras.

'The Mini is the least powerful car in this group, but with an unladen weight of 11.9 cwt it is easily the lightest. Thus it has respectable performance which is not far short of the newer Panda.

'The Mini's maximum speed is 81.3 mph and it takes 18.5 seconds to get from 0 to 60 mph. By absolute standards these figures are unremarkable but, because of the Mini's smallness and the driver's proximity to the ground, it feels quick.

'The engine is impressively flexible though nowadays it has to contend with much taller gearing in the quest for better economy and lower noise levels.

'With a wheel at each corner and minimum suspension travel, the Mini is but one step removed from a go-kart and feels it. In sheer handling agility the Mini makes the other cars in this group seem positively leviathan by comparison.'

'Above all, it's still fun.'

IX
The Mini in Competition

For what has become one of the world's most successful competition cars, the Mini's career got off to a slow start. The 1959 season was more than half completed when the model was announced—and hardly anybody showed an initial interest in its competition potential. In those days, races for small saloon cars were dominated by Doc Shepherd's Austin A40, which had a bigger, 948-cc, BMC A-series engine. The Mini also looked too low to be practical in rallying. Everybody was raising the suspension of rally cars at the time to cope with forest tracks that were replacing the open road, which was becoming too congested with normal traffic. As a result, Saab's agile 96 was beginning to oust Renault's low-slung Dauphine Gordini.

But before the 1959 racing season was over, Shepherd had decided to try his hand in a Mini because it was lighter than the A40. He had the Mini tuned by Don Moore from premises near his home—and doctor's practice—in Cambridge. Moore had been responsible for Shepherd's great success in the A40, which had a cylinder head by Harry Weslake, who was responsible for works development. Despite his age—Shepherd was well into his 60s (having started motor racing only when he felt too old for polo)—the flying doctor exploited the 848 cc Mini's handling to such effect that he won his class in a sprint at the Snetterton track in East Anglia. The general feeling remained, however, that the Mini was too low powered to stand much chance in circuit racing against the contemporary Ford Anglia 105E. The Ford's new overhead valve engine was already showing itself to have greater potential in Formula Junior racing than the BMC A-series unit. The only real drawbacks to the Anglia were that it weighed more than the Mini and had less forgiving handling with a live rear axle and rear-wheel-drive.

Then Mini development dithered in the face of a clash between BMC marketing policy, which dictated that all models should be prepared for competition, and Issigonis, who was totally against the idea. A compromise was reached in which the works Minis received little modification, Weslake's special cylinder heads being confined to private entrants such as Shepherd. As a result, works drivers did their best to avoid the Minis, aiming instead for the Austin-Healey 3000 sports car which, in any case, stood a much better chance of winning outright in top rallies. One of the Mini's few supporters, however, was influential: BMC Competitions Manager Marcus Chambers, who took an early version on the Viking Rally in Norway, returned with glowing reports of its handling and how the front-wheel-drive had enabled it to plough along on its sump guard. Then one of the new junior team members, Pat Moss (sister of Britain's fastest racing driver, Stirling Moss) won the low-key Knowldale Car Club Mini Miglia Rally late in 1959, with a man who was to be Chambers's successor, Stuart Turner, as co-driver. Already the Mini was winning friends, even if Turner did complain that it was very uncomfortable . . .

By the end of November 1959, BMC had prepared a team of three Minis—registered TMO 559, 560 and 561—as part of an eight-car assault on the RAC Rally. This event was just entering its 'forest' era after years of being held on less-testing tarmac roads. The drivers' lack of enthusiasm for the Mini was heightened when all three cars, driven by 'Tish' Ozanne, Alick Pitts and Ken James, had to retire when leaking oil seals made their clutches slip. The problem could be cured on the production line, so BMC were not too upset and decided that competition was good for the Mini, which was already earning a reputation for unreliability on the road. The strategy was then developed of insisting that works drivers, such as Peter Riley—nicknamed The Bear—had to serve an apprenticeship on the Mini before they could take their turn on the more highly-developed Big Healey.

Riley recalled years later that the Minis of that era had hardly any torque and needed a lot of revs to extract what little power they could generate—which, in turn, did not improve their reliability. The early cars also leaked a lot, which did not endear them to their drivers. It is worth noting that Saab's star performer, Eric Carlsson, who later married Pat Moss, reckoned then that the Mini would never make a rally car . . .

Gradually, Issigonis's objections were overruled and the Mini was given more power through engine modifications that were already being tried in the single-seater Formula Junior on Cooper cars. The Morley twins, Don and Erle, took time off from farming to win their class in the Geneva Rally in 1960, beating Carlsson's Saab in the process. Things were really looking up for the Mini! The new-found power brought its problems, however, with Riley recalling that the drivers had to learn new techniques. They discovered that while cornering, by yanking on the handbrake they could bring the tail skidding round and thus scramble through a tight bend quicker. This became the normal practice until a whole new breed of Scandinavian drivers, aiming to emulate Carlsson, developed a tortuous, but more controllable, way of taking such bends. They kept their right foot hard on the power and used the left for simultaneous braking. This meant that the front wheels of the Mini continued spinning as the rear wheels locked. The advantage was that the driver could then keep both hands on the wheel for more precise steering. This was of increasing importance on bumpy forest tracks.

Meanwhile, back on the race track, drivers such as Sir John Whitmore and John Handley were developing a cornering technique in which they hardly used the brakes, flinging their Minis sideways through bends with smoke pouring from the tortured front tyres. They had to keep the power on to prevent the cars from understeering off the course. The technique of slowing the machine and turning it at the same time was made practical by the fact that race track bends were not so sharp as, and much smoother than, rally track bends. One of the first problems encountered with this racing practice was that the centres of the wheels broke up, with the result that the wheel and tyre went flying off the car. Nobody was badly hurt when that happened, but you could almost hear Issigonis saying: 'I told you so'. BMC countered the problem by making their steel wheels stronger, but for a considerable time Minis were not allowed to compete until scrutineers had checked that their wheels carried RAC stamps denoting that they were of the later strengthened variety. Tyre wear then became a major problem, with the early cross-plies hard pressed to last even a ten-lap race.

During 1960, the British Racing and Sports Car Club ran a special championship for 'SupaTura' cars, and by mid-season nobody was surprised to see Shepherd leading in his A40. But the first Mini was already up to seventh place. From then on, the Mini became steadily more popular on the race track, even though Shepherd took the title with his A40.

The times were changing for works rally drivers, too. Until the early 1960s, they were usually more concerned with having a good time than the ultimate performance of winning a rally. But, first the French, and then the Scandinavians, changed all that, becoming far more professional in their attitude. As the British crews—BMC drivers included—relaxed on the beaches of the South of France before an international event, the French would be up in the Alps, practising hard. They were overjoyed when Panhards finished first, second and third in the 1961 Monte Carlo Rally, with the nearest Mini well down. By then,

Left: Full of hope and high spirits, the BMC works team line up at Abingdon en route for the 1961 Monte Carlo Rally with—from the left—Peter Garnier, sports editor of *The Autocar* and Rupert Jones with TMO 559, Tom Christie and Ninian Paterson with TMO 560, and Derek Astle and Steve Woolley with TMO 561. All were eliminated by accidents or illness, however, with TMO 561 giving the 850-cc Mini its works swansong by winning its class in the Tulip Rally soon after for Peter Riley and Tony Ambrose.

Turner was getting to grips with the organisation, as one of the first co-drivers to make pace notes—a process by which the results of intensive practice before any event were noted down, so that the navigator could relay the resultant information to the driver to help him take blind corners faster, for instance.

At the same time, John Cooper, whose family firm had won the world constructors' championship twice in succession with their Formula One cars, took over the running of BMC's works Formula Junior effort. Naturally, he suggested modifying the Mini's engine along similar lines for touring car races. BMC would need only to sell 1,000 of these machines to qualify—or homologate—the Mini for international events in which it had previously to run in tougher prototype classes if there were any modifications. Cooper was a close friend of Issigonis and eventually persuaded him that a purpose-built high-performance Mini would be better than a standard one with modifications. BMC's new chief, George Harriman, was happy to back an idea which looked like selling at least an extra 1,000 cars, so work went ahead. The arrangement was that Cooper would run a team of Minis in touring car races, alongside the Formula Junior cars, while the works competition department, housed in the MG and Austin-Healey factory at Abingdon, would run the rally cars. A similar arrangement where the Healey Motor Company (who had designed the Big Healey), ran racing cars, while Abingdon rallied the 3000, was working well.

Meanwhile the Mini was becoming ever more popular with club racers, particularly as a large amount of tuning gear was being marketed for it. By the time the 1961 season opened at Snetterton, there were enough Minis for the BRSCC to run a special 850-cc class, which Mick Clare won from John Aley. By Easter, Whitmore had given the Mini its first international win by running away with the 1,000-cc class in the Goodwood saloon car race.

Soon after, in April, the BRSCC was able to run the first-ever race for Minis only, in which Graham Burrows won with Kensington-piano-teacher Christable Carlisle stirring up the crowd with her car's antics. Saloon car racing was becoming a tremendous spectacle as Whitmore won at Aintree from Aley, after a tremendous dice in which Shepherd's Mini skated along on its roof for some distance! Nobody was hurt and the ancient doctor had the consolation of setting the fastest lap in his class at 68 mph—only 9 mph slower than the winning 3.8-litre Jaguar driven by Mike Parkes!

By the time the Mini-Cooper was announced in September 1961, Mini racing was firmly established. Cars such as the A40 soon disappeared, and even the Anglia was hard-pressed to keep pace, Minis attracting far more drivers because they were so easy to control.

By 1962, everybody who was anybody had a 1,000-cc engine in his or her Mini. The 850s were still going strong, but the spotlight tended to be on the larger-engined cars. The 850 had been outstandingly successful after a slow start, but the advent of the Cooper version left nobody unprepared—it simply meant that here was an engine with much of the basic work of tuning already carried out. For the next two years, the Mini-Cooper went from success to success with the tuning shops ever more busy carrying out further development.

The works concentrated on the Big Healey, but blooded their first really professional rally driver, the Finn, Rauno Aaltonen, on a 997-cc Mini Cooper. He was up to second place overall on the Monte Carlo Rally, behind Carlsson's Saab, when he overturned and was pulled from the blazing wreck by his co-driver, the Briton, Geoff Mabbs. At least the Mini had showed its paces . . . then Pat Moss, and Ann Wisdom (who was to marry Peter Riley) won the Tulip Rally and everybody was smiling as development continued apace throughout 1962. Downton Engineering were in the forefront of engine work and gained the respect of Issigonis, with the result that much of their experience went into the Mini-Cooper S.

Success was not confined to rallying of course. After Whitmore had won the British Saloon Car Championship with his 850-cc Mini in 1961, he joined the works Cooper team to support John Love, who drove Ken Tyrrell's works Formula Junior Coopers. Cooper's top mechanic, Ginger Devlin, was in charge of their Minis, with Whitmore becoming the more successful driver.

Above left: Rauno Aaltonen is pictured near Luceram in Geoff Mabbs's works-supported Mini-Cooper in the 1962 Monte Carlo Rally just before crashing and having to be pulled from the burning wreck by co-driver Mabbs. For Aaltonen it was the start of a long career in international rallying and for Mabbs a long association with the Janspeed tuning concern.

Above right: Hundreds of spectators turned out to watch the Glasgow contingent leave for the Monte Carlo Rally on a chilly January morning in 1962, Maurice Robertson and James Preston departing at 4.58 am in their Mini-Cooper before being sidelined following numerous punctures as their new studded tyres overheated on predominently dry roads.

Left: One of the most successful Mini-Coopers ever built was the November 1961 works car registered 737 ABL which took Pat Moss (right) and Ann Wisdom (left) to a Coupe des Dames in the 1962 Monte Carlo Rally before winning the Tulip and German rallies and taking third place in the Geneva for the same crew that year.

Above: Piano teacher Christabel Carlisle was one of the stars of early Mini racing in her Don Moore-prepared 850-cc car, pictured here showing strongly in one of the first rounds of the new European Touring Car championship at Mallory Park in July 1963 before having to retire when a wheel pulled out of its centre as she flung the hard-used car through Gerard's Bend.

Top right: Sir John Whitmore and Paddy Hopkirk began a long period of domination in the 1,300-cc touring car classes for the Mini-Cooper S by taking the class and sixth place overall as torrential rain swamped the track at Brands Hatch for the *Motor* six-hour race in July 1963.

Above right: Molyslip oil additives sponsored saloon car championships in the 1960s with Mini exponent Ken Costello (number 150) snatching victory in their up to 1,200-cc class from Bill McGovern's similar 1,071-cc Cooper S at Brands Hatch in March 1964.

In company with Formula Junior ace Jimmy Blumer, and saloon car specialist Bill Blydenstein, he dominated the 1,000-cc class in Europe, although back in Britain Mike Young managed to win the 1,000-cc class in the club championship from Mini drivers Rod Embley and Robs Lamplough. Stars in the 850-cc class included Mini drivers Barry Hall and Sheridan Thynne. The Mini stayed on top in the big events, though, with another Formula Junior driver, John Fenning, making his Janspeed car Whitmore's closest rival.

Such was the Mini's dominance in the 1,000-cc class that most British organisers switched to 1,300 cc in 1963 to give the opposition a chance. But the European Touring Car Championship, with its Auto Unions and Fiat Abarths, kept the smaller class, in which Aley's Mini-Cooper took second place, Rob Slotemaker winning their 1,300-cc division in a Downton Mini-Cooper S.

In Britain, Whitmore carried on his duel with Fenning, securing second place in the BRSCC saloon car championship behind Jack Sears, who had to use a combination of a Ford Cortina, Ford Galaxie and Lotus Cortina to the best advantage to take the title!

Top left/right: One of the fastest and most spectacular Mini drivers in the early 1960s was Mick Clare, pictured here demolishing a boiler house at Aintree in April 1964 with his Alexander Engineering 1275S after a furious dice with Mike Young's Ford Anglia and John Handley's Broadspeed Cooper S in the 1,300-cc saloon car race won by John Fitzpatrick's 1275-cc works car.

Opposite: A curly-haired youngster called Gerry Marshall takes his Mini to his first overall win in a BRSCC club meeting at Brands Hatch in April 1964. Behind the 22-second win from Peter Bevan's Austin A40 and a lap record of 1 min 4.8 seconds there lay a tale: the Mini, registered YCD 436, had been built from two halves of wrecked cars and was powered by a 998-cc short-stroke engine constructed around a prototype Riley Elf cylinder block. The car was subsequently crashed very heavily at Mallory Park, but Brian Claydon, of Newtune in Cambridge, managed to rebuild it by 10 am the day Marshall was pictured at the start of a career which would take him to the top in saloon car racing.

Other drivers were less consistent or had other commitments, such as in rallying. In the most glamorous race in Europe, at Spa, Patrick McNally, of *Autosport,* set the fastest lap in practice only to crash before the event. The small touring car class, however, fell to the Minis of De Barsey, Dubois and Aley in that order. In Britain's big saloon car race (the *Motor* Six-Hour at Brands Hatch), Whitmore was partnered by emergent BMC rally star, Paddy Hopkirk, from Northern Ireland, into sixth place overall. They scooped the 1,300-cc class and team prize, supported by John Rhodes in a Broadspeed Mini Cooper, and Slotemaker (eighth overall) plus the ladies' champions, Carlisle and the American journalist Denise McCluggage. Stars of the 1,000-cc class were Liz Jones, partnered by another front-line rally star, the Finn Timo Makinen.

The Mini-Cooper S, introduced soon after the start of the season, then began to dominate the 1,300-cc class as the Cooper had done in the 1,000-cc class before it. The first results were seen in rallying, however, as the works cars were more advanced in development than those of private owners. As soon as the Mini got its extra power, it also became a candidate for overall victory in rallying, such was the superiority of its handling over difficult surfaces. Hopkirk,

Above: Seven Minis started the *Motor* three-hour round of the European Touring Car championship at Mallory Park in May 1964 with the private entry of Tommy Weber and Mario Cabral pressing Warwick Banks (number two) and John Fitzpatrick (number one) hard until the Ken Tyrrell-run works cars drew away by dint of highly-organised pit work for Banks to win from Fitzpatrick with the nearest foreign opposition, Bjorn Rothstein's Saab 96, in fourth place.

partnered by Henry Liddon, cleaned up in the Tour de France, with one of the first 1,071-cc cars, registered 33 EJB. He won the touring car category in this event, which amounted to a rally based on hill climbs and race circuits, taking third overall with a class win in the process. This car then achieved lasting fame by taking the same crew to first place in the Monte Carlo Rally in January 1964.

The Monte was then the world's greatest rally and, with the Tour de France victory, and a touring car win by Aaltonen in the Alpine Rally, did much to boost Mini sales throughout Europe. The popularity of that first Monte Carlo Rally win was undoubtedly heightened by the fact that Ford of America, in search of a high-performance image, had openly declared that they would walk

Right: In a supporting race for 1,300-cc cars at Mallory Park in May 1964, John Fitzpatrick is pictured taking the Downton Engineering 'works' Mini-Cooper S to victory from Handley's Broadspeed 1275S.

Left: American lady journalist Denise McCluggage teamed up with BMC works driver Liz Jones in Alexander Engineering's new Mini-Cooper 1275S (Clare and his car being hors de combat), for Britain's longest race, the *Motor* six-hour, at Brands Hatch in June 1964. They are seen leading Ernesto Primroth's Jolly Club Alfa Romeo Giulia Ti Super and the 3.8-litre Jaguar of Chris Summers. The Mini was running well up the field—despite a five-minute penalty for rally girl Jones having taken a short cut!—when Miss McCluggage caught her elbow in the steering wheel while negotiating Paddock Bend and overturned. That left rally stars of the future Roger Clarke and Timo Makinen duelling furiously for first place in the 1,300-cc class with the Broadspeed 1275S of John Handley and Ralph Broad, who snatched the class win and sixth place overall when their rivals' Don Moore car blew up within sight of the finishing line.

all over the opposition with their massive Falcons! The Fords, and Carlsson's Saab, put up a stern resistance, but Hopkirk exploited the Mini's handling to such effect that he led Makinen, fourth, and Aaltonen, seventh, to the prestigious team prize at the same time.

Meanwhile the Mini racers regrouped with John Fitzpatrick joining the Cooper team from Broadspeed to replace Whitmore, who had gone to Ford. This left Ralph Broad and John Handley to contest both British and European events. Warwick Banks was signed to drive a 1,000-cc Cooper S for the Tyrrell team with Vernaeve in a 1275. Eventually Banks won the European championship from Fitzpatrick, who took the 1300-cc class in Britain. The chief opposition came from DKW in Europe and Young's Ford Anglia in Britain. Development was broadly in line with that on the fastest modified cars offered for road tests at the time.

British club racing was booming with crowds of more than 30,000 at winter meetings, let alone the summer ones! But as more and more meetings were organised all over the country, for frequently oversubscribed grids, the 850-cc saloon car class almost died; practically every ambitious small touring car racer had a Mini-Cooper of at least 1,000 cc. Several instances of wild driving were reported as a result of so many competitors having cars of such equal capability. In one event, at Mallory Park, the entire field was called in for a lecture by stewards! Two Mini drivers emerged as stars of the future: Bill McGovern in a Cooper 1275S and Gerry Marshall in a 999S. Jeff Goodliff was outstanding in a 1293-cc Vitafoam Mini-Cooper S with Steve Neal starring in an Arden Mini. Northern racing driver Harry Ratcliff managed to enlarge the engine of his Vitafoam Mini to 1,390 cc before substituting a 3.5-litre alloy-blocked Buick V8 in the boot, driving forward to the front wheels! Where the Minis faced much serious opposition, it came chiefly from Hillman Imps and the odd Ford Anglia.

All the opposition paled into insignificance when Makinen started the Monte Carlo Rally in 1965 with co-driver Paul Easter. In company with the rest of the field, they ran into a terrible blizzard near Chambery and the Mini-Cooper 1275S emerged as the only car not to lose time on the road—with 201 of the other 237 starters eliminated for being more than an hour late on arrival in Monaco. The Mini's task was made even more difficult by the fact that it was running first on the road and had to plough through snow drifts over its bonnet and roof high on occasion. Studded tyres were of immense help. The thirty-five survivors then had to take part in a 400-mile section in the Alps which proved even more difficult—but served only to increase Makinen's lead over Lucien Bianchi in a Citroen and Eugen Bohringer's Porsche. The French were furious at such a massive defeat and their anger heightened when Makinen and Easter were late for the formal prize presentations by Princess Grace when their Mini refused to start again!

The Minis then went on to win the European Rally Championship for Rauno Aaltonen and Tony Ambrose, who claimed five of the team's eight victories, Makinen and Hopkirk suffering from mechanical trouble or plain bad luck. The Irishman managed a third consecutive win in the Circuit of Ireland, however, for consolation. Apart from the magnificent Monte win, the highlight of the year was a duel between Makinen in a Big Healey and Aaltonen Mini on the RAC Rally. The race to prove which was the best rally car in the world was resolved only when the Mini proved itself better suited to clawing its way up snow-covered Welsh slopes.

Meanwhile the Ford opposition mounted in circuit racing with group two regulations in Britain allowing more scope for the bigger cars, which could be modified for a better power-to-weight ratio than the smaller ones. Nevertheless, Roy Pierpoint's victory in the BRSCC saloon car championship with his 4.7-litre Ford Mustang was a relatively narrow one from Banks in the works Mini-Cooper 999S. Rhodes finished third in the championship and won his class with the team's 1,293-cc car, despite intense competition from Broadspeed drivers Handley and Fitzpatrick, who had been forced to withdraw from Europe through lack of finance. The opposition there, particularly of very powerful twin cam Fiat Abarths, made such trips unattractive in any case. The British racing

Below left: One of the reasons for the near invincibility of the BMC works cars in international rallies against private opposition was that they could carry out vigorous and expensive testing. This 1,071-cc Mini-Cooper S is pictured undergoing such trials in 1964—and it is known to have survived in a slightly ragged state as it was driven by the author in autocross the following year!

Below right: BMC supported private entries in a variety of countries where sales might benefit, with the quasi-works 1275S of Poltinger and Merinsky winning its class and taking fifth place overall behind Paddy Hopkirk's winning Big Healey in the 1964 Austrian Alpine Rally.

Left: Long-time Mini front-runner Mike Sutcliffe chose a 970S for the RAC Rally in 1964, at 2,525 miles the longest to that date. It had 60 special stages totalling more than 400 miles as far north as Blair Atholl in Scotland in a format that was to continue successfully until the advent of fragile 'supercars' in the mid-1980s. The entry of 180 represented the best cars and drivers in the world with Hopkirk's works Mini running at number one—but the stages were far from ideal for the low-slung Minis. They were so rough in parts that all the works cars were eliminated, Sutcliffe's works-supported example suffered, typically, from a broken gearbox extension which let out all the oil. Eventually Tom Trana's Volvo won a war of attrition against Timo Makinen's second-placed Big Healey.

Left: Timo Makinen's Monte Carlo Rally win in 1965 took the spotlight away from a brilliant drive by 1964 victor Paddy Hopkirk, who won his class and finished 26th overall despite being handicapped for much of the event by broken front suspension parts!

Left: Timo Makinen takes a typically spectacular line on his way to victory in his 'local' rally, the 1965 1000 Lakes in Finland from fellow Finn, Rauno Aaltonen and Paddy Hopkirk, all in Mini-Cooper 1275S cars. In ability there was little to choose between the two Finns, Makinen usually attracting more publicity because of his extrovert personality, although Aaltonen won the European Championship that year—in effect a world title.

was very spectacular in any case as BMC had homologated a wide variety of Special Tuning gear, such as wide-rim wheels, limited-slip differentials, 649 high-lift camshafts, flat-top pistons and so on. This enabled private entrants to keep in close touch with the more professional teams and often led to more than that—with accidents being all too frequent. The Superspeed Anglias of Young and Chris Craft appeared to have great potential, but were handicapped in the 1,300-cc class by Ford's failure to homologate wide-rim wheels. Some measure of the Mini's continuing popularity in top-line saloon car racing could be seen in its drivers taking twenty-seven of the first forty places in the championship.

In club racing, however, Marshall was the only real star to emerge from massed ranks of Minis and Anglias which were often ill-prepared through available money being devoted to ever more-expensive tuning equipment rather than more basic attention. Meanwhile autocross, in which a wide variety of cars were raced over courses of around half a mile on suitably bumpy grass fields, was becoming so popular it was even televised. Needless to say, the Mini-Cooper S was one of the most prolific entrants, with John Gunn's 1275-cc example winning the national championship.

Meanwhile the French had re-written their regulations for the Monte Carlo Rally to make it possible only for a group one car (with very few modifications) to win overall. They firmly believed that sales of 5,000 cars a year, needed to homologate the 1,275-cc Mini Cooper S in this category, could never be achieved. But they were enraged to discover that such was the popularity of the 1275S through its Monte Carlo victories that 5,000 and more had, indeed, been sold in the previous year. And when the works team, led by Makinen, took the first three places, a mighty row developed. Eventually the regulations were revealed to have been rewritten again during the event to specifically exclude the Minis, alleging that their headlights did not dip properly, thus promoting the fourth-placed Citroen of Pauli Toivonen to first place. It is significant that after such a blatant disregard for natural justice that the Monte Carlo Rally lost much of its attraction for major manufacturers and with it its reputation as the world's greatest rally. As it was, the disqualification gave BMC more publicity than any hat trick of wins—and changed the whole pattern of the European Championship. BMC continued to enter Makinen in a group one Mini-Cooper 1275S only while an unsuccessful appeal to the French-dominated controlling body of the sport was heard. Makinen—by now recognised as the best rally driver in Europe—promptly won the group one category of the Tulip Rally before moving over to group two cars, which were more highly modified, leaving Sweden's Lillebor Nasenius to win the European title with a group one Opel Rekord.

Hopkirk, with his ill-fated third place on the Monte, a win in the Austrian Alpine Rally and a near-win in the Acropolis, was confirmed as the best driver in Britain. With the advent of the new Appendix J regulations covering both the Mini's groups, the Big Healey was rendered uncompetitive in major international rallies. BMC, therefore, concentrated on the Minis, mainly in Hydrolastic form. Some drivers, Makinen in particular, preferred the older 'dry' cars; he used one to win the 1000 Lakes Rally. Where Hydrolastic cars had to be used—

such as in group one—early troubles with the driveshafts were eliminated by scrapping the flexible rubber couplings and substituting more conventional Hardy Spicer universal joints.

As a competition car in either group one or group two form, the Mini-Cooper 1275S was proving unbeatable on speed alone. The only reason that it did not win more rallies that year was one of fragility. The most vulnerable spot on the Mini was the sump and, although years of development had gone into perfecting sump guards, an occasional fracture cost them the lead. People who had originally said the Mini was too low for rallying were still saying it . . .

The RAC Rally saw the works Minis going very well before a bearing in the drive train cost Makinen victory. It was a fault which had not shown up before because something else had broken first. As weak links in the chain were strengthened, new ones appeared, especially as more than 110 bhp was now being extracted from group two engines. Tyre development was also struggling to keep up with such outputs being poured through small diameter wheels.

Such problems did not deter club rally enthusiasts, however, who competed by the hundred in Minis. What they lacked in ground clearance, they made up with the Mini's amazing ability to plough through difficult terrain. Their cars were very competitive because, at the time, more powerful machinery had inferior traction, and, in the case of sports cars, no better ground clearance. The Mini also had the overwhelming attraction of being very cheap!

One-make domination was a different matter when it came to attracting crowds, causing great concern to the BRSCC, as organisers of the British Saloon Car Championship. They feared spectators would grow tired of watching Ford Mustangs win the big class, Lotus-Cortinas the middle class, and Minis the smaller classes. So they switched to the more liberal group five regulations. They led to domination in the big class for the ultra-lightweight Ford Falcons, originally built for the Monte Carlo Rally. Nothing changed among the middleweight Lotus-Cortinas, but the decision made life more difficult for Mini owners. The new rules allowed complete freedom so far as brakes were concerned, dramatic changes to suspension and running gear, and extensive engine development. The original type of engine had to be retained, but almost everything else could be changed, resulting in the immediate use of

Below left: Although Aaltonen won the European Rally Championship in 1965 he still had his share of bad luck, pictured here taking 14th place in the Alpine Rally after being misdirected by police while on his way to a probable overall victory and a coveted third consecutive Coupe des Alpes for an unpenalised run.

Below: During the early 1960s, John Aley became involved with an organisation called the Squadra Tartaruga in the European Touring Car Championship whose activities extended to encouraging cut-price racing in 850-cc Minis. Bill Blydenstein, who went on to become one of Britain's top competition preparation experts, is pictured here in one of the Squadra's cars, number 158, leading Steve Duncan in a similar Mini to take third place in the 850-cc class of the November 1965 Brands Hatch round of the hotly-contested Ilford Films saloon car championship. These cars were, in effect, the forerunners of Mini Se7en racers.

Right: Part of the reason for the Mini's great success in international competition was the fanatically-high standards of preparation in the BMC Competitions Department at Abingdon, Aaltonen's 1966 Monte Carlo Rally car, GRX 55D, being seen here alongside Raymond Baxter's similar car, GRX 195D, which went on to win the 1000 Lakes rally for Makinen in 1967. Part of the Mini's popularity with the BMC team could be attributed to the fact that these relatively simple little cars took only five weeks to build from scratch against seven for a Big Healey. At the labour rates and price scales prevailing in the 1980s, that would put the price of a competitive Mini at around £12,000, against ten times that amount for one of the modern supercars.

Right: The Mini Se7en Club opened Britain's racing season in 1966 with a saloon car festival at Brands Hatch in which Tony Lanfranchi, having been displaced by officialdom from the front row of the grid in the Speedwell Trophy race for 1,300-cc cars, could manage only second place to Ken Costello's pole-sitting Cripspeed Mini. Lanfranchi's blue and cream Cooper S was to become a familiar sight, entered by the indefatigable Alexander Engineering following the demise of their previous drivers, Clare and McCluggage.

special alloy cylinder heads, dry-sump lubrication and fuel injection, even superchargers. The transmission case had to be used but five-speed gearsets could now be fitted with limited-slip differentials. The bodywork had to remain the same above the hub line, but any width wheel could be used providing it did not protrude beyond the original wing line. As a result, suspension systems changed completely inside the body to accommodate new wheels, their extra width moving inwards rather than out. Initially, the Anglias benefited most under these regulations, running racing engines developed from the new Formula Three, which had replaced Formula Junior. They also had five-speed Hewland gearboxes to make better use of their relatively narrow power band and to cope with the higher outputs. Later in the season, a coil spring rear suspension system replaced their old-fashioned leaf springs to further improve handling. The Hillman Imps, with their Lotus Elite-inspired alloy engines, were also more susceptible to advanced degrees of tuning than the Minis. Most other cars also got an immediate advantage by using twin Weber carburettors on their four-port cylinder heads, whereas the BMC A-series unit, with its siamese porting, gave no such instant advance. It was not until well into the season that a four-port alloy head was developed for the Mini, and even then it did not work well.

Above left/right: With the advent of group two regulations in the British Saloon Car championship, more power could be extracted from the 1275S, while tyre and brake development lagged. Gordon Spice (picture one) is seen here with smoke pouring from the outside front wheel of his Mini at Crystal Palace in May 1966 as Lanfranchi spins after his car was rammed in the back by Harry Ratcliffe's brakeless Cooper S. The eventual race winner, John Rhodes (picture two) was a few lengths clear by that time, Spice following up to take second position from John Handley.

Left: It is every Finnish rally driver's ambition to win the 1000 Lakes—but to take this testing event three times in succession is almost beyond the realms of imagination! Needless to say the ever-spectacular Timo Makinen achieved that feat in 1966, before going on to an even more historic fourth win in 1967 . . .

Above: Paddy Hopkirk made the Circuit of Ireland almost his own like an Irish version of Makinen . . . except in 1966, when he had a problem: not enough time to complete the incredibly thorough reconnaisance for which he was famous even on home roads. And then he ran into another problem, with co-driver Terry Harryman, at about 4.30 am near Lough Eske in Donegal. As Paddy was to say later 'It was a good stage, six or eight miles long and we were going steadily because our times were quite fair, and I had marked this brow on the pace notes as absolutely flat. It was on a straight bit of road. Part of the trouble was that during practising we hadn't been able to try out all those brows and generally you mark them all flat if the road each side is straight and wide. There must be no kinks or anything.

'I approached it going as hard as I could, I suppose about 75 or 80 mph, but it was a funny brow and the car took right off and landed in the middle of the road, but very heavily on its sump guard. The rear end never seemed to come down and the front bounced but unfortunately it didn't bounce straight and the car went over to the left and flipped on to one side. In this position it demolished a tree of about 18 inches diameter by uprooting it with the roof, missed a rather strong-looking wall then put the wheels in the air and spun down the road upside down.

'This was my first really big shunt and the first time I had ever had time to think during one. I don't want to repeat it. When it was spinning upside down all I could see was sparks, and it was a wet night, too. I could feel the roof coming in on me and although I didn't notice it at the time, my door had come off which meant that the road was scraping my shoulder and elbow. But the roof coming down preoccupied me and I kept remembering other shunts I'd seen. All I could think of was getting out of the thing. When it flipped back on to its wheels after about 100 yards, Terry's door was jammed and it wasn't possible to climb out through the windscreen because the roof was crushed down to the bonnet and where the rear window had been the roof was level with the petrol tank. The top of the tanks had been filed off by the road and there was quite a lot of petrol about but we switched the ignition off and Terry, with great presence of mind, asked me if I was all right before the car had stopped. Then we just unbuckled our seat belts and climbed out. It would have been more difficult if it had rested on my side . . . I must say that a roll-over bar inside looks like an essential piece of equipment in future!' For the record, Tony Fall won the Circuit of Ireland that year in an identical works Mini and BMC fitted them with roll cages after that . . .

BMC's problems were made more acute by an economic climate in which credit was being severely restricted. Exports were of paramount importance, so what finance was available was concentrated on rallying, which, ironically, cost more because top-flight events were scattered all over Europe. As a result, support for circuit racing was cut back, with only Cooper retaining their BMC sponsorship. Even then, they were running Downton-prepared engines rather than works examples because the private concern had been able to invest more in development. Ralph Broad was badly hit through lack of finance and quickly switched to Ford, leaving John Rhodes and John Handley to team up for Cooper.

This left John Fitzpatrick driving a 1,000-cc Broadspeed Anglia, which went so well under the new regulations that he won the British championship by the narrowest of margins from Rhodes' 1,300-cc Mini. Young and Craft were usually faster than Rhodes in the 1,300-cc class, but it was not always the same Superspeed Anglia which won, and Rhodes was so often second that he finished higher in the championship than Young or Craft. The Hillman Imps prepared and entered by Alan Fraser also posed a far more vigorous threat to the Minis in the 1,000-cc class, outrunning all but Fitzpatrick.

In Europe, however, Hopkirk drove well in a Don Moore-prepared 1,000-cc Mini, with Vernaeve winning the 1,300-cc class in four European Touring Car Championship races, which had stuck to the group two regulations. British support for private entrants in Europe was understandably poor with no group-two races at home, other than the Snetterton round of the ETC. This meant there was little point in owning a group two Mini any more, as the extra money spent on travelling could have been better devoted to a bigger car, which would have stood more chance of overall victory. The classic example was the secondhand Falcon, the brakes of which were so much more effective than those of the heavier Mustang which shared the same power unit.

Club racing continued to boom with events for saloons proving the most popular. By that time, the Mini had been overshadowed in the 1,000-cc class by the Fraser Imps, although Dave Morgan stayed near the front on the way to Formula Three drives. The Mini still reigned supreme in the 1,300-cc class, however, with Chris Montague, Ratcliffe (having abandoned his Buick-Mini)

Above left: The BMC works team's only English driver, Tony Fall, was dropped for the Acropolis Rally in 1966—but given a works Mini-Cooper S, registered DJB 93B (Aaltonen's 1965 RAC Rally winner) as a consolation. He promptly won the Scottish Rally with it in June 1966 and was well on course to winning the Gulf London Rally soon after (on which works-entered cars were not allowed) when he overturned in one incident, then rolled end over end out of contention near the finish.

Above: Dubious penalties administered after the Acropolis Rally in 1966 relegated Paddy Hopkirk's works Mini-Cooper S from first to third place, leaving BMC and Hopkirk even more determined to win in 1967—a feat, duly accomplished, which gave them great satisfaction.

Above: Minis competing in the over 1,000-cc classes of club racing were becoming ever more sophisticated by August 1966 when Steve Neal's 1,400-cc Equipe Arden Cooper S was pictured leading Brian Cox's 1,293-cc example and Ken Costello's 140-bhp Piper eight-port headed Cripspeed Mini, Starting Grid Club entrant Mac Ross bringing up the rear. But after 10 laps, it was Cox who ended up in front because his tyres lasted better . . .

Top right: The British Saloon Car Championship was never more spectacular than in 1966 when tyre-smoking Minis battled it out behind Lotus Cortinas and Ford Mustangs. Here Paddy Hopkirk's works 1,293-cc Cooper S leads team mate John Handley.

Above right: When the Westover Special Saloon Car Championship was announced as a season-long title chase it meant just that. Mo Mendham is seen winning the last over-1,000-cc race of 1966—on Boxing Day—before preparing for the next round at Brands Hatch on January 8. Enthusiasm for club racing was running so high that more than 20,000 people turned out on a cold, wet, day to see drivers like Mendham in his ultra-light pop rivet-and-aluminium panel Mini-Cooper 1293S that scorned even seat belts as being excessively heavy.

and Mo Mendham among the more successful. Alec Poole provided much entertainment in a very fast Wolseley Hornet, which at least looked different from the average Mini! Already as much money was being spent on development of some cars as those in group five, to the concern of enthusiasts like John Aley. For a time he marketed very successful racers at only £400 each to show that you did not need to spend a fortune to be competitive. Other enthusiasts in the 750 Motor-Club who mourned the demise of the cheap 850-cc racing Minis organised their own Mini Se7en Formula for 1967. Broadly speaking, this formula required that cars taking part in its races should be either group C all-out racers or simple 850-cc Minis. In the cheaper class, a maximum capacity increase of 0.040 ins was allowed using only a standard 848-cc mini cylinder block. The head had to be a standard BMC A-series five-port casting, with any modification in respect of combustion spaces, valve and port sizes; there was also a choice of camshaft, valve gear and manifolds, but costs were contained by allowing only one carburettor no larger than a 1.5-inch SU. A four-speed transmission had to be retained with a ban on the expensive limited-slip differentials. Brakes were unrestricted partly as a safety measure and partly

Left: As the Mini Se7en Club progressed towards low-cost racing, formula libre Minis became popular on the modified front in 1967. Gerry Marshall is pictured here leading from start to finish at Brands Hatch in February 1967 in a special lightweight 850-cc car shared with Ken Ayres and built by Bill Blydenstein ... who was soon after to begin developing General Motors' works cars for Marshall to drive.

Left: Despite the debut of Ford's new Escort, John Rhodes had the 1,300-cc class of the British Saloon Car Championship well under control with his fuel-injected group five Mini-Cooper S in 1968. He is pictured cocking a wheel on the way to his first win that season at the Race of Champions meeting at Brands Hatch.

Left: BMC had cut back to two works Coopers for circuit racing in 1968, driven by John Rhodes and Steve Neal, but gave whatever support they could to private entries, such as that by John Handley. When he blew up his British Vitafoam Mini in practice for the Crystal Palace international in June 1968 they lent him the spare works car, with a taped V-sign on the radiator grille to denote its entrant. Handley promptly took Rhodes for the lead in the British Saloon Car Championship round, yielding only to Neal in a downpour on the last lap.

because racing Minis did not use them much in any case! In similar vein the standard saloon body had to retain steel doors. The suspension could be lowered to improve handling along with alternative dampers and anti-roll bars. But only BMC pressed-steel wheels were permitted. Thus started what was to become the longest-lived form of racing in Britain, and frequently the cheapest.

By 1966, kit cars that used the Mini's convenient subframe-mounted power unit and suspension in glass fibre bodies were becoming very popular. They combined better aerodynamics with lighter weight, the inconveniences of a

Right: Julian Vereker, of *Cars and Car Conversions* road test fame, sold his 'shopping Mini' to Peter Baldwin to win the 1969 Janspeed championship, although Peter—pictured here winning at Brands Hatch in April that year—said later it was not a very good road car with an engine that was happier at 10,000 rpm than 5,000. Below that it would not pull at all! Baldwin replaced the 850-cc 'screamer' next season with a 1,000-cc unit to win two more championships, the car being dubbed 'Baby B' by his mechanic.

Right: Harry Ratcliffe ran one of the most adventurous Minis in 1969 under the British Vita Racing banner, fitted with an eight-port fuel injection engine and the first beam axle rear end to save weight. He is pictured here setting a lap record of 1 min 47.8 seconds at Silverstone in May 1969 while winning the formula libre saloon car race by 54 seconds from opposition including Rob Mason, Richard Longman and Chris Buckley in other hot Minis.

generally-rougher finish paling into insignificance on the race track. It was one of these cars, a beetle-like Mini-Marcos (likened to an animated roller skate by the French) which hung on to finish the Le Mans 24-hour race as Ferrari crumbled in the face of a multi-million dollar blitz by exotic Ford V8-powered sports racers. For the French entrant of the £1,000 1,293-cc Mini-Cooper S-powered car, Jean-Louis Marnat, it was a dream come true; for his co-driver, Claude Ballot-Lena, the start of a long career in top touring cars, and for Britain, salvation because it was good for exports when no other British car

Left: Gordon Spice sold so many copies of *Encyclopedia Britannica* that he could afford to go Mini racing in 1965, before achieving startling results while sales director of Downton Engineering in 1966. By 1967 he had started his own highly-successful chain of motor accessory shops, before heading for the big time in Le Mans racing sports cars while still competing in the BMC Britax-Downton-Cooper team in 1969. Try as they might, other works Mini drivers, Handley, Rhodes and Neal, could not catch Spice or Broadspeed Escort driver Chris Craft at the Crystal Palace international meeting in May 1969.

Left: Readers of *Cars and Car Conversions* were kept entertained and well-informed by arch-Mini racer Clive Trickey, seen here competing in the Brands Hatch Mini festival in May 1969.

could finish. The 2,160 miles covered by the Mini-Marcos at 89 mph would have been good enough to win sixteen years earlier.

The next year, 1967, was one of the last really successful seasons in top-flight competition for the Mini, which had by then been honed to a fine pitch of development. In international rallying, the Porsche 911S, Lancia Fulvia HF and Renault Gordini were close to overhauling the Cooper 1275S. Nevertheless, new restraints on tyres—allowing only eight for the mountain tests in the Monte Carlo Rally, rather than a choice of hundreds—helped Aaltonen to BMC's third official win. Vic Elford's 911S and Ove Andersson's Fulvia provided the stiffest opposition. The European Rally Championship that year was divided into three classes, for group one, two and three cars, with no overall winner so most manufacturers, BMC included, gave it a miss and concentrated only on individual events.

Hopkirk hung on grimly with a battered car to give the Mini a great win in the very rough Acropolis Rally before Makinen landed a historic hat-trick in the 1000 Lakes. The Irish driver then kept up his fine form to win the Coupe des Alpes before taking victory in the Circuit of Ireland for a fifth time. Almost immediately he flew to America to partner Andrew Hedges in an old group two rally Mini, which beat the Lancias to win the 1,300-cc class in the Sebring 12-hour sports car race.

Aaltonen had less luck, despite devising all manner of gadgets to enable a Mini to compete in the notoriously wet and difficult East African Safari. Sadly, his car expired when the engine sucked in mud and water on monsoon-soaked roads . . .

An even more powerful fuel-injected Mini-Cooper 1275S was built for Makinen to contest the RAC Rally, but did not run when the event was cancelled because of a nationwide outbreak of foot-and-mouth disease among cattle!

Below: Former racing cyclist Dave Preece took to four wheels and mechanical power to become one of the stars in autocross. He is pictured here winning one of two runs in his Nagspeed car before having to give best to Irishman Ronnie McCartney in the Big Mini class at the Player's Number Six championship finals at Woburn Abbey in September 1969.

Left: Preece then went on to drive a works Mini 1275GT in Continental Rallycross with considerable success.

Left: Rob Mason drove one of the fastest Minis, prepared by Don Moore, in the 1970 Hepolite Glacier saloon car championship, chasing Roger Williamson's Anglia for the title all season before rolling the car at Mallory Park. Then Mason, pictured here taking fourth overall at Brands Hatch in August, had to be content with a class win.

Left: Wheels grew wider and engines wilder as group two racers took over the British Saloon Car Championship in 1971, Dave Morgan's Mini pictured here leading John Littler's 1300GT Escort in a battle for the 1,300-cc class at Silverstone in May.

Right: Irishman Alec Poole's Complan Mini represented the way Syd Enever, head of M.G.'s experimental department at Abingdon, was thinking when Lord Stokes shut down the BMC Competitions Department. Poole's Mini featured a 1,293-cc Cooper S engine with short connecting rods lowering the compression ratio to 8:1 and equipped with an alloy eight port cylinder head and Lucas fuel injection. A Holset turbocharger was attached to a special manifold where the normal carburettors would have been, with one short stub exhaust emerging through a hole in the top of the bonnet! Underbonnet heat was a major problem, two radiators being needed—one either side of the engine—with asbestos lagging to stop the throttle linkages from melting. Around 200 bhp was claimed from this unit for a car running on 13-inch × 8-inch front, and 13-inch × 7-inch rear wheels, from a Brabham formula two car. The overall weight was kept as low as possible with a British Vita beam rear end located by two radius arms and an A-bracket. The Complan Mini, rated at 1,800 cc, proved almost unbeatable in Ireland and is pictured here thrashing Mike Chittenden's twin-cam Anglia in the Hepolite Glacier saloon car race at Brands Hatch in June 1971 before Syd Enever's son Roger—like Poole a former BMC works driver—took it to overall victory at Silverstone from David Howes's 4.7-litre Ford Falcon.

The works Mini-Coopers had been using fuel injection all season in British races. The Superspeed Anglias generally had the edge on speed, but not reliability, with the result that Fitzpatrick's Broadspeed Anglia won the championship by a narrow margin from Rhodes. Neal also performed well in an Arden Mini-Cooper and Ratcliffe and Gordon Spice were the other Mini stars. The works Minis, driven by Rhodes and Handley, had an advantage on rivals in that Dunlop had developed a formula one-style tyre for them to cope with power outputs of around 105 bhp.

The 970S continued to be competitive in the odd European event, with Hedges, Vernaeve and rally man Tony Fall finishing Second to Elford's Porsche in the 84-hour Marathon de la Route at the Nurburgring.

The popularity of club racing was beginning to wane in Britain, but big fields were still the order of the day, with Minis dominant in the 1,300-cc class. Ken Costello ran away with the Redex saloon car championship, only Poole's Wolseley being able to beat him on the odd occasions its driver could find time

Top left: Bob Fox graduated from Mini Se7en racing to special saloon ranking to lead Ian Bax and Paul Butler in the *Daily Express* Trophy race at Crystal Palace in August 1971.

Top right: Club racing flourished at Lydden Hill thanks to organisers such as TEAC. Dave Foster is pictured here winning a race-long duel with David Enderby in the 850-cc event, one of 11 promoted in four hours on August 8, 1971!

Opposite: Mini racing went from strength to strength in the 1970s, with these two competitors occupying the minimum of track space at Llandow, South Wales, in August 1971.

to race it. The Imps and Anglias were generally on top in the 1,000-cc classes, although Janspeed worked wonders to graft an Anglia's racing SCA engine onto a BMC A-series transmission for Mabbs to run with the top opposition. Dave Morgan and Charles Carling were the other 1,000-cc Mini front-runners, with the up-and-coming Roger Williamson.

The Mini Se7en formula started well with a 1,300 C class won by Costello, a 1000 by Morgan and an 850 by Bob Riley, while the basic 850-cc class was taken by Bob Fox.

Meanwhile autocross went from strength to strength with more than 500 meetings in 1967 when Player's tobacco sponsorship in the Midlands extended to a national championship. Minis remained ever popular, with Charles Inch and Mike Dabbs winning their championships from stars such as Keith Aslett and Gerry Bristow.

The introduction of the Escort by Ford in January 1968 spelled trouble for the Mini in competition as this car could be made to take the same running gear as the bigger saloon, which had previously been confined to the next class above the Minis. In fact, two-litre Formula Two Cosworth FVA engines were inserted into front-line Escorts, with Porsches 911 also being accepted as a group five saloon car because it had a steel roof and two tiny rear seats! The lower-powered

Above: Peter Baldwin ran four Amal carburettors on his 1,000-cc Mini Baby B in the Hepolite Glacier championship in 1972, taking pole position at Brands Hatch in March—then having to be content with third position behind the Imps of Jeff Ward and Ray Calcutt when his front-mounted induction system iced up with the throttles wide open. Baldwin coped by switching the ignition on and off to negotiate corners . . .

Top right: Battle of the day at Cadwell Park in July 1972 was between Roger Saunders and Martin Sellicks in their 1,000-cc Minis during the Forward Trust special saloon car championship round—Saunders winning by the thickness of the trim he began shedding earlier.

Opposite: Baldwin's next Mini had a Cosworth Ford MAE one-litre 'screamer' and carried the number plate Baby B2 to victory in the Hepolite Glacier championship round at Brands Hatch in September 1972 from Mo Mendham's Mini and Jeff Ward's Imp.

1,300-cc Escort GT also presented a formidable proposition, but no more so than the Anglias before it, and Alan Fraser lost his Rootes backing, so the previously all-conquering Imps now appeared only infrequently. The overall result was that Rhodes's 1,300-cc works Cooper S won its class from Fitzpatrick's Escort in Britain, but could only manage third in the championship behind the new two-litre Escorts. Arden fuel-injected, 1,000-cc Minis proved very reliable, winning their class.

Interest, which had been flagging, revived in the European Touring Car Championship when it changed to group five regulations in 1968. Again reliability stood the works Minis in good stead, enabling Handley to win a new division one for 1,000-cc cars despite the rival Fiat-Abarths being much faster. Rhodes also managed to beat Tedora Zeccoli's Alfa Romeo GTA—an alloy-

bodied car which had been dominant in 1,600-cc form—in the 1,300-cc class. These cars, along with British Vita entries, were very highly developed, featuring crossflow eight-port cylinder heads and fuel injection.

This year also saw the decline of the Mini-Cooper in international rallying. Sir Donald Stokes, faced with having to make economies when British Leyland absorbed BMC, shut down the rally team for a time. Racing carried on, however, because it was officially a private operation and cost less. The decline of the Mini in rallying was no fault of the car, the drivers or the mechanics. The Mini-Cooper 1275S had simply run out of possibilities for major development in this area. It had kept ahead of its rivals in the previous five years, chiefly on a superior power-to-weight ratio. Now there were machines with a better combination—Porsche 911s, Lancia Fulvia HFs, and Renault Gordinis—with equally good drivers.

Top right: Mini racing continued to be well supported in 1974, in the face of the world oil crisis which caused a temporary ban on rallying. Clubman Alan Rogers is pictured here leading Colin Selvage in the *Kent Messenger* 1,000–cc special saloon car championship race at Brands Hatch in June.

Centre right: Reg Ward enlivens the Esso Uniflow special saloon car championship round at Brands Hatch in June 1974 with one of the first spaceframe Minis, powered by an 850-cc engine.

Below left: Peter Baldwin needed more power to stay at the front in special saloon racing in 1975 so he bought a Ford BDA-Mini engine and transmission, developed by crankshaft king Gordon Allen. He then installed it in Baby B3, with a new Clubman front to clear the induction system—and hence adopted the new number plate, Baby B4. He is pictured here winning his class in a BRSCC special saloon car championship race at Snetterton.

Below right: The Forward Trust series was one of the best-supported for special saloons in 1975, with Robin Bastable caught skipping over the chicane rumble strips at Thruxton in his 1,000-cc Mini.

But like the circuit racers, the rally Minis were still more reliable than the new cars at first. Early in the season, three works Minis took third, fourth and fifth places in the Monte Carlo Rally behind the leading Porsches. But by mid-season, Aaltonen could manage only fifth place in the Acropolis behind two Porsches and two Escorts, despite returning times as good as those of Hopkirk the previous year. And Renault were blooding a much more formidable new rally car, the space-framed Alpine . . .

The Mini continued to be one of the most popular cars in club racing, however, with Fox, for instance, rebuilding his Mini Se7en to take the free-formula class C in 1968. His chief opposition came from Imps driven by the experienced Keith Holland and McGovern, plus newcomers Peter Baldwin and Ginger Marshall. Terry Harmer won the 1,000-cc class and Geoff Wood the 1300s. Mick Osborne was a frequent winner on the way to taking the 850-cc Mini Se7en championship. In the other saloon car series, Peter Wilcox won the 1,000-cc class in the BARC's Osram-GEC championship, with another newcomer, Richard Longman, taking the 1300s, both in Mini-Cooper S cars; David Alexander won the Redex 1,300-cc class, and Ratcliffe the BRSCC Northern series. Handley and Rob Mason performed well in the odd event with a Don Moore Mini, along with Jonathan Buncombe. But already a new threat was emerging in very fast and highly-modified Vauxhall Vivas in the hands of drivers such as Gerry Marshall. A young Austrian driver called Niki Lauda was making his debut in a Mini Cooper S, however, on his way to a world championship.

Autocross continued to expand with Minis ever popular in the 1,300-cc classes, more than 700 meetings being held in 1968. It was also the first full year of Rallycross, a combination of the time trials that distinguished autocross, with an element on special stage rallying, in that events were held at motor racing circuits, partly on tarmac and partly on a loose surface. This new form of motor sport was conceived as a television spectacular, and attracted all the top rally drivers, both international and club, plus some racing drivers. Once more, Minis were to the fore, the chief opposition coming from Fords and Imps, plus Elford's Porsche.

During the next season, Rallycross continued to expand with BBC TV covering Lydden Hill and ITV Cadwell Park and Croft; top British drivers started to compete in Europe, where this new sport had become even more popular. Front-running Mini drivers included Hugh Wheldon and Keith Ripp in Coopers and Jeff Williamson in a Riley.

Autocross became the most popular type of event on the RAC calendar, with an increasing level of professionalism. Speeds went up at the same time, with lightweight Porsche-engined Volkswagen Beetles coming to the fore, although Minis—particularly those driven by Southern champion Graham Craker, Player's star Tony Skelton, and Williamson—were well up because these events still favoured cars with their power over the driven wheels.

The 1969 season was also the last for the group five regulations because, although development costs were soaring, the racing had stagnated into a Ford versus BMC battle in Britain and BMW versus Porsche in mainland Europe. No other manufacturer was able to produce anything really competitive, except Abarth in the European small-car class. The racing suffered further as few entrants felt like pouring money into what would be redundant machines.

In Britain, conflicting sponsorship demands led to British Leyland fielding two works' teams of Coopers: Rhodes and Handley in Cooper's cars (sponsored by Britax and Downton), and BL's own Arden-prepared cars driven by Spice and Neal. These 1,300-cc eight-port fuel-injected Minis, with another driven by Abingdon designer Syd Enever's son Roger, produced 130 bhp, and ran with light alloy bodywork and wide 12-inch diameter wheels covered by spats. The increase in wheel size was taken up by low-profile tyres so that the wheelarch—and hence the bodywork profile—did not have to be changed. The advantage was that the larger area of contact afforded by these tyres allowed them to run cooler, 10-inch wheels being retained in the wet where temperature did not rise too high. Long and short-stroke engines were used in a bid to keep up with the Escorts, the drivers generally favouring the long-stroke engines which gave more torque and only a little less power than the short-stroke units which revved at more than 8,500 rpm.

Nevertheless, the Escorts usually won the 1,300-cc class, but not the overall championship, which, to many people's surprise, fell to a 999-cc Arden Mini driven by Poole. His 115-bhp unit proved so reliable that he trounced the overstressed Escorts, the only consistent opposition coming from Mason in a Moore-tuned Mini. Other Mini stars included Colin Youle, and Barrie Williams in a British Vita car. Williams, a rally man who had won the Welsh international as long ago as 1964 with a Mini-Cooper, was destined to enjoy a long career into the 1980s.

Meanwhile, club rallying continued to flourish in a rather disjointed state. Events were divided into night rallies held on hopefully-deserted roads and stage rallies using competitive sections off the road—usually forest tracks. Tony Fisher was one of the early Mini stars, with Mike Sutcliffe and Mabbs; Logan Morrison, Alan and Sheila Taylor, and David Friswell came later—with Roger

Below left: British Leyland-powered Minis were struggling in special saloon racing in 1975. Stephen Hall's example, racing wheel to wheel for fifth place with Pat Mannion's Hillman Imp, was the first Mini home in the *Kent Messenger* race at Brands Hatch in June 1975.

Below right: Phil Winter faced formidable opposition in the over 1,300-cc class of the Forward Trust special saloon championship in 1975, hanging on well to take third place at Brands Hatch in September behind Nick Whiting's FVC Escort and Colin Hawker's 'Volkswagen' powered by a Cosworth DFV grand prix engine!

Clarke, who went on to become Britain's best rally driver with Ford. John Sprinzel, at one time a member of the works' BMC team and one of the original partners in Speedwell Engineering, temporarily forsook his Austin-Healey Sprite, transferring his well-known number plate, PMO 200, to a Mini-Cooper S. Later John Bloxham, with various co-drivers, disputed the *Motoring News* and RAC national championships with Cortina and Imp opposition, along with George Hill and Will Sparrow. By 1969, however, Minis on stage rallies faced many problems, not the least Escort-sized ruts!

The Mini continued to be a way into club racing for a large number of drivers although, for those with greater resources, an Imp allowed more scope for development as modified cars were very much the order of the day.

Longman emerged as the champion club racer of 1969, notching twenty-seven outright victories with his Mini-Cooper S in either 1300-cc or 1000-cc form. Along with Harmer, he was one of the leading exponents in swopping engines according to events. Ratcliffe and Mason were still going well, along with Fox and Brian Chatfield—whose efforts in Rallycross were works-supported.

Left: In the Radio One production saloon car championship, classes were divided on list prices, chiefly to Mazda's benefit—but British Leyland used the November round at Brands Hatch to try out the 1275GT. Peter Jopp's Henlys/*Evening Standard* car is pictured here alongside the disc jockey Emperor Rosko in a Mazda RX3 on the way to second in the up to £1,300 class won by a cut-price 1,600-cc Lada.

Left: Jopp then went on to contest the first round of the 1275GT Challenge at Snetterton in March 1976. He is seen battling for second place with John Woodcock in a race won by Alan Curnow.

Right: Mini 1000 racing was ever
popular in 1976, so much so that
there were two races at a Brands
Hatch meeting early in May—with
Ian Briggs and Colin Beckwith leading away the field in the consolation
event for those who had not qual-
ified for the main race.

Right: Rallycross Minis are pictured
enjoying a rare spot of mud in 1976
at Brands Hatch in January, with Viv
Potter leading Graham Strugnell
and Brian Pearce, James Leggate
bringing up the rear in an Escort.

The economy Mini championships still continued to be well-supported and
divided between free and not-so-free classes, with Longman the leading light in
Formula C and Paul Gaymer holding off Clive Trickey for Mini Se7en honours.
The M7C (club) as it was now known, also introduced a Mille Mini class to
coincide with the introduction of the 998-cc production cars.

The British Saloon Car Championship switched back to group two in 1970
in the hope that costs could be reduced—with Minis once more outclassed by

Left: Although many of the Minis that appeared in rallying in the 1970s bore Clubmen fronts, most were pure Cooper S underneath, this example built by Brian Powley being photographed before the Welsh International Rally in 1976.

Left: Motor mechanic Terry Kaby worked day and night on the remains of his brother Ralph's wrecked Mini for two years in the tiny garage beside his parents' farm cottage in Northamptonshire. Then it emerged with an eight-port head to take him to the top in international events. Kaby, who had started by servicing for Bob Freeborough, did it all on a shoestring during the 1976 season— in which he was pictured in the Forest of Dean National event. At the end of the season he found himself £15.50 in profit he had won so much prize money at a few pounds a time, plus all of £200 in sponsorship.

Fitzpatrick's Escort, now producing 150 bhp from 1,300 cc. The best Mini, Spice's works car prepared by Arden, eventually got up to 128 bhp for sixth place in the championship with Longman's Downton-engined ex-works car on 124 bhp as the only other Mini in contention; overall victory went to Bevan in an Imp-dominated smaller class.

Most saloon car races in Britain at that time were for what were called Special Saloons. Five championships were run for these hybrids, which had to retain some resemblance outwardly to normal cars, but featured almost unlimited mechanical modifications. Geoff Wood's 1,300-cc Vita car totted up thirty victories, more than anybody else, with Ken Walker's 1,000-cc Mini third on twenty-seven. Longman, Mason, Baldwin and Gaymer were other leading Mini exponents in this sphere, with Poole experimenting unsuccessfully with a turbocharged Mini featuring huge 'cotton reel' wheels. The chief problem was that it wouldn't steer with so much power and rubber! The Mille Mini class became known as the Mini Miglia to Mick Osborne's benefit, Len Brammer cleaning up the Mini Se7en class.

British Leyland provided the only works opposition to Ford in Rallycross, with Rhodes and Handley being joined by Williamson and Chatfield. Most success, however, went to Wheldon with fellow privateer Dave Preece.

Right: The Mini Jem, first built in 1967, took its inspiration from the Mini Marcos of two years earlier, featuring a Lotus Elite-style glass fibre bodyshell into which could be bolted Mini subframes and mechanical parts. Production continued under a succession of different manufacturers until 1975 with this example, powered by a 1,361-cc A-series engine, winning numerous modsports races in that era. Ian Hall is pictured taking the Mini Jem to a runaway win at Brands Hatch in May 1976, from former Mini driver Ian Bax's MG Midget, Simon Packford's Imp-powered Davrian on the right occupying fourth place.

Specials—frequently with Mini power—started to dominate autocross, which subsequently lost its Player's sponsorship because they looked nothing like normal cars. Then the crowds shrank and this form of sport declined. Minis continued to flourish in the saloon car classes, though, with Mark Smith, Brian and Tony Wilson, Mick Hill and Eric Nosek to the fore.

Rallycross gained Wills tobacco sponsorship for the 1971 season with Preece driving consistently in a works car to win their championship narrowly from Ray Houghton's Rippspeed Mini, with fellow Mini drivers David Angel, Ripp and Wheldon well up. By now most of the Minis were sporting Clubman fronts in deference to British Leyland help with running costs and the makers' marketing plans. These fronts were invariably made in one piece from glass fibre and, as the 1970s went on, started a trend in replacement parts for road Minis suffering from rusted wings . . .

The 1,300-cc Mini rallied by Sparrow and Raeburn also used one of these

Top left: Terry Grimwood, then deputy editor of *Cars and Car Conversions*, is pictured track testing Paul Taft's ultra-rapid Mini 1275GT at the end of the first season of the Leyland Challenge—and taking sixth place at the same time. Grimwood concluded that the secret to driving these Minis was to keep both front wheels on the track at all times . . .

Top right: Barry Hathaway, seen at Brands Hatch in January 1977, rapidly emerged as one of the stars of Rallycross in a Mini, bearing his old hot rod number 83.

Left: Graham Woskett, pictured at Snetterton in March 1977, proved one of the fastest Mini 850-cc drivers.

squared-off noses, and came within seconds of winning the Castrol/*Motoring News* championship despite being one of the few really competitive Minis left among dozens of Escorts in club rallying. The same combination took seventh place in the RAC championship.

The cost of a competitive front-running Escort had soared to ten times that of a new Mini as a result of the freedom allowed by Britain's new group two regulations, with the result that the saloon car championship declined dramatically. For the first time, fields were small and competitors complained of the cost as McGovern won the championship with his Imp again. Nobody could keep up with him in the small class, Escorts disputing the other classes, with only Buncombe in a Longman Mini and Mendham putting up any significant opposition.

Special saloon car racing tended to be more rewarding for Mini exponents, especially Good with his 1,300 cc car, and Jansen, who regularly beat the Imps with his 850 cc Mini. In the financially-sane area of Mini Miglia racing, field were as good as ever, with Graham Wenham taking the title from David Sambell, Brammer turning the tables on Osborne in the Mini Se7en championship.

The success of a one-make series for virtually standard Escort Mexicos led to the re-establishment of production saloon racing in 1972 with express intentions of reducing the cost of competition for a series featuring widely differing cars. At the same time a ban on advertising on cars had been lifted in an attempt to allow competitors to raise more money to cover running costs. The result was quite unlike what the organisers had intended: suddenly luridly-painted saloons appeared which looked and handled quite differently to those on the road. They also cost a lot more, despite the new group one racing being divided into categories according to showroom price. This was because manufacturers promptly homologated all sorts of expensive go-faster parts for cheap saloons: even in the cheapest class, a front-runner was likely to have a 'blueprinted' engine, legally-lowered suspension, racing tyres, limited-slip differential and an international-class driver. Once again, the Mini stood little chance, although a very standard one driven by John Worton thrilled the crowds again by displaying masses of understeer on narrow rims. Victory in this class went to a state-supported Moskvitch.

McGovern won again in group two, but Buncombe's Longman Mini-Cooper S shocked everybody by taking the 1,300 cc title from Vince Woodman's very fast, but unreliable, Escort. The Mini just wouldn't lie down and die in top-flight competition.

Meanwhile, in the budget class, the Mini Se7en Club continued with their very successful formulae. Osborne returned once more to the winner's rostrum with his 1,000-cc car, while the 850-cc cars made up for their relative lack of speed by providing very close bunched racing for Reg Armstrong to take their title.

Osborne's old opponent, Brammer had moved into special saloons, where Minis were still very popular. Along with Baldwin, his BMC-powered car enjoyed some success in the 1,000-cc classes against a welter of Ford-engined Minis. Mike Evans stuck to the A-series engine to out run the Imps for the Triplex championship and his class in the Hepolite-Glacier title race, but Fox switched to twin-cam power for his Mini, taking the 1,300-cc title from Longman, recently returned from a disastrous Formula Three debut. Harmer remained almost invincible at Brands Hatch . . .

By 1972, Rallycross had reached a crossroads, with a reduction in television appeal because the cars were becoming more like autocross specials; there was also a dearth of genuine rally stars to drive them because this sphere of motor sport activity was taking up far more time now that rallying was getting really professional. But while the television cameras remained, Rallycross cars enjoyed some measure of works support, with Preece, Pip Carrotte and Streat at the front in Minis. Angel, however, was more evident in autocross, which continued

Left: Problems in practice relegated Alan Curnow to last place on the grid for the British Saloon Championship's small car race at Oulton Park in April 1977—but he powered through a field including a 17-year-old novice, Martin Brundle, to take third place behind Richard Lloyd's Volkswagen Golf and winner Bernard Unett in a Chrysler Avenger. Curnow is pictured here passing sixth-placed John Burrows, racing his previous year's 1275GT Challenge car in group one trim.

Left: Most hot rod races took place on oval speedway tracks, with a budget class for Minis, called Mini-Rods. But occasionally these cars, which resembled Rallycross machines in many ways, ventured out on to the normal race circuits, Ray Rosser (number 152) disputing a Mini-Rod world championship qualifier at Brands Hatch in July 1977 with Richard Bunn and Clive Haynsford.

Left: Steve Soper heads for a win at Brands Hatch in July 1977—and the Mini 1275GT championship that year.

Above: Mini saloon expert Ginger Marshall started developing a beautifully-engineered Minivan—or Countryman, depending on which way you looked at it—in 1975. He took the Forward Trust special saloon championship with it in 1976, before increasing the power by substituting an Imp engine to drive the rear wheels in 1977. Marshall is pictured at Brands Hatch in August 1978 on his way to the Hitachi special saloon championship.

Top right: Mini Challenge cars were much better turned out once British Leyland had re-established patronage, with these immaculate examples of Roland Nix (inside, eventually second) and Mike Fry (outside, winner) disputing the lead at Oulton Park in July 1978.

Right: Steve Roberts, pictured breaking the lap record for 1,000-cc modified sports cars at Snetterton in June 1978 in the STP championship, went on to win the rival McVities title race that year with the works Mini-Marcos. It was prepared by D & H Fibreglass Techniques, which had taken over the manufacturing rights in 1975. This car was subsequently developed into the Midas kit car by D & H's former Jaguar works engineer chief Harold Dermott, to sell well into the 1980s.

on its own sweet way with ever smaller crowds. And in the RAC Rally, the highest-seeded Mini was number 64, driven by a star of the future, Russell Brookes . . .

In special saloon car racing a new super class was introduced in 1973 aimed at providing as attractive spectacle as the more extreme hybrids were drawn together; it also accommodated surplus group-two machinery now that the British Saloon Car Championship was going over to group one. This meant that Ford power became compulsory for continued success in the 1,300-cc class, although Brammer, Harmer, Ian Briggs, John Watts, Bob Jones and Ian Bax stayed with BMC power and enjoyed better reliability. So far as traditional special saloons were concerned, Crouch and Dineen shared an 850-cc Mini to win the Forward Trust series and take the runner's-up prize in the MCD competition that year. Mini Se7en racing seemed to provide an almost unlimited

Top left: Peter Baldwin had the misfortune to write-off Baby B4 in a high-speed accident at Mallory Park—so he built a new Mini, Baby B5, using the same Gordon Allen engine on Lucas fuel injection instead of carburettors. He is seen here with the new car at Brands Hatch in October 1978 on course for the Rivet Supplies special saloon championship.

Top right: Snetterton is the only British motor racing circuit with planning permission for night racing—an opportunity taken with an early evening start to one of the British Saloon Car championship rounds in 1979. Jon Mowatt's spot-lamp-bedecked Mini 1275GT is seen here battling it out with a Triumph Dolomite Sprint in an event which was none too popular with the group one brigade. But the spectators liked it and subsequently the classic of club racing, the Willhire 24-hour Race for production saloon cars was staged at this venue.

Centre left: Reg Ward's 850-cc spaceframe Mini proved so fast that the original patterns and moulds were sold to engineer John Maguire to put into production for special saloon car racing as Ward was interested only in building cars for himself. Meanwhile Peter Baldwin bought Ward's original car and converted it into Baby B6 using B5's mechanical components. He is pictured here in the paddock at Brands Hatch before giving the car its debut in the Wendy Wools special saloon championship in March 1980.

Below left: Trevor Smith is pictured taking his Mini to third place in the first round of the British Rallycross championship in January 1980—the day that Trevor Hopkins debuted his works Fiesta, a model that was to render the average Mini uncompetitive in such events because the Ford could use far more powerful engines.

supply of impecunious enthusiasts, notably Phil Spurling, who won the Miglia class and Mick Moss the 850 cc, other leading lights including Chris Tyrrell.

British Leyland concentrated on the Triumph Dolomite for group-one racing, leaving Rallycross and autocross as the other main area for competition Minis. Muriel Brooks proved almost uncatchable in group one of autocross with her 850-cc Mini, with Nick Garner and Roger Brunt winning Mini-only classes. Top-line Rallycross drivers were attracted abroad far more often, with Wheldon, Jesty, Airey and Preece enjoying success in Europe. At club level, Jesty's chief opposition came from Mini-men Ripp, Streat, Mick Bird and Keith Stones.

Most of the Rallycross Mini men—with the notable exceptions of Ripp, Bird, Nosek and Angel—switched to cars with more power in 1974 as an increased number of events were held on dry surfaces in the summer. But Muriel Brooks and Brunt stayed in the front in autocross.

Right: Minis have always proved popular in competitive driving tests, often held at such venues as office car parks deserted for the weekend. In their most specialised form, the tops are cut off these cars for better visibility over courses bearing some resemblance to the grand slaloms used for ski-ing.

Below: The 50th anniversary of the RAC Rally was commemorated in 1982 by a special tour of Britain for classic rally cars—with David Potter pictured starting one of the stages at Oulton Park in the ex-Paddy Hopkirk 1964 RAC Rally Cooper S. Hopkirk won the Golden Jubilee event in Timo Makinen's 1965 Monte Carlo Rally-winning Cooper S . . .

Quite the most incredible performance of the year came from a young Northamptonshire mechanic, Terry Kaby, who prepared Bob Freeborough's eight-port Mini. Kaby, who later became an international star, did all the driving as they took this long-outdated car to third place in class on the RAC Rally against such opposition as Sandro Munari in a Lancia Stratos and the eventual winner, Makinen in a works' Ford Escort RS1600.

Left: Minis continue to be popular in all manner of competitions with these two crews preparing to start the Beaujolais Run near Macon in 1982.

Mini specials continued to be popular in 1,300-cc special saloon car racing, but almost always with Ford BDA engines. Former motor cycle ace Paul Taft enjoyed a lot of success with a traditional Cooper S, however, winning his class in the Simoniz championship, Phil Winter, taking second in the Forward Trust, and Harmer staying in front at Brands Hatch. Dineen and Crouch's Mini also took its Simoniz class from David Enderby's similar car.

Mini Se7en racing tended to be concentrated in the south with two 850-cc championships, one won by Geoff Gilkes and the other by Tyrrell; the Mini Miglia series went to Russell Dell from Spurling.

At the same time Renault started a series of races worldwide for their supermini, the 5, with the result that by 1975 more than 800 of these little saloons were thrilling spectators in numerous export territories. Large fields were ensured by substantial subsidies. This gave British Leyland food for thought, so they experimented by entering the experienced Peter Jopp in a 1275GT in British production saloon car races. To everybody's surprise, Jopp won his class in the first race and became involved in numerous close dices after that, with an occasional placing. Greater things were to come . . .

Meanwhile plumber Graham Wenham won both Mini Se7en championships in 1975, plus a series run by the Thames Estuary Automobile Club. His car was based around a secondhand bodyshell; bought for £10, and prepared

Top left: Only the very best Minis remained competitive in Rallycross by 1982, with Trevor Reeves's famous 16-valve example leading Tony Drummond's group four Escort and Graham Strugnell's Gartrac Mini in the British Rallycross Grand Prix at Brands Hatch.

Top right: But Minicross produced a low-cost spectacle with at least four cars trying to get through one gap at Brands Hatch in December 1982.

Below left: With sponsorship from Continental companies, starting money and the late-lamented low-cost motor sport magazine *Auto Performance*, Graham Strugnell enjoyed several seasons of success in the Dutch Rallycross championship with his Gartrac Mini.

Below right: Once Reg Ward's spaceframe Mini design was put into production, these fabulous Maguire Minis became very popular in special saloon car racing, Peter Wartenberg's example being pictured in action at Brands Hatch in May 1983.

with the help of Mini Se7en stalwart Mark Derrick—a far cry from the professionalism that was endemic of the rest of circuit racing.

In special saloons, most Minis were now Ford-powered, although Gilkes substituted an Imp engine to beat all the Imps for their class in the Esso Uniflow championship! Conventional Minis were run by Harmer and Tony Westbrook among others.

In autocross, Nick Garner was king of the small Mini drivers, despite stern opposition from Derek Cleaver, Derek Piggott, Brunt and Terry Smith.

In Rallycross, Airey was the most consistently successful Mini driver, supported by Bird, Dave Baskerville, Trevor Reeves and Ripp.

Production car trials had long attracted Minis, but only with limited success when starts on steep slippery surfaces were needed with the weight transferance associated with front-wheel-drive. But RAC title holder Geoff Spencer managed to retain his championship for a second year and win the British Trials and Rally Drivers' Association title as well with his Cooper S.

Road rallies also had a reasonable number of Minis, notably that of Cyril Bolton, who went on to second place in the *Motoring News* championship in 1976 with Raeburn, and third in the BTRDA. Now the Mini's fortunes had been revived by the world oil crisis, British Leyland felt justified in promoting it in competition. Using the Renault 5 series as an example, they started a new championship for 1275GTs. The main problem was that the Mini Se7en Club's modified cars were faster than standard 1275GTs, so British Leyland framed

Left: Bruce Crosbie raced one of the last competitive Minis in 1983 hot rod racing, using a 1,480-cc A-series engine producing 108 bhp at the front wheels. This 86-mm stroke big bore engine was fed by a single 48DCOE Weber carburettor in a bodyshell that featured coil-sprung suspension all round with only 1.5 ins of movement. Once in front, Crosbie's naturally understeering machine proved very difficult to pass for what was virtually the standard car in Spedeworth events, the over-steering mark two rear-wheel-drive Escorts.

Below left: Alan Dignam's R6 Landar, pictured at the Historic Sports Car Club's classic sports car championship race at Donington in July 1983, represented one of the fastest Mini specials ever made. Around 50 Landars were built by a Birmingham cycle component manufacturer between 1963 and 1970. They had a spaceframe and glass fibre bodywork, which had a very low drag nose because the tall A-series power train was mounted in the back. Landars proved popular in the United States, winning the Sports Car Club of America's 1,300-cc championship, and achiev-ing a reputation as being something of a mini-Can Am racing car.

their regulations to allow a variety of Special Tuning parts to be used. These centred on the cylinder head, encouraging the extraction of more power by polishing, altering the combustion chamber shape, using a 539-based camshaft, free exhaust and 45DCOE Weber carburettor. Handling could be improved by the use of a negative-camber front-suspension kit. British Leyland were, quite naturally, also anxious to promote a smart image for these cars, so the rules stated that they had to retain standard trim such as radiator grilles and bumpers. This meant that the average Mini Se7en car tended to look very scruffy by comparison, so British Leyland took them under their wing by sponsoring their championships on condition that they reverted to radiator grilles and the normal brightwork!

As is inevitable with one-make series, there were many conflicting ways of interpreting the regulations, so much so that the series got off to a slow start, with Taft usually the most competitive driver; then his car was protested and found not to conform to the regulations, so that Roger Saunders won the championship from Malcolm Leggate with Alan Curnow third. Then Curnow's brother, Mike, won the Mini Miglia championship and overall championship for

Below right: Minis are useful for rather more than shopping as Mrs Lea Mylton-Thorley demonstrated while sprinting along the promenade in the class for Brighton and Hove Motor Club members in their speed trials of 1983.

Mini Se7en cars which carried a brand-new 1275GT as the prize! The Mini Se7en Club's 850-cc winner was Graham Wenham with Bob Addison first in the TEAC series.

Phil Darbyshire and Geoff Till also had some British Leyland encouragement in entering their 1275GT, prepared by Arden, in Britain's premier long-distance saloon car race, the Tourist Trophy at Silverstone. The crowd really took the Mini to their hearts as it circulated at the back of a field dominated by millions of pounds' worth of exotic racing BMWs and Jaguars . . . and Till won the Driver of the Day award when he pushed the Mini a mile from Abbey Curve to the pits for repairs when its fuel pump wire chafed through. A fifth place in class was their other reward.

Down among the special saloons, Enderby's Mini 850 performed well in the MCD 1,000-cc class and won its category in the Forward Trust championship, which was won overall by Ginger Marshall in an incredible Mini Countryman.

Autocross was dealt a near-mortal blow by the longest, hottest, summer Britain had known for years, which resulted in not only week after week of dust-racked racing, but a marked reluctance by farmers to hire out or lend fields for competition. The ruts that appeared in remaining tracks were also of no help to Minis. But Rallycross survived in better shape on permanent circuits, with Airey's Mini taking the TEAC title at Lydden with Gordon Rogers and Reeves among the front-runners.

The resurgence of the Mini 1275GT in group one racing provided one of the highlights of the 1977 season. Following experiments with a Mini-Cooper S, Longman switched to a 1275GT when the Cooper's homologation period ran out. British Leyland were of considerable help in qualifying various parts, such as twin SU carburettors, a special camshaft, a close-ratio gearbox, and 12-inch wheels, with Dunlop working wonders with tyres. Longman's 1275GT, supported by Curnow's similar car, very nearly beat the Chrysler Avenger of Bernard Unett, which had dominated group one for the previous three seasons. But eventually Longman, who beat Unett in the 1,300-cc class twice, had to be content with second in class, with Curnow third.

Leyland continued to support the three Mini championships, with Gaymer

Below left: Peter Baldwin continues to run away from the opposition in special saloon car racing, pictured here in winning form at Thruxton in October 1983.

Below right: Not even squally snow showers could stop the Mini Miglia Silver Jubilee brigade at Brands Hatch in March 1984, with Ian Gunn celebrating by taking sixth place behind winner Jim McDougall.

from the 1,000-cc class emerging as the overall champion. Saunders was ousted in the 1275GT category by a coming star, Steve Soper, with Mark Goodwin winning the 850-cc class.

Baldwin proved almost unbeatable in special saloon car races, winning the Esso Uniflow, Forward Trust and Century Supreme series with his Mini Clubman-based machine.

Rallycross continued to expand in 1977 at the expense of autocross, Minis battling it out with Escorts in both forms of off-road competition. Eventually Reeves emerged the victor from fellow Mini driver Angel in the Castrol/BTRDA Rallycross series.

Longman's persistence with the 1275GT really paid off in 1978, with an overall win in the RAC British Saloon car championship after rivals Richard Lloyd (Volkswagen Golf) and Tony Dron (Dolomite Sprint) were excluded from one round on grounds of non-eligibility. Longman, supported by British Leyland dealers Patrick Motors, won the 1,300-cc class in all but one round of the Tricentrol championship, despite stern opposition from Alfa Romeo, whose Alfasud now had a 1,300-cc engine, Chrysler's Avenger sinking into the background with Ford's Fiesta 1300S. It was a good win for the Mini, too, in that Leyland were able to switch much of their promotional budget behind it with the demise of the Dolomite in August. Tom Pitcher transferred from the Leyland Challenge in mid-season, with other Minis driven by Jim Burrows and Ben Johnson.

The Mini Challenge provided by far the best one-make racing in 1978,

Below left: Maguire Minis also made ideal hill-climb cars as Phil Crouch showed at Prescott in April 1984.

Below right: Simon Grattan follows Crouch up Prescott in April 1984 with his GTM—a Mini-based special that has a history going back to 1967 when it took the Racing Car Show by storm as the Cox-GTM. One of the chief advantages over the Mini-Marcos concept was that, like the Landar, the engine was mounted at the back which gave better traction (of particular significance in hill-climbing) and better aerodynamics.

Bottom left: Standard Mini-Cooper S cars continue to be competitive in production saloon car racing as Nigel Grant was about to show at Oulton Park in April 1984.

Bottom right: The one-day Coronation Rally at Eppynt, mid-Wales, was inspired by *Sporting Cars* editor Phil Young to cater for historic rally cars—and received enthusiastic support from the owners of ex-works Minis, including Paddy Hopkirk's 1965 Alpine and 1000 Lakes Cooper S, pictured here with Guy Smith about to start a stage in August 1984.

Right: The Unipower GT—pictured here being sprinted at Brighton in 1984 by Gerry Hulford—was one of the best Mini specials, standing only 41 inches high and produced by racing driver Andrew Hedges and Tim Powell between 1970 and 1974. The only trouble with the Unipower, which had a tubular steel chassis and glass fibre body, was that it was so well made **that** despite a relatively high price **its** manufacturers lost money on every one of the 75 made.

Right: Daily Mirror reporter and Northern clubman Allan Staniforth designed the Terrapin specifically **for sprints and hill climbs—and saw them win many awards before be-coming technical director of Naylor Cars, producing modern versions of the MG TF sports car.**

especially in the 850 and 1,000-cc classes, which invariably seemed to be oversubscribed. However, it was the large 1275-cc class which provided the overall champion Jerry Hampshire, Gaymer, Spurling, Wenham, Tyrrell, Steve Hall and Graham Woskett doing well, with the Graham Hill Memorial Series for novice drivers being won by Ken Brown's 1,000-cc car.

Special saloons were as popular as ever, Baldwin battling with Alan Humberstone's Ford-engined Imp to win the MCD Rivet Supply series, Steve Pengelly's Mini being runner-up in the Wendy Wools championship. By now the steel-bodied cars had been rendered uncompetitive by ultra-lightweight spaceframe racers, many carrying Mini panels. Mike Parkes took one of these

cars to the British Fusegear title in an acrimonious season. As a contrast, the
Hitachi series was free from dispute and won by Ginger Marshall's 'Minivan',
now powered by an Imp engine, with Reg Ward's Wadham Stringer Mini
winning the small class and taking second overall in the championship.

Rallycross continued to gain popularity, fields being made up mainly of
Escorts and Minis, with the odd Porsche, Sprite, Saab and Volkswagen for
variety. The top Mini men hardly changed, however, with Ripp and Reeves
winning major honours, alongside Ian Thompson, Richard Painton and Barry
Hathaway. Kentish driver Graham Strugnell took advantage of starting money
in mainland Europe to contest the Belgian series with his ultra-lightweight
1600-cc Mini.

Longman once again provided the highlight of the Mini year by winning the
group one British Saloon Car Championship from Curnow, which was good
enough to give British Leyland the manufacturers' championship, too. The only
problem was that the Mini was not an overall race-winner, that glory being
reserved for much bigger cars. Leyland, therefore, instigated a competition
programme with their Rover V8 . . .

Below left: Mini Challenge races
continue to enjoy unparalleled
popularity, with Ken Marston leading the Mini Se7ens at Brands
Hatch in March 1985 (picture one),
and Danny Allpress, John Davies
and Chris Lewis the Mini Miglias.

But the Mini's only real opposition came from Jon Dooley's Alfasud, in third place, with fourth-placed Jon Mowatt also racing his 1275GT in British rounds of the European Touring Car Championship.

The Mini Challenge seemed to be caught in a time warp between the old steel-bodied cars and the new spaceframe special saloons. The 1275GTs were similar to Longman's group one cars, except that they were not allowed the expensive group one limited-slip differential. Soper won the championship again, with Spurling taking the 1,000-cc category and Patrick Watts—who, like Soper, was to become a British Leyland works driver—won the 850-cc class.

Baldwin's Mini-Ford was still a long way ahead of the other special saloons, winning the Donington GT series, and taking second place in the Rivet Supply and Wendy Wools championships. British Leyland development engineer Charles Bernstein crowned many years of competition with immaculate machinery by winning the British Fusegear championship.

The Cooper S was still popular in production car trials, Richard Acres taking the BTRDA series, but the Mini's decline had started in Rallycross, despite the adoption of 16-valve twin overhead camshaft engines by Reeves and Painton. Minis won nine major events and Escorts 12, but only Painton's car could take a championship, at Lydden. Strugnell continued well in Europe, however.

The Mini's run of success in the British Saloon Car Championship ended in 1980 when a change in the regulations resulted in a higher minimum weight limit in the 1,300-cc class. As a result, Longman switched to Ford, with Curnow winning the class in a Fiesta from Dooley's Alfasud; Mowatt, still in a 1275GT, was third, the overall winner being Win Percy in a Mazda RX7.

Changes in regulations gave the Mini a short new lease of life in Rallycross, however. Classes were now divided at 1,600 cc, each on a knock-out basis with their own final, thus allowing the Minis to pick up points without ever facing the bigger more powerful cars until a Superfinal between the two classes. As a result, the Minis of Stud Nicolaou, Brian Peacock and Ian Thompson took class wins at Lydden with Reeves—in his twin-cam, 16-valve Mini—winning the overall championship. Barry Hathaway also won the Snetterton championship in a Mini. But soon he was to switch to a Fiesta powered by a similar engine to the special saloons, in company with other Rallycross stars.

These Ford BDA engines were proving very expensive to maintain in the special saloon series, resulting in depleted entries. But Baldwin won the Wendy Wools and BRSCC titles, and the 1,500-cc class in the Donington GT championship, with Paul Craymer's Mini-Ford runner up in the BARC series. Barry Reece's 850-cc Mini won its class in the Wendy Wools championship.

The far cheaper Mini-only series still attracted healthy grids, though, with Roland Nix winning the championship overall in his Miglia car prepared by Steve Harris, who won the 1275GT section from Watts, Baldwin competing in as many races as possible between commitments in special saloon competition. Jonathan Lewis scraped home in the 850-cc class from Russell Gray and Tyrrell, with John Meale winning the TEAC Mini Se7en championship, Gerald

Dale taking the Miglia category. Further indications of the Mini series popularity could be seen in Gordon Lovett winning the same club's Graham Hill Memorial championship with his 850-cc car, the 1,000-cc class going to John Simpson.

British Leyland naturally switched from the 1275GT championship to a Metro Challenge for 1980, the sleeker-shaped new car proving slightly faster. Many of the former Mini competitors changed too, leaving the Mini Se7en Club members to enjoy their unchanged series. No fewer than 111 Mini drivers competed in these races in 1980, with Chris Hampshire winning the national Mini 1000 Challenge from Dave Carvell, and Gary Hill the 850-cc category from Nigel Gaymer.

Several redundant 1275GT cars found their way into Modified Saloon Car racing for steel-bodied machines. One of these cars, driven by John Hopwood, took the spoils while Pengelly and Robert McIntyre did well with other 1275GTs.

Special saloon car grids continued to shrink at an alarming pace, but Baldwin battled on against Soper, now Fiat-mounted, in the Donington GT series. He won the 1,300-cc class and the overall championship in the Wendy Wools series, with Bill Richards's 850-cc Mini taking its class.

The expensive Fiesta dominated the small car classes in Rallycross, with Ripp winning the first of three consecutive Lloyds and Scottish national championships in one, the highest-placed Mini driver being Bruce Male in seventh position, although fifth-placed Reeves temporarily returned to his old 1,500-cc Mini when his new spaceframed Metro blew up. Strugnell carried on happily, however, with his exotic Gartrac-shelled Mini in Europe.

Minis had become scarce in top-line Rallycross by 1982, with only Strugnell, Tony Bardy and Ian Rawle appearing regularly, although Reeves reverted to his old faithful to take seventh place in the B final of the first British Rallycross Grand Prix at Brands Hatch.

The traditional Mini Challenge for 1000-cc and 850-cc cars was as successful as ever, though, with 117 competitors in 1982. Gerald Dale won the 850-cc title easily although the runner's-up slot was tightly contested to the end by Nigel Gaymer and Peter Allen. But Gaymer could do no better than second again in the TEAC Mini Se7en championship from Christopher Gould. The Miglia series featured a fine three-way tussle between Chris Lewis, Mike Fry and Hampshire, finishing in that order, with the TEAC Miglia title going to Jim McDougall.

Baldwin soldiered on in special saloons, beating fellow Mini driver Peter Bray in the Wendy Wools 1000 Plus title race, with McIntyre second in the *Cars and Car Conversions* Modsaloon Challenge to Barry Robinson's Imp.

Crowds throughout Britain were thrilled to see Hopkirk back in action, however, winning the first historic rally, the RAC's Golden Jubilee, in Makinen's 1965 Monte Carlo Rally-winning Mini Cooper S!

Meanwhile, Minicross events which had been held for bargain basement 850-cc cars, expanded into a formula four in Rallycross proper during 1983, with Chris Greenwood winning their title from Mark Lord. The Mini got nowhere in the up to 1,300-cc formula three, but Terry Sowden took his 1,600-cc example to first place in the formula two, from fellow Mini drivers Ian Sandwell and Ivan Gill! Another Mini exponent, Len Payne, also won the 1,600-cc class at Lydden.

Right, opposite right/below: Realising the Mini 1275GT was entering its last year of homologation for international events, Mike Smith developed his budget-priced example to test in the 1985 Coronation Rally at Eppynt (picture one), taking care not to risk jumping the notoriously-dangerous Deer's Leap (picture two), like Adrian Wildsmith and Julie McGowan, before repairing to the roads used in the Monte Carlo Rally of old, to raise tremendous enthusiasm from the nostalgic French crowds at the Rally D'Antibes in October 1985 (picture three), with a car which cost a fraction of the price of the winning Lancia 037.

The perennial Mini Challenges continued as ever on the race track, with Chris Lewis taking the Miglia title from Mike Fry and Stephen Hall, Chris Gould winning the 850-cc series from Barbara Cowell, with Jonathan Thompson third.

Renewed links with the manufacturers led to the Mini races being grouped under the banner of the Austin Mini Silver Jubilee Challenge in 1984, with Mini Seven Club chairman Mike Fry carrying off the Miglia and Southern area spoils! Lewis was second, also managing to win the Mini Se7en Challenge, southern area and Lydden titles, with sixth place in the Miglia southern races for good measure. Other front-runners as the Minis raced on towards a half century on the track were Jim McDougall, Gerald Dale, Cowell, Garry Hall and Steve Mole.

Then just as rally enthusiasts had given up hope of ever seeing a Mini again in anything other than a historic event or the most mundane club trial, housing officer Mike Smith from Northamptonshire converted his 1275GT, which had been contesting the Duckham's road car series on the race track, into an international group A rally car! In the grand old manner, he drove down to the South of France with co-driver Keith Baud, his tools and two spare wheels packed in the boot. Then this car, bought as a wreck for £125, took on the world's finest multi-million pound machinery in the Rally D'Antibes, held over the same roads as the Cooper S had excelled twenty years earlier. In the last year of its homologation, this incredible 1275GT managed to finish what amounted to a 1250 km road race in last place! The French crowds went wild with appreciation as more than two-thirds of the field were eliminated in an event won by a Lancia 037 supercar. There was no killing off the Mini in competition!

X
Buying a Mini

It goes without saying that Minis are among the most practical modern classics to buy: apart from their ready availability in the showroom, the only parts that are not obtainable for even the oldest examples are relatively minor items of trim which can be substituted by spares for new cars. The Mini-Cooper, and Cooper S cars can be the exception when it comes to mechanical spares, but such is the interest in these machines that new parts are frequently being remanufactured for them and existing areas of difficulty are rapidly being eliminated. Providing that absolute originality is not vital to a purchaser, the availability and low cost of most parts for a secondhand Mini can make it a far more practical proposition than any of its peers, although the cost of labour needed for repairs and professional restoration is relatively high in relation to the cost of the car.

This is because the most common cause of trouble in Minis of more than about five years is corrosion. Although the body looks simple, in fact box-like, it is difficult to repair properly. In many cases, a sound, secondhand, bodyshell is a cheaper proposition than repairing a badly-corroded shell. The reason is that apart from the opening panels—the doors, bonnet and bootlid—the only part of the bodyshell that is bolted on is the rear valence under the bumper. Everything else has to be welded, with the relative light weight of the metal requiring a high degree of skill if the replacement panels are to be made to fit properly. Few jobs are simple on a corroded Mini's bodywork, and most of them are vital for safety.

Corrosion—which can be successfully delayed, even stopped, by careful application of preservatives—attacks in a manner as classic as the Mini itself: all round the perimeter where water and road debris is thrown up, underneath and in the seams where panels are joined, especially in areas subject to stress.

As compensation, the price of replacement panels varies from very cheap to only moderate. Very few are expensive by modern standards, because there is such a continuing demand for them. As a result, numerous independent suppliers produce both replacement panels and repair sections and, of course, ARG still supply a comprehensive range of spares for a car which is still in production. In general, the cheaper a part, the less likely it is to fit properly, costing more, perhaps, in labour to adapt, or 'fettle', than might be saved. In addition, because so many Minis are still bought as economical runabouts rather than modern-day classics, the cheaper body parts are often deliberately designed to facilitate cut-price repairs that are not necessarily the best. The common incidence of flanges that are intended to fit over the rotten roots or original panels well illustrates this points. The correct way to repair a Mini body is to cut away the complete corroded section and replace it with a new panel. Obviously it takes longer to cut away the roots as well, but if they are not removed there is a considerable risk of the repair being not only unsightly, but unsound.

The best example in this case is outer sills that pop rivet over the top of rusty originals. These are downright dangerous as they are intended to deceive inexperienced eyes into believing that the car is structurally sound.

Right and right below: No matter whether it looks disreputable (picture one), or careful attempts have been made to restore it (picture two), old Minis can need a lot of work to put them right.

Beware of any plastic body filler, especially around seams, in a secondhand Mini. There is no telling when it is removed what trouble might lie underneath. Fortunately the presence of such filler under the panel can often be detected by a rippling effect which can be seen when viewed in strong light longitudinally along the panel. Alternatively, if no seam is visible where there ought to be one, the car should be treated with extreme caution. More conclusively, a magnet can be run along a suspect surface to discover whether, in fact, the panel is all metal, or just coated, even made, from body-filler. The correct way to fill minor imperfections in a Mini's body is relatively expensive, the lead loading process needing skilled labour. On the good side, the selection of replacement panels and repair sections for Minis is probably the largest and widest ranging for any car. The only Minis which are likely to present problems when it comes to finding replacement panels are the rarer variants, such as the Wolseley Hornet and Riley Elf. Odd items, such as the bootlids of the early cars, with their large indentations for the hinged number plate, are almost impossible to obtain now because later lids are a direct substitute. This is only a problem, of course, if originality is of paramount importance.

From the point of view of security, the first area to check on a prospective secondhand purchase is the outer and inner sills and doorstep. Replacement parts are exceptionally cheap because corrosion here is common, but they are expensive to fit. If corrosion in this area has been neglected for long, the adjacent floorpan can be affected, too. Again panels need not be expensive, but they can cost a lot to fit.

Left: The Mini-Cooper bought by *Practical Classics* magazine provided all the problems you might expect to encounter in restoring an old Mini—and took more than two years of skilled labour as a result.

Right: Replacement trim can be a major problem, particularly if you want to end up with a car as immaculate as this Riley Elf.

The next most vulnerable area for rot in the basic bodyshell that is vital for safety is the back. The rear valence acts as an efficient mud scoop. The road debris it collects harbours moisture and eventually it starts to rot the metal. The valence itself is easily replaced, but it serves only as a decoration. It conceals reinforcement panels which also rot away and add to replacement bills. Removal will reveal two further skins, the floorpan, and the panel on which the luggage boot lid hinges. These parts tend to rot and the hinge panel, in particular, is subject to flexing stresses. Should the entire boot floor need replacement, the pressing is very expensive and costs a lot to fit.

Inevitably, rot in this area will have affected the rear suspension subframe, if it is original, and if it has been replaced recently, be suspicious of its mountings. Both the subframe and the mountings in the bodyshell are vital to safety: in extreme cases, where corrosion has been neglected or the repair bodged, the back wheels have been known to part from the rest of the car! Early warning signs, apart from the visual ones, can be clonks, bangs and squeaks from the back as the subframe loosens itself over a relatively long period and starts to move about. Again, repairs are relatively expensive, not the least because they ought to include a suspension and brake overhaul at the same time. Hydrolastic cars, of course, need more parts and time to fit them because of the interconnecting pipes. The front subframe suffers less than the back from corrosion, but still needs careful inspection and preservation or replacement.

Above: Interior trim, particularly for a Mini-Cooper like that pictured here, can be even more difficult to find if originality is vital.

Left: Under the paint, the way a Mini bodyshell is constructed.

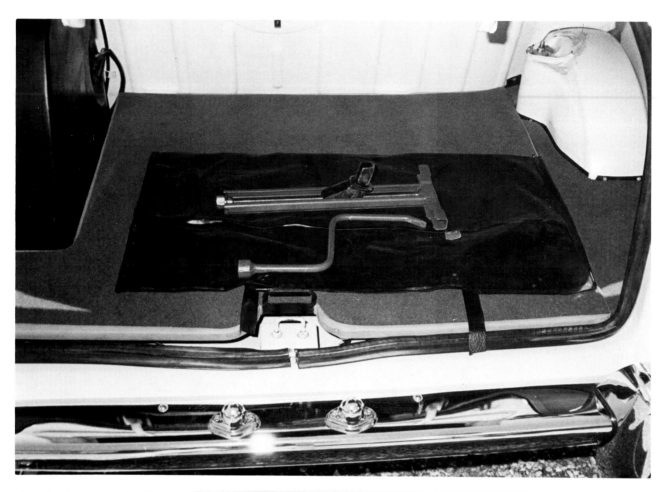

Above: A well-kept original toolkit is rare and all the more attractive as a result.

Right: Rust holes in the top of the scuttle can be repaired with a certain amount of dexterity.

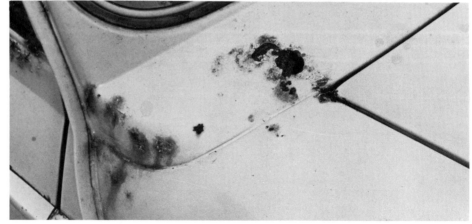

The next most common area for corrosion is around the door hinges, especially at their roots. Like the boot lid support panel, it is a stressful place. A quick glance at earlier cars with exposed hinges can often confirm such a diagnosis!

The A-shaped panel which holds the static base of the hinge on these cars, has an outer skin and inner support with reinforcement plates to take the weight of the door. The outer panel is the last line of defence against corrosion, and if it looks to have been affected it is almost certain that the inner panel has suffered, too. Again, because they are such common problem areas, these parts are produced in large quantities and are relatively cheap—but this often conceals more advanced decay around the top of the bulkhead and the corner of the windscreen panel. The inner A-panel incorporates a splash guard ... which usually rots away as well. Hinge troubles, other than worn pins, almost inevitably lead to major surgery, which, of course, is expensive.

Left: Rust around the guttering is unsightly but extremely easy to eradicate.

Above: But such rot around the back is like the tip of an iceberg of corrosion.

On later cars with concealed hinges, the mountings are single-skinned and easier to repair, but lack of lubrication leading to stiff hinges can cause so much stress that the plates crack. Neglect of this sort can result in trouble with the door frame as well, which usually means that the entire door has to be replaced.

Other common areas for corrosion in the basic bodyshell are the outer edges of the centre crossmember, rust usually advancing rapidly around the jacking point in the sill. The bottom of the pockets beside the back seats tends to rot out, and is awkward to reach for repairs. The floor beneath the back seat and the heel areas need to be checked—they take the stress from the rear subframe. The point at which the rear wheelarch joins the side panel corrodes as well as the damper mounting points in the boot. The battery box and its seams suffer and weeping fuel tanks are expensive to replace. The more exposed tanks on the vans, pick-ups and estates are vulnerable, of course, but the tank inside a normal Mini rots from both the inside and the outside because of condensation and the water content in petrol.

The rear quarter panel itself is also a common rot area, especially at the bottom joint with the wheelarch. These panels are quite cheap, but need extensive welding to fit. The rear panels have a tendency, in addition, to corrosion under the top edges where the metal is thinner, and has been stressed when originally pressed.

The channel section trim on the seams joining body panels is a frequent rust area, and very easily replaced—but the roof gulley is not. Other difficult areas are the flitch panels inside the front wings, which rot at the bottom.

The wings themselves are easy to replace, which is fortunate as mud builds up around the headlamp aperture and, like the rear valence, starts a corrosive cycle. The backs and tops of the front wings are even more vulnerable to road debris, contributing to the door fixing problems.

Above and left: Filler (picture one), especially when covered with paint, may hide a great deal of corrosion, with a door about to drop off in this case (picture two).

Right: The sills are the most important structural part of a Mini—so they must be sound, not corroded like these dangerous items.

Right: Bootlids suffer from rot around the hinges just like the front bulkhead.

Right: The boot hinge mounting panels can suffer, too.

The doors rot at the bottom, and on early models, under the window channeling. Replacement skins are available, but difficult and often uneconomic to fit. Bootlids also rot away from their frame and need replacement as a complete unit. Bonnets present less of a financial problem because their construction is simpler. The front panels around the bumper and the bottom of the wing are not only cheap but relatively easy to replace. But complete glass fibre front ends to replace all the outer panels in front of the bulkhead reduce rigidity; it is essential to fit strong tubular supports between the bulkhead and the front subframe mounting points in this case. Such replacement can be attractive when the cost of a complete metal front end for a Clubman is considered.

Left: Common corrosion around the front lights looks bad, but is relatively easy to rectify.

Replacing worn, damaged or missing trim—especially that for the interior—can be more difficult. In general, hardly any Cooper, Riley or Wolseley trim is still available, and it is difficult to buy many parts for cars more than five years old. More recent trim can be substituted, of course, but—with classic car prices heavily dependent on originality—it may well detract from the value of a car. As Minis, particularly Coopers, appreciate in value, it is inevitable that the situation will improve. Small items of trim—such as badges—are already being remanufactured because there is sufficient demand. But it may be a long time (and may be never) before it is worth remanufacturing some plastic items, such is the initial tooling cost. Metal can always be restored at a price, but there may be no original-looking substitute for plastic parts. Therefore the standard of the interior of a secondhand Mini can be of far greater importance than might be immediately obvious.

The same philosophy may soon apply to the Hydrolastic cars. This form of suspension develops leaks in old age as faults occur in the Hydrolastic units, pipes (especially their connections) and pressure valves. Pumping up sagging suspension is often only a temporary cure. Trouble may also arise because the Cooper S Hydrolastic units, for instance, are no longer available. Hydrolastic cars can be converted to dry specification, but it is a costly process. Sagging suspension on the 'dry' cars is, by contrast, relatively cheap to repair. The rubber cones—which deteriorate with age—can be readily replaced as can other parts such as the suspension trumpets and knuckles. Squeaking noises from rather low-looking suspension can often be caused by the trumpet's Nylon seating having been worn through. Neglect can lead to the trailing arm pivot pins seizing in their plain outer bearings, which then turn and wear an oval hole in the arm. Crab tracking, or odd camber angles, can be caused by the radius arm having been distorted through the wheel striking a kerb or similar immovable object. Minis fitted with wider-than-standard wheels, or spacers, also wear out their wheel bearings much faster. Shock absorbers present few problems although they do need replacing when they are worn, of course; and their mounting rubbers, especially at the back, need far more frequent replacement on cars used over rough surfaces.

Front suspension parts are relatively cheap although, naturally, they can add up to a lot if everything needs replacing. The tie rods at the front frequently suffer from impacts, but they can be either straightened successfully or replaced. The rubber bearings in the upper arms are often neglected, but can be quite cheap to replace, especially if other related work is going on at the same time. The same applies to the rubber bushes in the lower arms, and to the swivel pins at the top and bottom of the hubs. The hubs and drive flanges are quite durable, but they can be scored and damaged if worn wheel bearings are not replaced.

The main problems at the front of a Mini are likely to revolve around the constant velocity joints, which are expensive to replace. Knocks on full lock herald their demise—and with so much dependent on their condition, it is worth fitting only new replacement units. Knocks on acceleration or the overrun on cars made before May 1973 can be caused by their rubber couplings starting to break up. Worn or torn gaiters in the joints need instant replacement in the lucky event of the joint not having suffered from the ingress of dirt. Trouble with the steering can result from the column pinch bolt loosening, with consequent clonking as a warning.

Above left: The wooden trim stuck on the sides of Mini estate cars can become exposed to all the ills of bare wood left outside when strong sunlight cracks its protective varnish.

Above: The rear bed of a Mini pickup usually spends a lot of time unprotected and does a lot of hard work—so look for rot around the wheelarches and edges, and for damage caused by heavy objects.

Left: And thereby hangs a tail . . .

By Mini standards, the brakes are costly to repair and replace. Wear is the most common fault, of course, but back plates on drum brakes can rot away through not having been kept clean. In this case, an accumulation of road debris holds damp. Worn drums are expensive enough, but discs cost even more, especially for Coopers. Anything to do with the hydraulic side is costly, with corrosion causing caliper pistons to seize as the most common condition. Heavy-handed attempts with crude tools to move seized adjusters often leaves them rounded off, which may not look serious, but can cost a great deal to rectify.

Steel wheels give few problems on Minis other than if they are damaged by kerbing; but the alloy ones can suffer badly from corrosion if neglected. Cars still fitted with Denovo wheels and tyres are less than popular because of problems with replacement cost for rubber that wears quickly and provides poor handling in any case.

The electrical side of a Mini is easier to repair than that of many other classics because it is relatively modern. But new looms are expensive and, because they suffer little from corrosion, a good secondhand one can save quite a lot of money—providing it has all its original fittings in good condition. Otherwise changing a loom can be a tedious and expensive business.

Engine and gearbox problems on anything other than a 997-cc Cooper or S type are quite straightforward as parts are readily available, or alternatively, units from other related vehicles are easily adapted. If originality is important, it is worth checking that a prospective purchase has its original type of unit, however! The engine should run at between 15 psi and 60 psi oil pressure when hot, according to revs, with a water temperature of 70°C, 20–25 psi being the absolute minimum on the Cooper S. A normal running figure of 40 psi is acceptable with most Minis, except the S, which ought to have at least 50 psi under such circumstances.

Smokey exhausts are not to be tolerated even if it is accepted that the A-series unit is a tough one which will run a long time in a worn condition. The new valve guides and piston rings usually needed are not cheap. Cam followers, rockers and timing chains are cheaper except on the Cooper S, which needs rebushing. If an engine is giving trouble with oil leaks other than of a simple nature—from the rocker cover, for instance—it is often cheaper in the long run to remove the entire unit for rectification rather than to waste time fiddling with it in the car.

Be wary of noises from the transmission, as worn gears are not only expensive to replace but can damage the casings, which will add considerably to the bill. Synchromesh wear is common, particularly on the second ratio, and whines are usually traceable to bearings which wear quite quickly. Needless to say, parts for the later all-synchromesh gearbox are cheaper and more readily available than for the earlier transmissions. It is also wise to be very suspicious of any automatic transmission as lack of maintenance can lead to very expensive repairs, sometimes costing more than the car is worth. The main problem here is that the oil, shared with the engine, should be changed frequently and is often neglected.

As a consolation, none of these problems are so severe as those encountered with almost any other classic car, partly because the Mini has always been so popular and most items are priced roughly in keeping with the original cost of the car—which has always been very economical!

XI
Restoring a Mini

One of the strengths of a Mini when it comes to restoration—whether total or just one small area—is that it is so small. It takes up little room and most components are relatively light, which makes them far easier to handle. Room to work, particularly under the bonnet, is rather restricted, but after 25 years and five million cars, there are a large number of special tools which can be hired in Europe to help.

Although many quite big jobs, such as changing a clutch, can be carried out without removing the engine and transmission, it is still advisable to take them out if major work on the body is needed. There seems little point in welding in all manner of new panels, respraying a car, and then leaving it with a scruffy engine bay. In any case, the power train has to come out for extensive panel repairs at the front.

There are two ways of removing a Mini's engine and transmission: either by disconnecting the battery, taking off the bonnet, uncoupling the controls, driveshafts and supplies, and lifting it out with a hoist; or by disconnecting the supplies, unbolting the front subframe and lifting the front of the car clear of the power train, which with the subframe and radiator, remains as a unit. In general, the second method is only the best if nothing other than major mechanical work is intended. If work on the bodyshell is needed, it is usually far better to leave the front subframe and wheels in place so that the powerless car can be wheeled about, rather than left immobile on blocks. And if extensive panelwork replacements are taking place at the front, it is necessary to leave the subframe and wheels in place as datum points. It is worth bearing in mind also that if much metal is removed from the front that the subframe should not be allowed to move: this means either supporting the car firmly with blocks at its original ride height or attaching temporary, but strong, supports between the front of the subframe and the top of the bulkhead, assuming that the back of the subframe will be remaining in place while the panels are changed and repaired. Such is the extent of the panelwork which will be required in this case that it is relatively quick and easy to fabricate two tubular supports to bolt in place rather like the legs of a spaceframe. They can also be bought readymade as they are needed to help retain rigidity when a glass fibre front is fitted to a Mini. Ironically, once a

Mini has had new panels fitted, and everything is sprayed in a smart new coat of paint, the best thing to do is to remove the front subframe, refit the power train, then lift the car back over the resultant ensemble. Otherwise, there is a far greater risk of damaging the new paint, craning the unit back into the close quarters of the engine compartment.

Corrosion at the front of a Mini almost invariably means fitting new wings. These are easily removed by either drilling out the spotwelds—once they have been located under a mass of paint—or by chiselling, making sure not to cut out too much metal which will be needed as roots for the replacement wings. If the bonnet is removed while this is being done, carefully mark its mounting points so that it can be returned to exactly the original position—assuming that it fitted well in the first place. It is difficult enough to give Mini panels a decent closing gap, let alone if you have no fixed point at which to start. The front shroud and valence are quite easy to replace, although welding is still necessary, but, again, they need a reference point in the bonnet, as well as the wings. When corroded panels are being removed it is essential to go to great lengths to retain any bits and pieces of trim as such parts may now be unobtainable, especially if the car is a Riley or a Wolseley. Repair sections are available for the headlight flanges which rust out at a rapid rate, but they seem hardly worthwhile; if the wing is that rusty, the rest of the metal will not have long to go and it is cheaper to replace the lot. But it is worth considering replacing headlamp wells with plastic components which are almost corrosion-free, plus wing liners which do a lot to delay further rust. More advanced corrosion starts in the bottom front corners of the flitch plates and continues below the shock absorber mountings.

Right and opposite page: Lifting an engine out from above, or dropping it out underneath a Mini, involves a decision on what needs doing to the rest of the car. If total restoration is involved, it is best to follow the latter course after paintwork has been completed. The operative (in picture two) is using buckets to contain loose chains on the hoist, for fear of damaging the freshly-sprayed paint.

Above: The entire front of a Mini's bodywork is relatively easy to remove.

Right: The rear subframe drops out like the front one, but often with more difficulty because the mounting bolts become far more corroded as there is no oil seepage from the power train to protect them.

When repairing or replacing components so fundamental as these inner wing sections, it is vital to buy the replacement panels first. It may be necessary to marry up parts of new panels with parts of the old if the original pattern is no longer available. This is always likely to be the case with some of the early panels: when a manufacturer knows that late-pattern panels can be substituted, it is frequently not worthwhile having the earlier ones remade. By classic car standards, the Mini's panels are quite simple, so it is not a difficult task to tailor new parts to repair or replace old, accepting that a reasonable degree of metalworking skill is needed in the first instance to tackle so much welding.

One of the more difficult examples is when rust strikes at the windscreen roots, around the scuttle top and under the rubber sealing for the glass. Replacement panels commonly have to be fettled ready to let into the old. The golden rule here, of course, is to cut back beyond any sign of corrosion so that it does not provide an easy start when the car is turned to normal. Again, accurate datum points should be preserved and notes made of measurements before any parts are finally welded into place.

The A-panels in front of the doors are a common trouble point and, in the case of the early, exposed-hinge, cars, both inner, and outer, panels should be replaced in view of the additional stress placed on the eventually-unseen inner plate. If the doors fit well initially, line up the new panel with the door held in place at its normal shutting gap, rather than replace the panels and then try to make the door fit the resultant gap. Kits are available to replace the hingepins on early cars if that is all that is causing trouble. Doors—which frequently rust through at the bottom, can be reskinned, but it is a relatively difficult process because they are lapped all round. Only very skilled panel beaters can reskin a door without ripples or marks, so it is worth searching for good secondhand ones or buying new; the same strictures apply to the bootlid, which often suffers damage, or rusts around its frame. Beware also, in obtaining replacement panels that you select the right type of bonnet. Not all hinge points are the same.

Further problems arise with the doors on vans and estate cars. Their hinges are not adjustable once in place so it is vital to make sure that the doors fit properly before final welding. In the same way, bootlid hinge support panels need very accurate alignment because there is very little adjustment on the hinges once a new part is fixed in place.

The sills, which are frequently corroded on older Minis, are, fortunately, quite easy to replace. Purely cosmetic repairs are to be avoided like the plague. It is vital that not only the entire three-part structure is replaced, but that all the corroded metal is removed. Otherwise, rusty roots attract new corrosion at an unprecedented rate. Some very early Minis had rigid foam injected into the sills to ward off rust, which gives off toxic fumes when heated. Great care should be taken when replacing sills on these cars—which dated around the first three or four years of the 1960s—to chisel away the old metal and scrape out all the remaining foam, which might have become lodged on the inside of the box sections which run down to the sills. Replacement sills often do not include items such as jacking points, but these are easily fabricated. Care should be taken to preserve the efficiency of built-in drainage slots in the sills for obvious reasons. Replacement of the rear quarter panel needs a lot of patience for trial and error fitting, and it is worth repairing the inner seat pocket at the same time. This part, which is important to the car's structure, frequently rots away at the bottom when its drain hole (feeding straight into the footwell!) becomes clogged; and it is far easier to repair when the attendant quarter panel is off the car.

Below: It is essential to go to great lengths to preserve the chrome waist strips of cars like the Wolseley Hornet and Riley Elf because replacements are often impossible to obtain.

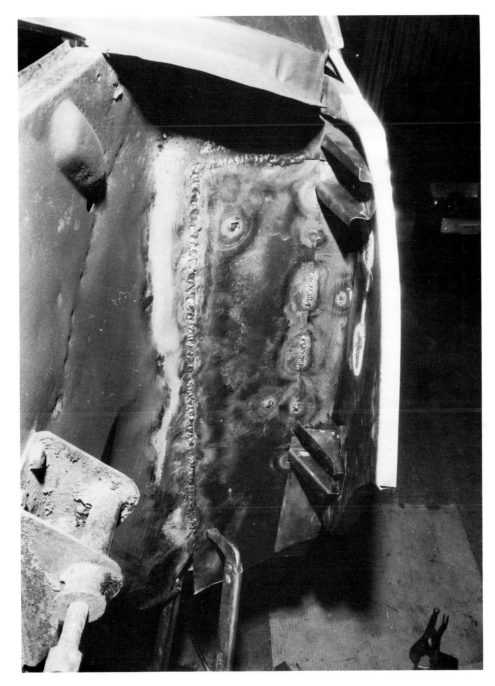

Left: Fresh metal to replace corroded sections—such as at the back of the front wing area—can be cut from sheet steel because it will be concealed when the work is completed.

Repairing the back of a Mini's bodywork follows the same lines as the front, except that it is imperative to remove the fuel tank or tanks, and the battery (for all welding repairs), to avoid the risk of explosion. A petrol tank can remain potentially lethal even after it has been drained due to the retention of fumes. The best way to deal with this danger is to have the tank steam-cleaned, removing sediment which will have built up at the same time.

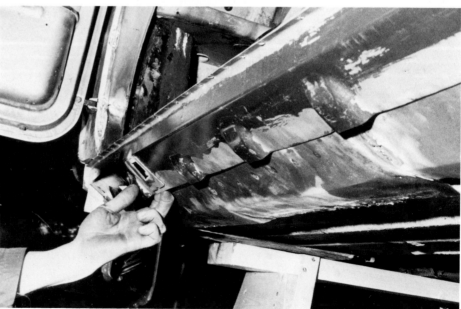

Above and right: It is not only essential to replace corroded sills (picture one) with new panels (picture two), but to keep the drainage slots free to help avoid a repetition of the failure.

With rust causing so many problems in the bodyshell, it is well worth priming and then painting the expanses of bare new metal to inhibit corrosion before the top coats are applied. Few people realise that primer is porous and will only delay the onset of rust for a short time if no top coat is applied.

As long obsolete Hydrolastic systems deteriorate, a conversion to 'dry' suspension becomes ever more attractive. Obviously the best way to do this is to buy all new parts, the only problem being the cost. An alternative method is to buy the parts secondhand, which is more practical so far as the front is concerned than the back, where the common incidence of rust in the subframe makes sound parts rare. It is possible to repair this expensive frame, but only if its vertical webbing has not deteriorated. For ultimate economy, it is possible to adapt many of the 'wet' suspension parts to work with rubber cones—including the precious rear subframe. The front subframe of the Hydrolastic cars has to be replaced during such a conversion in any case, using the pre-1976 part with 'twin-bolt' fittings. The top shock absorber brackets are needed as well, bolting through holes already drilled in the inner wings although they may be covered in dirt or underseal. Two new top arms are needed as well because the Hydrolastic versions are shaped differently and give a much stiffer ride. It is also necessary to chisel out the bump stop locating holes to accept the lower shock absorber pins. The bump stops can be discarded because they are already located in the dry frame. Obviously, it is wise to overhaul the rest of the replacement suspension at the same time!

Below: Interior of the *Practical Classics* Mini-Cooper, with much of the floor and bulkhead having been replaced.

If a Hydrolastic rear frame is to be modified, the displacer retaining lugs will need to be reshaped to locate the rubber cones. The radius arms need to be changed because the knuckle joint seating lug is in a different position and the axle stubs vary, too. It is important to set the toe in at 0.062 ins if handling is not to be compromised. New brake pipes are always a good idea, and the handbrake cables are different, as well. The front and rear ride height on dry cars can be varied by cutting down the small knuckle or packing it with washers: it works on a ratio of 3:1, 0.25 ins off the knuckle resulting in a ride height of 0.75 ins lower. The back end follows the same principles with a 5:1 ratio. Hydrolastic suspension can be pumped up or let down, with standard datum points at 12.5 ins from the hub centre to the wheelarch at the front, and 13.5 ins at the back. Never attempt to vary the pressure yourself. The fluid is contained at very high pressure and should only be adjusted with special tools, normally held by a main agent. Such attention is cheap and the car can be driven to and from premises for such work with the suspension deflated providing the speed is kept down to about 30 mph. For work on the dry suspension you need a special rubber cone compressor.

Replacing a subframe is not difficult although it can be surprisingly heavy if you have not handled one before. The main problem centres around removing nuts and bolts which will inevitably be badly corroded. Repositioning the arms and trumpets in the new subframe can be tricky as well. The most successful way is to detach the knuckle from the trumpet and position it, with the cup and seal in the arm before reassembly, making sure that the cup has been driven completely home. Then lay the trumpet loosely in place, position the radius arm and screw on its inner nut, remembering to thread the handbrake cable through the frame. Next lift the arm and trumpet, and juggle them until the knuckle stub enters the end of the trumpet. You may need a lot of patience . . .

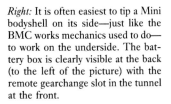
Right: It is often easiest to tip a Mini bodyshell on its side—just like the BMC works mechanics used to do—to work on the underside. The battery box is clearly visible at the back (to the left of the picture) with the remote gearchange slot in the tunnel at the front.

Above: It is well worth injecting a substance such as Finnigan's Waxoyl into closed box sections to combat further corrosion.

Left: The rear suspension of a Mini—in this case a Hydrolastic one—as it should look . . .

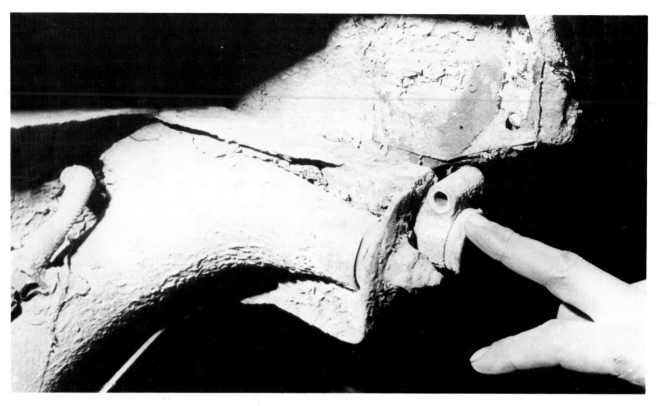

Above: The rear radius arm fixing as it often looks on disassembly . . .

It is a good idea also to reassemble the subframe onto the bodywork using only anti-corrosive nuts and bolts in case it has to come off again, and to smear the freshly cleaned brake back plates with high melting-point grease—especially around the adjusters—to combat further corrosion.

Obviously no compromises can be made in the braking system: any parts which have deteriorated need to be replaced by new ones. This applies also to the discs. It is not worth skimming them to remove scores or marks because they are far too thin for such treatment.

So far as the engine is concerned, the A-series unit is very durable, with timing chain wear on hard-used, or high-mileage examples as the most common problem. The chains are not difficult to replace. Overheating can cause head gasket trouble and burned exhaust valves can be a weak point if the car is driven hard for hours after a lengthy period pottering around towns. This condition is usually heralded by pops and bangs through the exhaust system on the overrun.

Listen for bearing rumble on high-mileage cars, and if the engine is being overhauled for any other reason, it is always worth being suspicious of the centre main bearing. It always seems to be the one that goes first and it is a good idea to replace it as a precaution. Slimy yellow deposits or foaming in the oil filler are a good indication of worn bores or valve guides. Eventually low compression makes starting difficult. Trouble when tuning SU carburettors can often be caused by air getting in from wear at the point where the linkage runs into the body. It is easily cured, however.

Minor work (as extensive as a top overhaul) can be carried out with the engine and transmission remaining in the car: it is simply a case of how good you are at fiddling. Leaving the power train *in situ* can be especially attractive with a Hydrolastic car, but—at the other extreme—competition Minis with detachable glass fibre fronts allow a good mechanic to remove the unit in as little as 15 minutes! Whichever way you do it, it is worth taking off the grille as it just gets in the way and risks being damaged.

Two of the most awkward areas around a Mini engine are the bottom radiator hose—which usually needs to be unclipped for draining—and the exhaust manifold flange, which is particularly difficult to refix for a good seal with the engine still in the car. There are tricks, too, like disconnecting the speedometer drive at the instrument end rather than fiddling about beside the gearbox while the engine is halfway out on a hoist. A wise rule when removing an engine for any reason is to check the gear linkage carefully because any slack is magnified at the other end, making it much more precise if it is cured first!

One of the most difficult jobs is removing the flywheel, which should be torqued on at 130 lb/ft. Always keep the engine at top dead centre on cylinders one and four while working on the flywheel. All the clutch parts are stamped with the letter A; this acts as a guide while lining up to ensure good balance, and if it is not followed there is a risk that the C-shaped retaining washer might fall into the flywheel groove while it is being removed. You really are in a jam then! The primary gear oil seal should always be changed when working on the clutch, too.

Below: It is wise to use new plated corrosion-resistant nuts and bolts on reassembly.

Above: At least the rocker gear is easy
to reach for adjustment . . .

Mini oil pumps are also notorious for wearing quickly, probably because the
shared oil supply carried little bits of metal from gear wear. Remember also to
check the oil pressure relief valve for wear. Fit new parts if it is suspect and a
new spring is a good idea in any case for safety. You should also check the valve
guides for wear. Virtually any movement between a new valve stem and the guide
spells trouble. Neglected oil changes can also lead to rocker shaft wear, so check
for grooving and for dishing or pitting on the rocker face pads. If the cylinder
head needs any work it is also a good idea to have it planed flat.

Working on the trim of a Mini is quite straightforward—with the better the
quality of the replacement trim, the easier! A good rule in this case is to try to
work to mirror images, doing one side at a time, so that you have the original, or
accurate, side as a pattern. This is particularly important while replacing the
wood on an estate car.

Left and below left: Oh so precious ... the upholstery of a Mini-Cooper.

Providing you have a reasonable degree of skill at welding, however, there is nothing too formidable about restoring a Mini, especially as everything is so small and easy to handle. If you are not such a good welder, there is likely to be a man or a firm nearby that is quite capable. Mini owners are lucky in that people of average, conscientious, ability make a very good job of restoration which might be impractical on more exotic cars.

As a general guide, while examining a stripped engine, bore wear and ovality should not exceed 0.008 ins and crankshaft journal wear must be no more than 0.0015 ins; otherwise a rebore or regrind is necessary. It is worth considering having an engine balanced at such a stage, not only for better performance, but for a far longer potential life than the normal 60,000 miles or so.

XII

Preparing a Mini for Competition

It is essential to have a clear idea of what sort of competition you intend to enter before you start preparing a Mini, because the necessary modifications are becoming so specialised. The cheapest outright racing Minis are undoubtedly Challenge cars on the circuits and Minicross cars off the road; the most expensive, potentially, are the big-engined Minis in special saloon car racing and the Rallycross cars.

The heart of a competition car is obviously the engine, and the power and torque which can be extracted from it. In the case of the Mini, engines divide into two sectors: the small bore units (848 cc, 997, 998, 1098), and big bore (1275 and all S types). The greatest gains, especially in terms of horsepower, can be made from the small bore engines because they have a relatively old-fashioned cylinder head design in which the heart-shaped combustion chamber shrouds the inlet valves, which are on the small side anyway. The remaining engines were given the bigger bore partly to get round this problem and partly to avoid using an even longer stroke which would compromise higher revs with larger capacities. More modern engines, such as those produced by Ford initially for the Anglia in 1959, are ultimately better suited to competition work except when the older long-stroke A-series units can remain competitive because they provide so much torque. Juggling cylinder heads can be a rewarding pastime when building competition Mini engines, with the head of a 998-cc or 1098-cc engine giving 848-cc units an instant extra 5–6 bhp. But it is no good trying a Cooper S head in such circumstances because the valves are too big and would foul the block face without extensive surgery. The biggest potential gains are to be made in reshaping combustion chambers, and increasing valve sizes, in conjunction with better fuel induction and free-flow exhaust systems.

The initial decisions involve regulations covering the type of competition that is attractive in relation to the price which can be afforded. It is pointless spending a great deal of money on a small-bore unit if it is easier to achieve the same result at no great cost by substituting a big bore engine. Ultimately, of course, the higher the degree of tuning, the less reliable an engine becomes. There is no simple guide to bolting on bigger carburettors either. The

Above: Competition Minis—such as this Se7en racer driven by Terry Grimwood at Brands Hatch in December 1983—frequently use negative camber at the front for better handling.

distribution of fuel droplets between each of the four cylinders is critical. This means that it can be more beneficial, for instance, to use two 1.25-inch SU carburettors rather than one 1.5-inch instrument; and there may be no improvement to be gained from using two 1.5-inch SUs because the engine cannot take any more of the mixture than they can pass. In general, exhaust changes work much better after the inlets have been improved, and the better the shape of the combustion chambers, the more response there is to fitting a hotter camshaft. The simple substitution of a richer needle in a single carburettor small bore engine can also liberate a little more power at consequent cost to the fuel consumption. Ram pipes of good smooth design to replace air filters can be advantageous providing the engine is not required to work in, say, a dusty atmosphere, where bore wear can be accelerated out of all proportion to the advantage gained. SU carburettors are to be recommended in economy installations, not only because they are efficient, but because there are hundreds of needles available for them. For a long time in Mini Challenge racing, however, the Fish carburettor reigned supreme because it works so well in a single installation. For ultimate power, however, the more sophisticated carburettors, such as the Weber, will provide the most power, although the similar Dellorto units can gain on flexibility. Split Webers—in which one choke is blanked off and the other serves two of the cylinders through a straight tract—have long been favourites for engines where cost is of secondary importance to maximum power at high revs. The same theory applies to the quadrupal Amal set-ups and fuel injection. As a general guide, a 40-mm Weber or Dellorto works well with an 848 or 1000-cc engine producing up to 75 bhp; after that a 45-mm carburettor is desirable. The combinations are endless, though. In Rallycross events, during which a Mini can still be competitive, particularly on wet and slippery surfaces, the ultimate induction on a five-port head has been found to be a single 50DCOE Weber; this is because torque is even more important than maximum power for cars on which everything depends on who is first into the first corner. Front-wheel-drive is more difficult to get off the line than rear-wheel or four-wheel-drive, so wheelspin has to be avoided for maximum traction. That makes torque all-important, and more so when fractions of a second can be saved by being able to stay in the same gear for much of an event. Maximum power is far more important in circuit racing, particularly on a dry surface, providing the gearing takes advantage of an engine's power band.

Above: Heart of the A-series engine—a standard 848-cc cylinder head in this case.

Left: When the entire front end of a Mini is detachable—as in the case of this Se7en racer—accessibility is vastly improved. This car has been fitted with an auxiliary forward-facing water radiator on the right with an oil cooler next to it; the 'serpents' trunk' on the left is to help cool the driver!

Above: Bulkheads have to be sealed against fuel and acid spillage on competition cars, and it is wise to isolate the fuel tank and filler from the bodywork in case of rupture during an accident.

Right: Spartan interior of a Mini Se7en racer, with warning lights on top of the instrument box, securely-lidded battery helping counter-balance the weight of the driver, and key ignition out of harm's way on the floor.

Above: Compulsory roll cages make injury, even when a car overturns, a rare occurrence today.

Left: Early rally cars, such as this Mini-Cooper driven by Glasgow starters Jim and Bill Morrison in the 1962 Monte Carlo Rally, were remarkably standard in their preparation.

Below: The Mini-Cooper S as used by Rauno Aaltonen to take fourth place in the 1964 Alpine Rally used the lighting equipment that caused so much trouble in the Monte Carlo Rally nearly two years later.

Above and right: The Mini-Cooper 1275S with which Timo Makinen won the 1966 Munich-Vienna-Budapest Rally was subsequently rebuilt with numerous Rauno Aaltonen-inspired devices for an unsuccessful tilt at the 1967 East African Safari Rally through obstacles such as deep mud and water.

The bottom end of an A-series engine, other than that of a 997-cc Cooper, rarely gives problems, with the Cooper S crankshafts best at withstanding a lot of power and revs. The 1275GT engine has to be regarded as a cheap substitute, but a worthy one because its crank made up for the strength lost to the more expensive S by having journals 0.125 ins bigger. The cylinder head casting is also similar to that of the last batch of S heads, which had slightly smaller valves to improve reliability. The S head has always been on a cracking limit between its valves. Cylinder heads marketed by the Longman tuning firm have worked wonders by having inclined valves to get over the limitations on space. At a great deal of extra expense, Arden's eight-port alloy head, with inlets one side and exhaust at the other, gave more power, followed by the exotic, but rather heavy, 16-valve twin overhead camshaft Motorspeed conversion on Rallycross Minis which took power into new realms with outputs as high as 180–190 bhp from 1,600 cc. Special saloon racing Minis—which bear a close resemblance to Rallycross cars in basic construction—have opted for the Ford BDA engine grafted on to the Mini transmission as a more economical way of gaining an instant 160 bhp from 1,300 cc against around 125 for an eight-port A-series head. When taken beyond about 140 bhp, the Mini transmission has to be replaced by special straight cut gears such as those marketed by Jack Knight featuring ultra-quick motor cycle-style dog clutch engagement. Flywheels can be machined down to 18–19 lb in weight before it is necessary to adopt special steel competition ones to half the weight again.

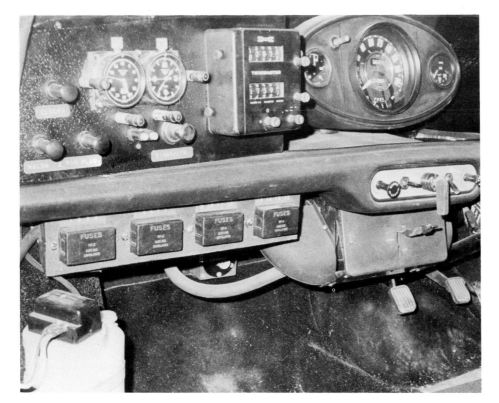

Left and below: Interior of Rauno Aaltonen's 1966 Tulip Rally-winning Mini-Cooper S reflected this Finnish driver's constant search for a new gadget which would help him to victory.

Right: The expensive split Weber set-up used on BMC works rally cars before fuel injection.

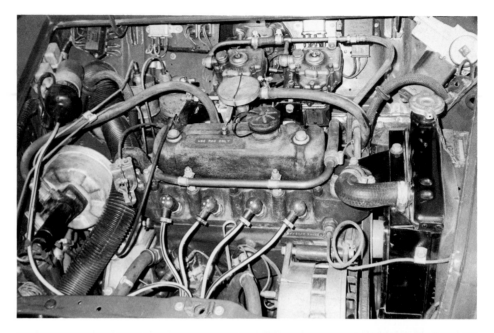

Right: Works rally cars had detachable transparent headlamp covers and padded covers for the spotlights to protect them from flying stones on rough stages. The spotlights and their mounting bars were also made quickly detachable from 1965 with a caravan socket to unplug their wiring loom.

In more mundane applications, a wide variety of camshafts are available, distinguished chiefly by whether they are pin drive (for pre-1971 pattern oil pumps) or spider drive for the later pumps. A golden rule when rebuilding is always to use new cam followers because they are highly-stressed components. They should not be lightened either! Cooper S type duplex timing chains are better than single drive, with gear trains being available for the ultimate engines. But another essential modification if an 848-cc cylinder block is being used is to have cam bearings fitted or else the cam will wear its way out. Later 1275 blocks are particularly attractive because they have a thicker bottom flange for oil security. The Cooper S-style fully-floating gudgeon pin connecting rods are the best at the bottom of an engine, with pistons presenting no real problem other than price. The special long-stroke cranks needed for extra-large A-series engines make the Ford conversion more attractive providing regulations allow its use. The long centre branch exhaust manifold of Cooper S-type was long the hot Mini favourite, until more recent three-into-one systems have been made to work better.

Above: It is important to site as much weight as possible over the driven wheels of a Rallycross car, so the battery and fuel tank has been mounted on the bulkhead of this Mini ... curiously, just where Sir Alec Issigonis first visualised them.

But none of this work is really worthwhile unless the engine is in perfect condition to start with. Beware always of distributor drive wear, which can go unnoticed and cost a lot of power. In the same vein the water and oil cooling system has to be in first-class condition, with a works blanking plate in place of the thermostat promoting better water circulation and an S-type water radiator better than normal because it has 16 gills to the inch against 14. Ford-powered Minis in particular need a front-mounted radiator because of the lack of space for this conversion under the bonnet, alleviated only by using a Clubman-style front at the expense of aerodynamics. The later spider-type oil pumps are better and it is essential to use a central oil pick-up in the sump to avoid bearing starvation if the ultimate dry-sump lubrication is not being used. Straight-cut gears are not only expensive, but very noisy, and limited-slip differentials add considerably to the cost; in many cases they also make a car very difficult and unpleasant to drive, needing to be warmed up properly before they work well and then only with a lot of snatch.

Below: BMC works rally cars with eight-port cylinder heads used four Amal carburettors for a time.

Above: The five-port Mini engine in this GTM rally car has to use a long, involved, exhaust system to avoid reducing the available torque by saving complexity on short pipes.

Left: Classic trials competitor T. R. Limpkin—pictured on the Land's End in 1984—carries two spare wheels on the nose of his Mini to help combat the notorious weight transfer which handicaps front-wheel-drive cars trying to take off on steep loose surfaces.

A Mini's ride height has a major effect on handling, with lowering offering even more stability. Lowering a Mini by conventional means gives more negative camber at the front, or more positive as it goes up for off-road work. Negative camber promotes oversteer, positive understeer. Increasing the toe-in at the back reduces understeer, with consequent results the other way. At the same time, more castor angle on the front wheels increases the self-centring action on the steering. Beam axles have become popular on competition Minis in recent years because they save a lot of weight, promote the use of softer and more efficient coil spring suspension systems as a result, and keep wide wheels at a more consistent attitude to the surface. But the good old drum brakes are still the favourites at the back of cars which are lightly loaded; in fact, for years special saloon racing Minis ran without back brakes because they promoted instability, until scrutineers objected! Massive four-pot caliper, ventilated disc front equipment is necessary on the highest-performance cars, however, with Cooper S discs still excellent for more normal machinery.

When Minis were still used extensively for rallying, seam welded and gusseted shells and subframes were popular: the labour content was high but the advantages never better demonstrated than when a friend was involved in a head-on collision in his Cooper with a similar, standard, car. Needless to say, the seam-welded car stood up to the impact far better! Such preparation can still be beneficial to off-road cars using steel shells, although ultimate grass track and Rallycross Minis now feature spaceframes like special saloons. Where steel panels have to be retained, the floor is cut away, the body dropped over the new lightweight frame, and then replaced with alloy sheeting. In some cases the floor is raised to door bottom level for improved suspension mounting. Deseaming of such shells is popular because it saves 40 sq in in frontal area and promotes a cleaner airflow. Glass fibre panels are used on the even lighter special saloons. Rose-jointed suspension provides a wide range of adjustment with wheels of 13 inches diameter that accept readily-available competition rubber shared with Escorts and the like. The maximum practical width in these cases seems to be up to 10 inches, with half that being a must for road use when normal suspension geometry is retained. Mini Challenge cars have to stick to 5 inches in the 850-cc class and 6.5 inches for 1,000-cc cars.

XIII

Interchangeability of Spare Parts

Mini parts of all ages can be swopped around like Meccano providing some modification is acceptable. Major items, such as complete power trains, or suspension systems, present little problem providing Hydrolastic does not come into the equation! It is when smaller parts are involved that trouble can arise, such as the extreme difficulty in fitting big-valve cylinder heads to small bore engines. The basic decision to be taken, of course, is whether you want to improve the performance of your Mini, or just to keep it running. If the latter is the case, the general policy should be the younger the substitute the better! Otherwise, such was the rate of attrition to the bodyshells of the 1100 and 1300 range of small saloons that they can form the best source of supply for BMC or British Leyland A-series power trains which can be dropped straight into a Mini. Obviously the performance of an 848-cc car will be substantially improved by either a 1,098-cc or a 1,275-cc engine, so the braking will have to be uprated, too. The larger 1.5-inch SU carburettor and inlet manifold used on these cars can be a worthwhile substitute on a Mini as well, giving a little extra performance at a low price.

Varying gains can be made by swopping cylinder heads, with those stamped 2A629 being directly interchangeable between the 848-cc Mini, the Austin A35, Austin A40 and Morris Minor. Heads marked 12A1458, without the boss at the front for a water temperature gauge are similar to the 2A629 and fit the later 848-cc cars and the 998-cc Mini. Heads bearing the code 12G185 are rare, coming from the 997-cc Cooper, but will serve as a big-valve adaptation for the 848-cc and 998-cc cars. The similar 12G202 cylinder head is far more common, belonging to the Austin and Morris 1100 saloons. Almost as rare as the 997-cc Cooper head is the 12G206 casting (for the early MG 1100) which was essentially an improved version of the 12G202. But 998-cc Mini owners searching for more performance could be well advised to look for the larger valve 12G295 head for a 998-cc Cooper, MG1100, Mark II MG Midget or Mark III Austin-Healey Sprite. So far as big bore engines are concerned, the nine-stud cylinder head coded 12G940 from the Mini 1275GT, Austin and Morris 1300 saloons, Mark III MG Midget, Mark IV Austin or Austin Healey Sprite, and 1300-cc Morris Marina saloon car be modified to the same

Above: All the parts that went to make up a Mini in 1959 . . . many of them still interchangeable with those of today.

Below: Combustion chambers are frequently modified on alternative cylinder heads.

specification, or replaced by, the 11-stud 12G940 head from the Austin 1300GT saloon, MG 1300 Mark II and the later Cooper S. The AEG165 Mini-Cooper S head can also be used in place of the 11-stud 12G940 casting. The Austin Allegro saloon which replaced the 1300 range is also a good source of such spare parts, as will be Austin and MG Metros with their complete A-plus engine and transmission when they reach scrapyards in sufficient quantities. But beware, although stud centres are the same for all A-series engines, the big bore units' water passages do not line up with those on small bore cars, apart from the problem with valves.

Above: Swopping a complete power train on its subframe is one of the easiest ways of interchanging wearing parts on a Mini.

Transmissions can be swopped with equal dexterity, the close-ratio all-synchromesh Austin 1300GT box being in great demand as a cheaper alternative to the Cooper unit. By far the most common final drive ratios are the 3.765:1, 3.647 and 3.444. Trouble can arise, however, when people try to swop the cogs around rather than entire units. On the crash first gear baulk ring synchromesh boxes, for instance, there were two distinct helix angles, the A type made until 1964 and the less acute B type which followed. The B type gears are much better, ironing out a tendency to jump out of mesh, and featuring needle-roller bearings on the second and third ratios instead of plain ones. They also have a caged roller instead of a sleeved roller on the first motion shaft and can be substituted directly for the A type gears as the casings are sufficiently similar. The casing was changed, however, for the all-synchromesh gearbox in 1968, so that these transmissions have to stay as a unit. It is possible to transfer the remote gearchange to an older fashioned gearbox, but far easier to substitute the rod-change box made from 1973, which has a remote change as standard.

Above and right: Standard Valve covers (picture one) are prone to leakage, so more rigid substitutes, such as this one by Mini Sport of Padiham (picture two), are popular.

Above: Ultimate road-going conversion on a Mini—a Lotus twin cam engine which necessitates the use of a Clubman front to cover the twin Weber carburettors.

Great difficulties arise when updating a Mini's brakes. The Cooper and 1275GT discs have their own special drive flanges, hubs and constant velocity joints, plus the caliper, of course. But they also need a master cylinder with a bigger reservoir. There is a danger that if a Cooper S braking conversion is carried out on an 848-cc Mini, for instance, without changing the master cylinder that the entire supply of fluid will be absorbed, leaving no braking power! This may not be immediately apparent when the pads are new, but can occur suddenly when they are worn. All Cooper and Cooper S cars and the 1275GT also had longer travel brake pedals and cylinder pushrods, so these have to be matched up as well. Fitting the discs from an 1100 or a 1300 saloon is not the easy way out either, because they have different constant velocity joints and the 12-inch wheels fitted as standard can present vivid problems with the bodywork! In addition, Cooper S wheels cannot be bolted straight on to other Minis because they have a different offset and will foul the bodywork.

Steering assemblies differ between those made with the wider turning circle before the Mark II Mini and those with the tighter radius which followed. The later steering arms took the track rod ends nearer the hubs and there were differences in the racks, too. This means the entire system has to stay together.

Body panels are more straightforward with differences in outline and detail accommodated mainly by modifying newer components to follow the pattern of the old, with the same provision for the interior. In these cases, the appearance of originality is the only real difficulty.

The electrical systems in all Minis are basically the same although early ones were positive earth and later ones negative ground. There is a considerable advantage in charging to be gained from substituting an alternator from the later cars for the earlier dynamo. In essence it is simply a case of reversing the battery's position, and the positive and negative wires on the coil and heater motor, and finding a new fan belt to run with the pulley of the alternator, which bolts on with its normal brackets in place of the dynamo. Accessories, such as ammeters, electronic ignition, clocks, radios and stereo, and rev counters may have to be replaced, though, if their polarity cannot be reversed.

XIV

The Men Behind the Mini

One of the most remarkable things about the Mini was that, in reality, only two men were responsible for it: Sir Alex Issigonis, the designer, and Sir Leonard Lord (later Lord Lambury) who commissioned it. Although they worked in great harmony during the Mini's gestation, their personalities were far from similar. Lord was an abrasive Yorkshireman with a genius for production engineering, renowned for his ready use of rough language; Issigonis, a Briton of Greek and German descent, was, and still is, a complex personality, a brilliant, eccentric intellectual.

It was only in one major aspect of their personalities that they were alike. They were both great individualists who insisted on being absolute masters of their work. Lord, as chairman of BMC, was one of the last motor industry leaders to exercise total control and Issigonis, as chief designer, refused to work with the committees which have since become dominant.

Issigonis was probably the only designer that Lord looked up to: he interfered in the work of almost every other one with whom he had contact. Lord, born in 1896, and educated at Coventry's famous Bablake School, served his engineering apprenticeship at the Courtauld's fibre works before spending the 1914–18 war at the Coventry Ordnance Factory. Following a period at the Daimler motor works in the city, he joined the Coventry branch of Hotchkiss, the French engineering firm, in 1922. Hotchkiss, which had won an order to supply engines for Morris cars, was promptly bought out by Morris in 1923.

It was then that Lord made his name with such strokes of inspiration as producing Continental metric thread bolts with Whitworth heads to fit British spanners, which enabled the French-designed machinery to be adapted quickly to British engineering needs. Lord did not survive on such genius alone, however. He displayed such an unrelenting talent for streamlining all aspects of production that he was soon transferred to the ailing Wolseley concern to modernise their plant in 1927 before reaching the top of the Morris empire as managing director at the main factory in Cowley, near Oxford, in 1932. This was despite Lord's personality clashing almost violently with the boss, William Morris. On the one hand, Morris wanted to give Lord free rein, but with the other he interfered in almost everything Lord did. It was inevitable that such an explosive relationship would not last, and Lord, bent on revenge, joined Morris's greatest rival, Austin, in 1938.

Meanwhile, Alexander Arnold Constantine Issigonis, born in Smyrna, Turkey, in 1906, had been evacuated with his engineer father and his mother as British nationals during a period of unrest in 1922. His father died as their ship docked in Malta, leaving the 16-year-old Issigonis to be brought up by his mother in London in much-reduced circumstances. It was during this period

Right: Eccentric genius . . . Sir Alec Issigonis, the man who designed the Mini.

that they felt penniless and the young Issigonis became obsessed with making the most out of the least in everything he did. Already it was evident that he had an outstanding talent for drawing, but funds would not stretch to art school, so Issigonis joined the 'poor man's university'—Battersea Polytechnic—having displayed a fascination for engines. Soon after leaving college, having failed to matriculate, Issigonis, with his mother, departed on the great Continental tour, then almost compulsory for upper middle class students about to start their working life. This was despite their still reduced circumstances, and endowed Issigonis with an abiding love for everything European, especially French and Italian. As a young man of extreme passions, he then decided never to visit America because it represented everything he disliked: excesses of size, abundance of leisure time, and a distinct lack of historic architecture. On his return from the grand tour, Issigonis plunged headlong into working for Edward Gillet, whose firm made automatic clutches.

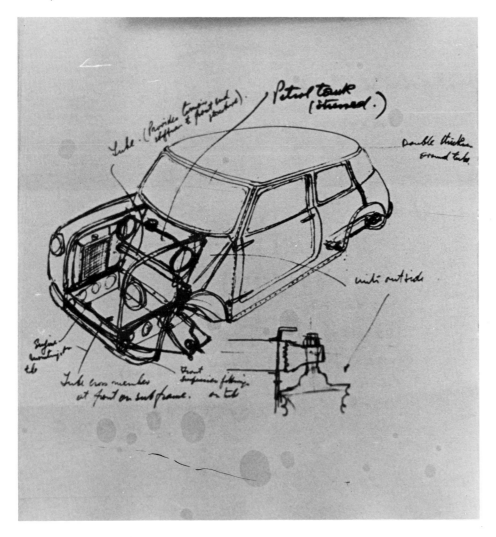

(Left and overleaf): Issigonis sketched out his ideas and then used his small team to put them into practice.

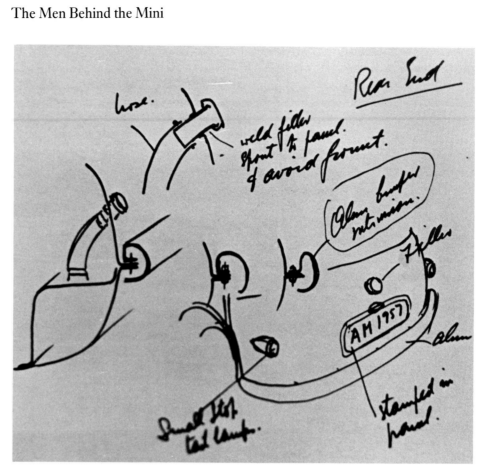

Below: Draughtsmen transferred Issigonis's creations into concept drawings.

In his limited leisure time, Issigonis raced a supercharged Austin Seven Ulster which reflected a new obsession for making one thing do at least two jobs: the rather floppy chassis was braced by being firmly tied to the engine compartment's sidewalls, forming a structure so rigid that the supercharger could be held in place solely by the radiator cowl rather than heavy brackets. It was while working for Gillet (and developing a lifelong passion for automatic transmission), that Issigonis started making his own racing car, a lightweight special, with a friend, George Dowson. His work, as Gillet's only draughtsman, took him into contact with all manner of motor manufacturers, and led in 1934 to similar work in the design office of Humber. Issigonis was inspired by William Heynes, and disappointed when he left in 1935 to become Jaguar's chief engineer.

One of the areas in which Issigonis was to be dismayed was when he was told that there was no hope of Humber adopting the rubber suspension he was developing in his Lightweight Special, because the parent firm, Rootes, owned a leaf spring makers. As soon as Issigonis was offered the chance to show his ideas on suspension, he joined Morris Motors at Cowley in 1936. But when he found that he was to be hired to work on back axles only, he refused point blank. Such was his evident talent, however, that he was mollified by being allowed to design the far more important front suspension. Issigonis did not like Lord's new system inspired by the American General Motors, of making one man responsible for the engine, one for the chassis, one for the brakes, one for the front suspension, and so on. But, for once, he had to compromise, because independent front suspension was a vital development and here was the chance to design it. Years later he was to display his continuing dislike of General Motors and the American way of life by having a large poster of GM's proving ground in a prominent place in his toilet!

Left: The first Mini as Issigonis visualised it in 1958 with a simple Minivan-style front and no brightwork other than bumpers.

Right: The Mini as Issigonis did not visualise it in 1959 . . . bedecked and gaudy.

When the Lightweight Special at last appeared in 1938, it bristled with ingenious features such as all-independent rubber suspension, and—powered by a works Austin Seven side value engine—proceeded to dominate the 750-cc class in British hill climbs and sprints before and just after the 1939–45 war. Part of the reason was that its weight was a scant 5 cwt and served notice that Issigonis would have nothing to do with anything which was big, heavy and uneconomical. He cited American cars as being the worst examples of this, and remained a fan of tiny four-cylinder engines like that of the Ulster, for the rest of his life. For anything more powerful, he dreamed of harnessing steam in place of expensive fuel like petrol.

Already his design work was having a profound effect on the British motor industry. His independent front suspension by unequal length wishbones and coil springs, with rack and pinion steering, was widely adopted, remaining in service with British Leyland into the 1980s.

Lord, meantime, engaged in a price war with new models ranged against those of Morris—now known as the Nuffield Group—until the two giants had to merge into BMC in 1952, with Lord firmly in charge. By then, Issigonis had designed his first complete production car, the Morris Minor, which even Austin's greatest advocate, Lord, had to concede was a brilliant success. Issigonis, however, was disappointed in the Minor, saying that it had too many compromises and the only thing really good about it was that its 14-inch wheels showed that everybody else's 16-inch wheels were too big. He had wanted to use a new flat four-cylinder engine that he had designed and front-wheel-drive as a way of liberating more space for passengers. He was not keen on its 'American' styling, either, saying that all styling meant was adding weight—which was the enemy. Issigonis saw unparalleled beauty in machinery which was purely functional.

Above: Issigonis did not mind unusual cars such as this courtesy bus intended for plush holiday hotels.

Left: One of Issigonis's favourite machines was this Mini-Moke with a second engine in the back.

One of Lord's first actions, in a period of intense rationalisation to make BMC more profitable, was to replace the Morris Minor's engine with the A-series unit from the rival Austin A30. Issigonis recognised the improvement, but left to join Alvis when offered the chance to design a completely new car.

The job appealed to him partly because he could work with a small staff. He disliked being part of a large staff, even in charge of it, because he could not supervise so many people adequately, and thought this might be the case at BMC. To Issigonis, who constantly used other engineers, and even journalists, as sounding boards, personal contact was everything. He insisted on getting hold of the man who mattered most and thrashing out any problem which interested him in an atmosphere of hilarity and intellectual fervour—even when debating the qualities of a rubber bush.

Filled with an overwhelming sense of curiosity and enthusiasm for originality, he designed his only big car, as that was what Alvis needed as a hedge against defence contracts falling flat. And then his engine, an overhead camshaft 3.5-litre V8 was really just two advanced four-cylinder engines put together . . . and perhaps the most significant part of the design was that it was, in 1954, the first car in the world to have hydraulic interconnection between front and rear wheels under a system patented by the rubber engineer Alec Moulton. But Alvis got their defence work and the car progressed no further than the prototype stage, so Issigonis went back to BMC at Lord's calling in 1956, having been promised an almost free hand with design. By then, Lord's health was failing and he no longer interfered so much in design, so their relationship stabilised. Lord's brief for the Mini to simply use any engine on his production lines became famous.

Brooking no interference from committees, and working without a personal assistant on the basis that such luxuries made you slacken pace, Issigonis had the Mini designed and built in two years against the motor industry norm of seven.

For Lord, his last great work safely in production, retirement came on his 65th birthday in 1961, although he remained a director and subsequently honorary president of BMC and British Leyland until his death in 1967. Issigonis, meantime, carried on designing cars such as the Austin and Morris 1100 series, which were to become the top sellers in Britain, and the larger 1800 in 1964 of which he was proud because it offered so much space inside. But it still had a small boot because he considered anything else an unwarranted extravagence, much preferring the Mini's fold down lid as a platform to transport odd-shaped articles. His views on the Riley Elf and Wolseley Hornet have never been made public.

Always his cars were front-engined, Issigonis proclaiming that rear-engined cars like the Volkswagen were dangerously unstable and mid-engined machinery purely for playboys. His eternal quest was to reduce the size of the working parts, such as the engine. He was gratified that automatic transmission for small cars became a reality at last on the Mini, and continued to drive them as personal transport. Issigonis refused to have one long-suffering example serviced while developing longer service intervals. Then he became very enthusiastic about the idea of using two engines, one at the front and one at the back, controlled by two gearlevers, transporting friends and journalists around in a twin-engined Mini Moke. Later he worked on ways of making a gearless car, driving a Mini with a 1,500-cc engine and a torque converter, but no real gearbox, just a control for going forward, backwards, or ticking over in neutral. He maintained opposition to streamlining for small cars, saying it was just an extension of styling, and emphasising that such vehicles spent 80 per cent of their time in traffic, so they did not need to carry the extra weight of a sleeker shape.

Above and opposite page: The Mini as stylists visualised it in 1958 . . . on its way to becoming an Austin-Morris 1100, with a Morris Minor for comparison.

He was a great advocate of disc brakes and overjoyed when the Mini-Cooper got them—and disappointed when the rubber belts, pioneered by the German firm Glas, were not used in an overhead cam engine on grounds of cost.

Issigonis carried on a campaign against in-car entertainment refusing to have his vehicles fitted with a radio, which he considered a distraction while driving. He was also prone to inform passengers that the Chinese had a law against talking to the driver . . .

Once out of a car, he seemed incapable of relaxation, smoking cigarettes furiously, uttering statements in staccato rushes, prefixing them with 'I insist absolutely . . .' and ending them often with 'Hmmm,' and a question mark as his mind raced ahead to something new. He appeared a habitual worrier, with his attention hardly ever leaving BMC business, whereas in his younger days he was often reprimanded for sketching parts of his Lightweight Special during company time. And then he would relax with a fury, on holiday at L'Hermitage in Monte Carlo, a monument to the ornate and ostentatious side of life he disdained.

In conversation, his huge, expansive, hands were seldom still, as he issued statements like a machine gun, showing a great love for shocking the listener.

When required by company policy to retire at 65, Issigonis held a leaving party, then carried on working . . . and he was still working as a design consultant for Austin Rover until just before his death, aged 81, in October 1988.

He proclaimed, on the one hand: 'If one pioneers something, and it is not copied, then it's a failure,' and, on the other: 'Small cars are so boring, they are ghastly, they all look the same because they are designed by committees trying to copy the Mini.'

XV
Thirty Years a Mini

The Mini's days were numbered when Prime Minister Margaret Thatcher moved Graham Day (later Sir Graham), a 52-year-old Canadian company doctor, into State-supported British Leyland to hack the company back into shape. Virtually everybody working for the ailing car maker assumed it would die of old age at almost any time. The only thing going for it in their eyes was a continuing demand—which they thought would soon evaporate because the basic design was so old.

But as Day forged links with Honda of Japan, first to build a stop-gap, medium-sized, car under licence, and then to undertake more ambitious joint

Below: Rover reverted to traditional British Racing Green for one of their most popular limited-edition models, the Racing.

car development, he realized that the Mini was still making a profit; and precious little else at BL could boast of that.

At the same time, there was an ever-increasing demand for Minis from the Japanese, who regarded these charming little cars as instant antiques! Not only did they rise in value, in the manner of all antiques, but they were perfectly practical to use in the meantime . . .

One of Day's first decisions was to revive the Mini, by expanding the

Right: Mini Moke production continued in Portugal during the 1980s, this Mini 25 limited-edition model fetching a premium while plying for hire at Praia de Rocha on the Algarve.

Right: Open-topped versions of the Mini had been produced for years by firms such as Ludgate Design and Development in Kent, before Rover produced a cabriolet version of the Mayfair in 1992.

policy of launching limited edition models which would increase its exclusive appeal at minimal investment.

The existing two Mini models had been given a new look for the 1986 model year. Outside, the City's wheel arch extensions, bumpers and door handles were now finished in grey, and the Mayfair got full wheel trims. Inside, the City took the Mayfair's instrument panel, while the Mayfair received a rev counter and trim changes. Side indicators became standard on both models. This was only the beginning.

In January 1986, the Chelsea became Austin Rover's latest limited edition Mini. It was based on the City, with Targa red coachwork and red and silver coachlining. The Chelsea logo was seen in red script on the light grey seat backrests, which were set off with red piping.

A production run of 1,500 started as the 5,000,000th Mini left the production lines in February 1986. It was handed over to TV personality Noel Edmonds, chairman of the Stars Organization for Spastics charity.

Soon after, in June 1986, Day began to take the group upmarket by changing the battle-weary name BL to the Rover Group, a symbol of solid prosperity. The Piccadilly, limited to a run of 2,500, coincided with this name change. In reality, it was half-way between the City and the Mayfair, finished in Cashmere Gold, with bright bumpers and door handles and full diameter wheel trims. Inside the trim was claret, dark and

Above: The lower-cost City took on the Sprite name—pioneered on BMC's small sports cars between the 1950s and 1980, and carried on a limited-edition Mini in the early 1980s—for the 1993 model year. Improvements to the specification included the standard fitting of a passenger door mirror, boot mat, front door bins, new trim and colour schemes, and an optional alarm and engine immobilizer. Like all 1993-model Minis, the Sprite received new Metro-style front seats, VIN chassis code etched glass to help deter thieves, and—for the first time since 1959—an internal bonnet release!

Right: The top-of-the-range Mini Mayfair included as standard the security-conscious features of the Sprite, such as the alarm, immobilizer, etched glass and internal bonnet release, locking nuts for its alloy wheels, with a chrome-effect grille and new bootlid badging.

Below: The Mini Mayfair's interior was much modernized for 1993 with a full-width walnut facia carrying a radio/cassette in the centre, rather than above the passenger's knees, and the option of full leather trim. The Cooper edition was basically the same, except that it did not have the leather.

Above: A team of Mini-Coopers—not including the author's which exploded before it left England!—helped make the London-to-Italy Classic Marathon the most famous historic rally in the world. Terry Langridge and Mike Rosum's Cooper S is seen braving the local hazards while crossing the Franco-Italian border on the first marathon in 1988.

Left: Big name drivers, such as Paddy Hopkirk, were hired to help publicize the marathon by early sponsors Pirelli. Hopkirk is pictured here reunited with a Mini-Cooper S at the 1989 start on London Bridge.

light chocolate, with a Piccadilly logo on the seats and bootlid.

By this time the Mini had become a cult car in Japan. It led to an Austin Rover sales boom, 200 per cent ahead of the previous year, and providing two-thirds of total British exports to Japan.

In January 1987, 700 examples of the latest 4,000 production run limited edition Mini, the Park Lane, were earmarked for Japan. The black paintwork was set off with Park Lane striping, decals and bright metal trim. Inside, the car had coffee-beige, black and velvet seats and door trims.

As the Japanese demand was boosted by a parallel one from France, Day confirmed the decision to keep the Mini in production, which meant a commitment to this 'good little earner' until at least 1991.

It was pressure from Austin Rover France, and market research in Britain—which showed that 70 per cent of the Mini domestic sales were to women aged between 25 and 39—which most strongly influenced Day's decision. He was also beginning to feel the effect of a 'Minis have feelings, too' poster and TV advertising campaign. Sales rose 21 per cent as the result of this campaign, the first for five years, as market research revealed that many people thought that Mini production had already been halted!

In the meantime, the Mini Moke had undergone a similar process, being saved, effectively, by a retired BL executive, Jack Lambert. He stayed on in

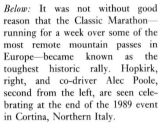

Below: It was not without good reason that the Classic Marathon—running for a week over some of the most remote mountain passes in Europe—became known as the toughest historic rally. Hopkirk, right, and co-driver Alec Poole, second from the left, are seen celebrating at the end of the 1989 event in Cortina, Northern Italy.

Above: Journalist Jeremy Coulter bought the ex-Mike Smith Rally d'Antibes 1275GT and campaigned it extensively in Britain during the late 1980s. He is seen here during the 1989 Coronation Rally, chasing Paul Howcroft's Lotus Elan 26R.

Left: Jeremy Coulter also built an 850 cc Mini to compete in the Monte Carlo Challenge, a winter version of the Classic Marathon confined to pre-1963 cars. He is pictured here leaving Rheims, northern France, in the long run to the Mediterranean from the Glasgow start of the first historic Monte in 1990.

Right: During the early 1990s, the Longleat Stages—a historic rally based at the West Country wildlife park—became Britain's premier single-day event. Its slippery tarmac proved ideal for Minis, the Cooper S of Cecil Offley and Peter Valentine taking 11th place in 1990.

Right: Gary Hall and Allan Dodge—pictured at Nova Lavante in northern Italy—switched from Mini racing to rallying for the 1990 Classic Marathon, finishing a creditable eighth behind Paddy Hopkirk's winning Mini.

1984 as a consultant to see what could be salvaged after Mini Moke production became uneconomic in Australia. This occurred partly because the Australians had insisted on using 13 in wheels, which meant producing special trailing arms for the rear suspension, a special steering rack and revising the shape of the rear mudguards. It also meant that a final drive ratio was needed that could not be shared with any other model.

Production was switched to Portugal, where there was spare capacity at a former MAN truck plant at Vendas Novas, 100 miles north of Lisbon. Once a surplus of 40 kits in Portugal and another 260 in Britain had been used up, Lambert evolved a new Moke using standard Mini parts, including a low-compression 998 cc engine, normal 3.4:1 final drive, 12 in wheels and suspension. These parts could then be shipped to Portugal ready-assembled, further cutting costs. This enabled production to continue, with a target of 2,000 Mokes a year.

So far as the Mini was concerned, Rover continued the limited edition theme in May 1987, with an Advantage, again based on the City. It had a diamond white body with white wheeltrims and full-length 'tennis net' side stripes incorporating an Advantage tennis ball logo. Tinted glass, a passenger door mirror, and opening rear quarter lights were fitted. The interior featured

Below: Jeremy Coulter, pictured here in Belgium, went on to demonstrate the ability of the Mini-Cooper S by winning the 1991 European Rally Championship.

flint grey trim overlaid with jade green pinstripe check and a tennis ball logo. A rev counter was fitted as standard on the 2,500 cars produced for Britain, with a further 1,975 going to France, Germany, Belgium and Holland, plus 200 for Japan.

Austin Rover's Japanese market doubled again in 1987, with Minis providing 98 per cent of its 2,325 sales. The trend was to convert standard Minis to a mock Mini-Cooper specification, with white roof and bolt-on rally accessories. Japanese emission regulations were exceptionally strong,

Right: The 1991 Monte Carlo Challenge became an absolute classic, snow feet deep packing much of the route through the Alps. Belgium's Alain de Falle is seen demonstrating the advantages of a Mini 850's front-wheel drive while climbing the Ballon d'Alsace in central France.

Right: A Mini for all occasions . . . Mike Feetham and Paul Brace are pictured with their ex-Marathon Mini on the 1991 Longleat Stages.

requiring the fitting of a three-way catalytic converter.

Autocar's Tokyo correspondent, Peter Nunn, reported:

'A Mini represents the very height of cool in Japan. The Japanese have an affection for the Mini like no other nation on earth. Not even the

Left: Britain's RAC joined the ranks of historic rally organizers by running their own international event at the beginning of 1991. Winner Timo Makinen, in Bob Young's ex-works Cooper S, is pictured taking a winning lead at the Prescott hill climb.

Below: The Stelvio Pass in northern Italy became the climax of the Classic Marathon, dwarfing Mike van Thiel's Mini-Cooper S, seen rounding the 42nd hairpin on the right *en route* to the 10,000 ft summit in the 1991 event.

British, who invented it, love it as much.

'The Mini has always been a good seller in Japan—but nowadays it's treated almost like royalty. The surprise is the attraction the car also has for the young, streetwise, Japanese boys. For them, the Mini is an affordable dream—compact, fun to drive, and, most important of all, cheap to buy.

'The older the Mini, the better. Indeed, Austin Rover Japan, is successfully capitalizing on the retro boom by importing the Mini in ever-increasing numbers. Besides a new Mayfair or Special Edition Mini, ARJ can offer you dozens of authentic-looking 1960s parts to make your Mini appear like one from the halcyon days.

'Remember the Paddy Hopkirk accelerator pedal, the Mini-Cooper roof rack and the large Mini centre speedo with little Smith's gauges either side? Believe it or not, these, plus a host of other add-ons, are all available from the official importers, who, privately, seem as bemused by the Mini's cult following as anyone else.'

Meanwhile, Honda dealer John Cooper—responsible for the original Mini-Cooper—had been making money for 18 months selling tuning kits to the Japanese. 'It's barmy really,' said Cooper. 'My son, Mike, went to Japan the other year on a Honda trip. He was in a hotel with all these Honda people,

Right: Irish ace Ronnie McCartney storms the Stelvio to win the 1991 Classic Marathon in Dr Beatty Crawford's Mini-Cooper S.

Left: Masaaki Kawahara and Yarawa Hirano—pictured in the Austrian Dolomites—shipped their Mini-Cooper S all the way from Japan to Britain to compete in the 1991 Classic Marathon.

Left: Italian-based Mini-Cooper S driver Richard Martin-Hurst used his local knowledge to good effect during the 1991 Classic Marathon, excelling on tough navigational sections.

Above: Classic Marathon atmosphere . . . with winners McCartney *(left of the centre Mini)*, and Crawford *(right)* celebrating victory at Cortina with second-placed Coulter (Mini to the left), and third-placed Healey drivers Donal McBride and Austin Frazer, backed by the yellow-clad marshals who made it possible.

Right: The Targa Rusticana was resurrected as Britain's top road rally when confined to historic cars . . . and Minis proved ideal for demanding night sections in the twisting Welsh lanes around its base in Llandrindod Wells. Richard Martin-Hurst is pictured here during the 1991 Targa.

and a procession of Minis arrived. He told the drivers, "I'm not John Cooper, he's my father!" But they were still impressed and asked him to sign the paintwork of their cars.'

Austin Rover responded by producing 2,000 Mini Designers, using a 1960s Mary Quant theme featuring tinted glass and black and white trim.

Four special editions were launched in 1989 to celebrate the Mini's thirtieth anniversary: the Racing and Flame came in traditional sporting green and red with white roof panels, chrome bumpers and rev counter, with pastel-coloured Special Equipment versions finished in white with a rose pink roof or a sky blue one, plus a Thirty, 2,000 in red, 1,000 in black, to help the Mayfair celebrate the model's forthcoming anniversary. Interiors were trimmed in what was called Lightning fabric with zigzags woven through it and occasional leather panels. Minilite-style wheels and a chrome grille and bumper completed the ensemble.

While trying a Mini City for size, 6 ft 7 in road tester Russell Bulgin complained about the 'sadistic seats,' but reported in *Autocar & Motor*—the two magazines had been amalgamated following the demise of *Motor*—in March 1989:

'In its latest cheapo City guise, this Mini is the only Rover product available for less than five thousand quid. But it doesn't feel skimpy. The interior is a predominantly grey tone, with a neat dash, a modicum of switchgear—including the daffy pull-on heater control, same as it ever was—cloth and vinyl seats, carpet, heated rear window and that's about it. The optional radio sits above the passenger's shins which means that you need a reach like Frank Bruno to flip stations.

'Outside, the 1989 Mini City is the prettiest model yet. All the exterior acne which used to ring the Mini in strips of penny dreadful chrome is now finished in a slick grey sheen, right down to the door handles . . .

'The good news is that the Mini still feels like a Mini. It's back where it started, as a small car that makes big cars look stupid. Mini-handling is still brilliant . . . I can't think of a modern car which places so much emphasis on steering response.

Left: Jeremy Coulter's public relations partner John Brigden, who represents Rover's British Heritage Museum, is also a rally fan . . . he is seen here competing in the classic Kent Forestry Stages in 1991.

Right: Mini stars of the 1960s were attracted when the Historic Rally Car Register, one of the prime moving forces behind the Classic Marathon, ran the Britannia International Rally in 1991 before thousands of spectators lining the route for the world championship RAC Rally. Sweden's Lars-Ingvar Ytterbring is seen storming the famous Sutton Park water splash in Birmingham.

Right: The Monte Carlo Challenge became ever bigger and more popular, especially when the liberation of East Germany allowed competitors like Alain de Falle to start from Berlin's Brandenburg Gate.

'The great thing about the Mini City is that it no longer pretends to be anything other than a Mini. It celebrates its heritage every time you get stuck into a zigzag road with an ability to snake through gaps most cyclists would think twice about.'

Left: The tarmac tests of the RAC's International Rally were considered too gentle . . . so, with Charrington's sponsorship, the event moved into the forests in 1992. Timo Makinen enjoys classical Welsh forest track action with one of his most famous 1960s co-drivers, Paul Easter.

Left: There's still a lot of enjoyment with a Mini Moke, especially when it meets Mini the Mouse, as this competitor demonstrates on the hugely popular Run-to-Euro Disney, from various starting points in Britain to the Paris pleasure park, in 1992.

Meanwhile John Cooper introduced a thirtieth anniversary model based on the Racing special edition. It had twin 1.25 in SU carburettors and a Janspeed cylinder head with polished rocker cover, 1.2 in rather than 1.1 in inlet and exhaust valves, and a 9.75:1 compression ratio. Steel valve inserts were fitted to combat unleaded fuel with special guides. Running a throaty twin box exhaust, quoted outputs were 64 bph at 6,000 rpm with 62 lb/ft of torque at 3,500 rpm.

The 3.1:1 final drive ratio proved rather a handicap to acceleration, 13.2 sec being needed for 0–60 mph, with 18.8 for the standing quarter mile. But a top speed of 85 mph made it a realistic proposition in modern traffic, with a reasonably frugal 30 mpg.

Autocar & Motor reported in June 1989:

'As the figures indicate, stirring the soul involves, first, vigorously stirring the pot . . . to get the scenery rushing by it is necessary to use all the available revs.

'Cooper had partially contributed to eyebrow-raising levels of grip. The inclusion of 12 in alloy Minilite look-alike wheels and Pirelli Cinturato CN54 145 70 SR12 rubber goes a long way towards keeping the Mini in the list of cars you would choose for a hard drive on narrow, twisting, country lanes.

'Handling is deliciously neutral. Initial turn-in is excellent, with the direct, positive-feel (read tending towards heavy) steering offering an exact indication of what the front wheels are up to. It makes an invigorating change from the occasionally over-assisted, slightly-vague, steering of some modern front-drive cars . . .

'The Mini shows its age when it comes to ride quality. But just when you thought the human endurance test would sour a blooming romance, you discover that mid-corner potholes, cat's eyes, dips, jumps and cracks

Right: Father-and-son Mini-Cooper S team Nick and Tom Barrow lift an exuberant wheel during the famous Modave stage in Belgium on the 1992 Classic Marathon.

don't toss this Mini off-line and into the shrubbery. That, in a nutshell, describes the driver-Mini relationship.'

Autocar & Motor were full of comparisons when they tested a Mayfair as part of their Mini thirtieth anniversary celebrations in August 1989. They noted that the original engine had been uprated to 998 cc and could now run on unleaded petrol, with an extra 4 bph and 6 lb/ft of torque. That 10 per cent extra was easily cancelled out by more than that in kerb weight—at 1,498

Left: By 1992 the Classic Marathon was searching for new challenges, the Belgian Mini-Cooper S of Alain Lopes and Jean-Louis Goblet, taking in Czechoslovakia—as it was then— as part of the fun.

Below: Mini Seven racing, as popular as ever, provides some of the most competitive fields in British club racing. Graham Lloyd's Seven is seen leading a gaggle at Mallory Park in 1992.

Above left and right: The spirit of Mini racing was never better illustrated than when Welsh veteran Len Brammer planted his Miglia on its roof during practice at Donington in 1992, then—with more than a little help from his friends—carried on racing the next day.

lb—and it was no surprise that the Mayfair was substantially slower through the gears than *Autocar*'s original test machine. Not only did the 1989 car refuse to pull from 10 mph in top—a task the first Mini performed without problem—but also the 30–50 mph time in top was more than 7 sec slower at 21.5 sec. This was because of a 20 per cent rise in gearing which made for quieter motorway cruising (with a 78 mph maximum speed) and led to the best part of 40 mpg for the average owner, 38 on test.

Such was the Japanese demand for Mini-Coopers and their look-alikes, that Rover adapted the Thirty to take a 61 bhp catalyst-equipped version of the MG Metro's 1,275 cc A-series engine in July 1990, tuned in the manner of John Cooper's earlier Racing version. Performance was in the order of 92 mph flat out, with an 11.2 sec 0–60 mph time. Green was added to the red and black colour schemes, with white stripes on either side of the bonnet for the first 1,000 (optional after that), in the manner of the 1960s works Minis. Rover had negotiated with the TKM group for the exclusive rights to market the Cooper name, which had been vacated by John Cooper when he sold his Cooper Car Company garages to TKM. The new Minis could then carry John Cooper's signature on the bonnet stripes!

This new Cooper was expected to account for one-third of all Mini sales to Japan. The way was then open for John Cooper to produce a conversion for this car to give it the equivalent performance to that of the fabled 1,275 cc Cooper S.

The result was an outstanding success as the Mini's worldwide exports continued to soar. No less than 12,100 were sold in Japan with the best figures in Europe since 1981. Total Mini exports were 31,655, from 46,045 British cars sold abroad, making it by far the best-selling model!

As Peter Nunn explained in *CAR* magazine in March 1992:

'There are several reasons why the Mini has such a cult following in Japan: one, its small, well-proportioned, size makes it eminently well-suited to driving on narrow Japanese roads. Two, there's its English character and timeless looks. Plus, it's cute, fun to drive and easy to park (an important point in a place like Tokyo).

'That it's a living legend, whose styling has remained essentially unchanged for 32 years, is another reason why the Japanese are so fascinated by it. Going on normal Japanese model cycles, a car such as the Civic would have gone through eight different permutations by now, but the ground-breaking Mini, the precursor of all modern superminis, remains fundamentally the same after all these years.'

It was then left to John Cooper to produce an S version of the new Metro-engined Cooper. It followed the familiar Janspeed/Cooper lines with the addition of an air cooler and a reversion of the original 3.44:1 final drive ration. In company with an increase in power to 78 bhp at 6,000 rpm and torque to 78 lb/ft at 3,250 rpm, the 0–60 mph time dropped to around 10 sec with a maximum speed of close to 100 mph. There was a sports handling pack, too, using low-profile Dunlop SP Sport 165/60 R12 tyres and adjustable shock absorbers.

Performance Car—a modern version of the old *Hot Car*—were full of nostalgia when they tested a new Mini-Cooper S in July 1991. Peter Tomalin wrote:

'Imagine the sharp intake of breath if the Prime Minister were to drop his trousers in full view of Mary Whitehouse, the Archbishop of Canterbury, Cliff Richard and the Singing Nun. That's the sound of the Cooper's twin SU carburettors at full suck.

'If you're used to a GTi, an SRi or any other i, the gasp and the gurgle of the Cooper will come as a surprise. Like the fact that it can outcorner

Left: Minis are still great fun in Rallycross as this competitor demonstrates at Lydden in 1992.

and outhandle just about any of the modern superminis. Or the fact that on the right road it's more than the lot of 'em rolled together.'

Not long afterwards these Minis had to be updated to comply with the new Japanese emission regulations, which meant that they needed a three-way controlled catalytic converter. The answer was to fit a fuel-injected version of

Right: Irish rally front-runner Frank Fennel bought the Coulter European championship Mini-Cooper S and continued campaigning it in the 1992 Rally Britannia.

Right: The 1993 historic Monte Carlo proved to be as big a challenge as ever, and Patrick Hesnard was glad to reach the finish in his Mini 850.

Left: Paul Loveridge and Graham Ford, pictured in the Coronation Rally at Pembrey, were early leaders in the 1993 Autostorica historic rally championship.

Left: Just as it used to be . . . the power house of Tom Seal's Mini-Cooper S at scrutineering for the 1993 Charrington's International Rally.

Right: BBC *Top Gear* presenter Tiff Needell storms through the Yorkshire forests with journalist Ian Bond in Seal's Mini-Cooper S during the 1993 Charrington's International Rally.

the 1,275 cc Metro engine, giving 63 bhp at 5,700 rpm and 70 lb/ft of torque at 3,900 rpm in standard Cooper—now 1.3i—form. Top gear acceleration from 30–50 mph dropped from 12.2 sec to 10.3, but the 0–60 mph time increased from 11.2 sec to 11.5. Never mind, it would still do 92 mph! John Cooper would then market a Cooper Si pack similar to his earlier conversion, giving 77 bhp—enough for a claimed 10.2 sec 0–60 mph time and 98 mph.

Rachel Butler wrote of the 1.3i in *CAR* magazine in March 1992:

> 'In the driving—around town at least—the new car does feel nippier. But at speed on the motorway it seemed to be noisier than the carburetted version.'

As Rover Group managing director Kevin Morley told the new magazine *Mini World* in its winter 1991 edition:

> 'When I joined Rover in 1986, there were suggestions within the company to stop producing the Mini. I immediately stated that I thought this a horrendous thing to do, but the news that we were thinking of stopping production leaked out and both Sir Graham Day and myself were inundated with letters and calls saying "Don't do it!" And these were from people who were buying new Minis, not just nostalgic enthusiasts.
>
> 'Basically the customer has kept the Mini going and continues to do so. But back in 1986 when we dropped the idea of stopping production, it was obvious that we should start developing the product again: hence the Coopers, hence the limited editions and hence the new one with three-way catalyst and fuel injection which will take us into 1992 and beyond.'

Minis continue to go from strength to strength in competition as our pictures and captions show, not the least because of the recent upsurge in interest in historic rallying, where the Mini-Cooper S fits in perfectly with the Pre-1965 regulations used in international events.

As the second edition of this book went to press, it was evident that you can't keep a good Mini down!

XVI

The Mini Clubs

By far the oldest-established club for Mini owners and enthusiasts is the Mini Se7en Racing Club, which can trace its roots to 1961—but caters, of course, purely for the competition world. It was not until 1979 that a cohesive club aimed at catering for all forms of Mini interest emerged in the Mini Owners' Club run by Chris Cheal, whose earlier interests included the small BMC and British Leyland Midget and Sprite sports cars. Since then the Mini Owners' Club has flourished in Britain and the rest of Europe, its steady growth receiving full British Leyland, and subsequently Austin-Rover Group, approval.

Benefits listed for club members include insurance obtained at lower than normal rates through club brokers, and an agreed valuation scheme for vehicles subject to claims, plus special discount rates on new, secondhand and reconditioned spares from Mini specialists. The club produces a quarterly magazine which includes not only articles on individual cars, and diagnosis of potential faults and problems, but free advertising of spares for sale.

Social meetings are held throughout the country with a national annual rally to enable all members to meet. The Mini-Cooper Club operates along similar lines, catering not only for Cooper owners, but embracing all Minis.

The first Mini Se7en Club was formed in 1961 by competition enthusiasts, continuing in slightly erratic form until it instigated the Mini Se7en formula for low-cost racing in 1966 as the price of competing in saloon car racing soared. It then developed into the Mini Se7en Racing Centre and Mini Se7en London Centre before they amalgamated to form today's Mini Se7en Racing Club in 1974. Such has been the success of this competition club that it not only organises its popular championships but runs a social programme with further get-togethers at race circuits.

The Thames Estuary Automobile Club (TEAC) dates to 1951 when it was founded in Southend, where it still has its own clubhouse and bar on the seafront. Initially the club was involved in rally organisation, going on to circuit racing, mainly centred now at Lydden in Kent. It was at Lydden that it became involved in the start of televised Rallycross and now takes in Minicross as well.

A number of other smaller clubs cater for individual interest in the Mini and its variants, particularly the specials that use Mini components in glass fibre bodyshells.

Above: A dazzling array of ex-works competition cars at a Mini-Cooper Club Rally in 1984.

Right: Bustling scenes at a Mini Owners' Club rally in 1985.

Left and below: Interest at club rallies has never been higher than in cars like the last works Mini, registered SOH 878H, used by John Handley and Alec Poole in the 1970 84-hour Marathon de la Route at the Nurburgring (picture one), and the 125S that took Paddy Hopkirk to second place in the 1967 Rally of the Flowers.

These include the Mini Sportscar Club specialising in the GTM, Hustler, McCoy, Midas, Mini Marcos, Mini Jem, Nimrod, Nomad and Status. Social events are high on their list of activities, with a magazine devoted to articles of interest on these cars.

Other specialised clubs include the Mini Moke Club, the Nimrod Register, the Scamp Owners' Club, the Riley Elf and Wolseley Hornet Owners' Club and the Crayford Convertible Club which maintains a high level of interest in the numerous Minis converted by this old-established firm.

Contact addresses are: Mini Owners' Club: Chris Cheal, 18 Mercia Close, Coton Green, Tamworth, Staffs; Mini-Cooper Club: Joyce Holman, 1 Weaver's Cottage, Church Hill, West Hoathly, Sussex; Mini Se7en Racing Club: Mrs Heather Beckwith, 141 Walton Drive, Terriers, High Wycombe, Bucks; TEAC: Miss B. Kaye, Wheelbase, 111 Eastern Esplanade, Southend-on-Sea, Essex; Mini Sportscar Club: Mark Burgess, Bank House, Summerhill, Chislehurst, Kent; Mini Moke Club: Paul Beard, 7 Oakdene, Hartlebury Park, Stourport, Worcs; Nimrod Register: Nigel Talbot, 24 Tything Way, Wincanton, Somerset; Scamp Owners' Club: R. F. Cake, 25 Deanland End, Rowlands Castle, Hants; The Riley Elf and Wolseley Hornet Owners' Club: Andrew Penfold, 97 Highfield Road, Yeovil, Somerset; The Crayford Convertible Club: Rory Cronin, 68 Manor Road, Worthing, West Sussex.

XVII
Your Mini Logbook

Austin Seven, Austin 850, Morris Mini-Minor

Introduced August 1959, from Austin chassis number A/A2S7 101, Morris M/A2S4 101.

Engine

Four cylinders, in-line, overhead valves CUBIC CAPACITY 848 cc; BORE AND STROKE 62.94 mm × 68.26 mm; MAX POWER 34 bhp at 5,500 rpm; MAX TORQUE 44 lb/ft at 2,900 rpm.

Chassis

WHEELBASE 6 FT 8 INS; WEIGHT 1288 lb; DIMENSIONS 6 ft 8 ins; FRONT TRACK 3 ft 11.75 ins; REAR TRACK 3 ft 9.875 ins; LENGTH 10 ft; WIDTH 4 ft 7 ins; HEIGHT 4 ft 5 ins; FRONT SUSPENSION wishbone and rubber, tie rod; REAR SUSPENSION, trailing arm and rubber; BRAKES drum all round; STEERING rack and pinion; GEARING (overall) 3.765:1, 5.317, 8.176, 13.657, reverse 13.657; TYRES AND WHEELS 10 ins × 3.5 ins.

Austin Minivan, Morris Minivan

As Mini saloon except WHEELBASE 7 ft 0.15 ins, LENGTH 10 ft 9.875 ins.

Austin Mini Countryman, Morris Mini Traveller

As Minivan.

Austin Mini Pick Up, Morris Mini Pick Up

As Minivan.

Austin Mini Cooper, Morris Mini Cooper

Engine

BORE AND STROKE 62.43 mm × 81.28 mm; CUBIC CAPACITY 997 cc; MAX POWER 55 bhp at 6,000 rpm; MAX TORQUE 44 lb/ft at 3,600 rpm.

Chassis

As Mini saloons, except BRAKES disc front, drum rear; GEARING (overall) 3.765:1, 5.11, 7.21, 12.05.

Wolseley Hornet and Riley Elf Mark 1

As Mini saloons except overall LENGTH 10 ft 10.3 ins; WEIGHT 1520 lb.

Wolseley Hornet and Riley Elf Mark II

As mark I except engine BORE AND STROKE 64.58 mm × 83.72 mm; CUBIC CAPACITY 998 cc; MAX POWER 38 bhp at 5,250 rpm; MAX TORQUE 52 lb/ft at 2,700 rpm.

Mini-Cooper S

As Mini-Cooper except ENGINE (1071 cc) BORE AND STROKE 70.64 mm × 68.26 mm; (970 cc) 70.64 mm × 61.91 mm; (1275 cc) 70.64 mm × 81.33 mm; MAX POWER (1071 cc) 70 bhp at 6,200 rpm; (970 cc) 65 hbp at 6,500 rpm; (1275 cc) 76 bhp at 5,800 rpm; MAX TORQUE (1071 cc) 62 lb/ft at 4,500 rpm; (970 cc) 55 lb/ft at 3,500 rpm; (1275 cc) 79 lb/ft at 3,000 rpm; GEARING: 3.77:1, 5.1, 7.21, 12.04; optional 3.44:1, 4.67, 6.59, 11.02; optional 3.77:1, 4.67, 6.7, 9.66; optional 3.44:1 4.27, 6.13, 8.84; WHEELS 10 ins × 4.5 ins.

Mini-Cooper Mark II

As per Mini-Cooper, except engine, BORE AND STROKE 64.58 mm × 83.72 mm, CUBIC CAPACITY 998 cc; MAX POWER 55 bhp at 5,800 rpm, MAX TORQUE 57 lb/ft at 3,000 rpm.

Mini Moke

As Mini saloons except WEIGHT 1279 lb; DIMENSIONS wheelbase 6 ft 7.9 ins; FRONT TRACK 3 ft 11.45 ins; REAR TRACK 3 ft 9.85 ins; LENGTH 10 ft; WIDTH 4 ft 5.55 ins; HEIGHT (hood erect) 4 ft 5 ins; GEARING (overall) 3.44:1, 4.86, 7.47. 12.48.

Left: The 1959 Austin Seven.

Left: The 1962 Morris Mini Super de Luxe.

Left: The 1964 Austin Cooper.

Above: The 1967 Riley Elf mark III.

Right: The 1964 Mini-Moke.

Right: The 1960 Morris Minivan.

Right: The 1961 Morris Mini-Traveller.

Mini Mark II

As Mini saloons except engine (home market) as Riley Elf and Wolseley Hornet; (export) BORE AND STROKE 70.64 mm × 68.26 mm; CUBIC CAPACITY 1275 cc; MAX POWER 60 bhp at 5,250 rpm, MAX TORQUE 69 lb/ft at 2,500 rpm; GEARING (overall) 3.44:1, 4.86, 7.47, 12.48.

Mini Clubman

As Mini saloons except LENGTH 11 ft 1.875 ins.

Mini 1275GT

As Mini Clubman except engine BORE AND STROKE 70.64 mm × 81.33 mm; CUBIC CAPACITY 1275 cc; MAX POWER 59 bhp at 5,300 rpm; MAX TORQUE 65 lb/ft at 2,550 rpm; BRAKES disc front, drum rear; WHEELS AND TYRES 10 ins × 4.5 ins; GEARING (overall) 3.65:1, 5.22, 8.10, 12.87, later 3.44:1, 4.92, 7.63, 12.13

Mini Clubman 1100

As Mini Clubman except engine BORE AND STROKE 64.5 mm × 83.7 mm; CUBIC CAPACITY 1098 cc; MAX POWER 50 bhp at 5,100 rpm; MAX TORQUE 60 lb/ft at 2,500 rpm.

Mini 1275GT

As 1275GT but from 1974 with WHEELS AND TYRES 12 ins × 4.5 ins.

Mini 1000HL

As Mini 998 cc except MAX POWER 39 bhp at 4,750 rpm; MAX TORQUE 52 lb/ft at 2,000 rpm.

Mini 1000HLE

As Mini 1000HL except GEARING 2.95:1, 4.23, 6.54, 10.4.

Mini City E

As Mini 850, except gearing as Mini 1000HLE.

Mini City

As Mini City E except WHEELS AND TYRES 12 ins × 4.5 ins; BRAKES disc front, drum rear.

The 1967 Austin-Cooper 1275S.

The 1979 Mini 850.

The 1979 Mini 1275GT.

The 1983 Mini Sprite.

Mini Mayfair
As 1000HLE, from 1989 MAX POWER 43 bhp; MAX TORQUE 58 lb/ft.

Mini-Cooper
From 1990, as Mini Mayfair except BORE AND STROKE 70.64 mm x 81.33 mm; CUBIC CAPACITY 1,275 cc; MAX POWER 61 bhp.

Mini 1.3i
As Mini-Cooper (1990 model) except fuel injection, MAX POWER 63 bhp at 5,700 rpm; MAX TORQUE 70 lb/ft at 3,900 rpm.

Mini Sprite
As Mini City.

Index

Index of Illustrations